The State of Being Stateless

The State of Being Stateless

An Account of South Asia

Edited by

PAULA BANERJEE

ANASUA BASU RAY CHAUDHURY

ATIG GHOSH

With a Foreword by

RANABIR SAMADDAR

Orient BlackSwan

THE STATE OF BEING STATELESS

ORIENT BLACKSWAN PRIVATE LIMITED

Registered Office
3-6-752 Himayatnagar, Hyderabad 500 029, Telangana, India
e-mail: centraloffice@orientblackswan.com

Other Offices
Bengaluru, Bhopal, Chennai, Guwahati, Hyderabad, Jaipur, Kolkata, Lucknow, Mumbai, New Delhi, Noida, Patna, Vijayawada

This book first published 2015
Paperback edition first published 2019

028594

ISBN 978-93-5287-466-8

Typeset in
Warnock Pro 10.5/13
by PrePSol Enterprises Pvt. Ltd, Haryana

Printed in India at
Yash Printographics, Noida

Published by
Orient Blackswan Private Limited
3-6-752 Himayatnagar, Hyderabad 500 029, Telangana, India
e-mail: info@orientblackswan.com

Dedicated to Professor Ranabir Samaddar,
who is the soul behind this book

Contents

Contents

Foreword

With this volume on statelessness in India, one phase of Calcutta Research Group's (CRG's) work in forced migration studies spanning more than a decade comes to a close. In 2002 it published—though not first—the most extensive volume on refugees in West Bengal, the institutional practices of their protection, and the production of the refugee identity (Bose 2000). Within one year or so of that publication it followed up its work on West Bengal refugees with the first comprehensive account of refugees in post-Independence India and the history of her asylum practices; in other words, the first account of the post-colonial regime of care and power (Samaddar 2003). Researching on the edges of ethics, law and history, the study of refugees in India produced a framework that was distinctly post-colonial and critical, but at the same time engaging and challenging the dominant paradigms of refugee studies, refugee law and refugee protection policies. It produced a framework that attracted wide readership, reviews, appreciation, comments, and encouraged many others to study in that frame. Insights gained from these two researches helped CRG to undertake the first systematic study of internal displacement in South Asia, the relevance of United Nations (UN) Guiding Principles, and the relevance of the Internally Displaced Person (IDP) issue to studies on forced migration (in 2005). The study of the IDPs, attending governmental practices, legal definitions and their limit, and finally the massive nature of the internal population flows also helped forced migration researchers to see refugee movements in a new and broader light, beyond the existing international legal framework or a dominantly cultural framework that limits our understanding to only symbols and identities.

These three studies set a critical, post-colonial mode of investigation that is now part of the valued methods in forced migration studies. Strong empirical base; historical understanding of issues in question; critical legal theory; gender-sensitive approach; deploying the concept of border as method of study; understanding of the epochal significance of issues of colonialism, partitions, borders and boundaries, and neo-liberal developmentalism, are some of the aspects of this critical post-colonial mode. This mode too studies subjectivity; this too accepts refugee subjecthood as expressed in literature, songs, music, etc. as important aspects of study. But in place of sterile and limited textual reading of these subject experiences, these researches showed how to study subjectivity materially, grounded in historical experiences.

An important stage in the evolution of this critical mode came when CRG published an empirical study of select camps of IDPs in South Asia with emphasis on mapping the voices of IDPs in camps (CRG 2006). The report broke many myths on laws, their efficacy and relevance; the comparative roles of development projects and violence in producing IDPs, etc. The study also helped CRG conceptualise the notion of *massive and mixed flows of populations.* These studies also helped CRG to anchor refugee studies firmly in forced migration studies. The results were seen in CRG's works in the early years of this decade when it undertook collective studies on two themes: the specific nature of protracted displacement and the governmental technologies that produce the identity of the migrant. Both these studies are available in book form and online (CRG 2006; Samaddar 2003). All in all, these CRG studies have deepened our understanding of human rights and justice.

The present volume on statelessness is to be seen in this perspective of a more than decade-long work on forced migration. Readers acquainted with its earlier studies will find the same unique method, selection of case studies, genealogical orientation, and a critical, post-colonial mode of investigation. Statelessness is seen here less as a positive definition, that is, a definition that sets complete conditions for statelessness. It is seen here more as refraction of a positive reality known as citizenship, citizenship as an institution that always—to use the word of a philosopher—

'incompletes' itself. Statelessness has a definition that always even if unknowingly bases itself on a kind of displacement of a reality—the reality of state, nationality, citizenship. Therefore, the studies this book offers are studies of permanent incompleteness—a reality that always seems to fall short of a hyper-reality, and therefore the ideal reality, of citizenship, entitlements, legal protection, full proof identity, solemn recognitions by courts of law, and the avowals by the State.

In this volume statelessness is more a situation, a condition, or a set of conditions that make what can be called a *limit situation* and *limit experience*, by which we mean *situated at the limits, and experience of the limits of a situation, at the same time limits of an experience and situation we have defined in this case as citizenship.* Such an understanding must at one point of time brush against the positivism of law. It is up to law (in this case international law) to live up to these refracted, displaced realities, whose function is to tell the society the limits of the assured knowledge of institutions like border, state, citizenship, rights, humanitarianism, constitution, etc. If the subject of the State is the citizen, the stateless is the alien.

We can thus say: the citizen is the defence of the visibility of Constitution; the alien is the shadow, its prey. The citizen exists in the alien as the savage form. Citizen is articulate; the alien inaudible, silent. Yet the more interesting question will be: What are the ways in which the alien overcomes the two obstacles of inaudibility and invisibility? To understand this life world of the stateless, forced migration studies will have to adopt the strategy of interrogating alterity. The same principle of interrogation will be valuable in studying actual conditions of statelessness in the post-colonial world.

There is no doubt that the study of stateless population groups will become increasingly significant in forced migration studies. As states once again go to wars, come up and go down in history; countries fight newer forms of colonialism; newer forms of decolonisation occur; and borders and boundaries play havoc with settled configurations, the number of stateless population will increase. We may see a reduction of de jure statelessness, but a rise in de facto stateless population around the world. It may also become increasingly difficult to distinguish between a refugee group and a stateless group. Newer identity practices imposed by States may produce stateless condition. If the preceding century was a century of partitions, this century may become known as the century of stateless people.

Ranabir Samaddar
Director, Mahanirban Calcutta Research Group

Publisher's Acknowledgements

We acknowledge with thanks the permissions received from the following:

Mahanirban Calcutta Research Group for material from the following papers that have been reproduced in Chapters 1, 3, 4, 5, 6 and 7:

- 'A Brief Report on "Mapping the Stateless in India": 2 Phase'
- 'A Report on the Tenth Annual Orientation Course on Forced Migration 2012'
- 'Executive Summary of the Report on "The State of Being Stateless: A Case Study of the Chakmas of Arunachal Pradesh"'
- 'Module D: Statelessness in South Asia (Concept Note, Suggested Readings, and Assignments)'
- 'Statelessness: Concept Note'
- 'Statelessness: Events and Announcements'
- Anasua Basu Ray Chaudhury, 'Unheard Voices: The Stateless Chakmas in Arunachal Pradesh', *Refugee Watch Online*, 28 February 2011
- Mahanirban Calcutta Research Group and International Committee of the Red Cross, 'Research on the Humanitarian Aspects along the Indo-Bangladesh Border'
- Raghu Amay Karnad, Rajeev Dhavan and Bhairav Acharya, 'Protecting the Forgotten and Excluded: Statelessness in South Asia'
- Subhas Ranjan Chakrabarty, 'Silence Under Freedom: The Story of Democracy in the Darjeeling Hills', in Ranabir Samaddar (ed.), *The Politics of Autonomy: Indian Experiences*, New Delhi: Sage Publications, 2005 (in Chapter 7)

Astral International (P) Ltd. for Table 5.3: 'District-Wise Distribution of Chakma Population in Arunachal Pradesh (in Approximate Terms)'. Originally published in Monirul Hussain M. (ed.), *Coming out of Violence: Essays on Ethnicity, Conflict Resolution and Peace Process in North-East India*, New Delhi: Astral International (P) Ltd., 2005, p. 90.

Abbreviations

AAPSU	All-Arunachal Pradesh Students' Union
AASU	All Assam Students' Union
ABSU	All Bodo Students' Union
ACHR	Asian Centre for Human Rights
ACR	Arunachal Citizens' Right
AESDU	All East Siang District Students' Union
AHURA	Association of Human Rights Activists (Bhutan)
AIADMK	All-India Anna Dravida Munnetra Kazhagam
AIFB	All-India Forward Bloc
AMSU	All Mishmi Students' Union
APITRO	Arunachal Pradesh Indigenous Tribal Rights (Protection) Organization
BBEECC	Bharat-Bangladesh Enclave Exchange Coordination Committee
BDR	Bangladesh Rifles
BJP	Bharatiya Janata Party
BPL	Below Poverty Line
BPP	Bhutan People's Party
BSF	Border Security Force
CBDP/TSI	Community Based Development Programme/ Transitional Solutions Initiatives
CCRCAP	Committee for Citizenship Rights of the Chakmas of Arunachal Pradesh
CERAK	Ceylon Repatriates Association, Kodaikanal
CHT	Chittagong Hill Tracts
CIC	Ceylon Indian Congress
CID	Crime Investigation Department
CPI(M)	Communist Party of India (Marxist)

CRG	Calcutta Research Group
CWC	Ceylon Workers Congress
CYMA	Central Young Mizo Association
DC	deputy commissioner
DGHC	Darjeeling Gorkha Hill Council
DMK	Dravida Munnetra Kazhagam
EPIC	Electoral Photo-Identity Card
GJMM	Gorkha Janmukti Morcha
GNLF	Gorkha National Liberation Front
GTA	Gorkhaland Territorial Administration
ICCPR	International Covenant on Civil and Political Rights
IDP	Internally Displaced Person
ILP	Inner Line Permit
IOM	International Organization for Migration
IPFB	Indian People's Forward Bloc
ISLAND	Indo-Sri Lanka Development (Trust)
JVP	Janatha Vimukthi Peramuna
KSU	Khasi Students' Union
KTP	Khristian Thalai Pawl
LPC	Land Possession Certificate
LSC	Land Settlement Certificate
LTTE	Liberation Tigers of Tamil Eelam
LTV	Long-Term Visa
MGYA	Mizoram Gorkha Youth Association
MLA	Member of Legislative Assembly
MMWS	Mizoram Muslim Welfare Society
MNF	Mizo National Front
MP	Member of Parliament
MZP	Mizo Zirlai Pawl
NEFA	North East Frontier Agency
NEITF	North East Indigenous/Tribal Peoples' Forum
NGO	non-governmental organisation
NHRC	National Human Rights Commission
NIC	National Identity Card
NMA	Non-Medical Assistant
OAU	Organization of African Unity
OBC	Other Backward Class

OfERR	Organisation for Eelam Refugee Rehabilitation
PAN	Permanent Account Number
PDS	Public Distribution System
PF	Provident Fund
PHC	primary health centre
PoK	Pakistan Occupied Kashmir
PRC	Permanent Resident Certificate
RBA	Royal Bhutan Army
RDC	Refugee Deportation Council
REPCO	Repatriates Cooperative Finance and Development (Bank)
RGGVY	Rajiv Gandhi Grameen Vidyutikaran Yojana
SLS	Seemant Lok Sangathan
ST	Scheduled Tribe
TANTEA	Tamil Nadu Tea Plantation Corporation Limited
TKP	Thalai Khristian Pawl
TRP	Temporary Residence Permit
UDHR	Universal Declaration of Human Rights
UFFR	United Front Federation for Repatriates
UID	Unique Identification Number
UN	United Nations
UNHCR	United Nations High Commissioner for Refugees
UNIFRONT	United Front for Repatriate Workers
UNO	United Nations Organization
UNP	United National Party
USAID	United States Agency for International Development
YMA	Young Mizo Association

The Grid

The Stateless and the Citizen

PAULA BANERJEE, ANASUA BASU RAY CHAUDHURY and ATIG GHOSH

> For the purpose of this Convention, the term 'stateless person' means a person who is not considered as a national by any State under the operation of its law. (Convention Relating to the Status of Stateless Persons', Chapter 1, Article 1.1, in Okoth-Obbo [2007: 68])

One of the great ironies of international law is that the 'other' of a citizen is neither a refugee nor a person who has dual or multiple citizenships but a stateless person. And a great fallacy of international law of statelessness is that a stateless person is defined by his/her lack. Yet to claim any legal correctives or rights the stateless person has to cite definite attributes. How can a lack be defined by attributes? This fallacy of law has given rise to animated debates between jurists, legal and rights-based activists, and social scientists. The backdrop of our present volume is this conversation that has been happening over the last few decades between lawyers and social scientists about the compulsions and the limitations of laws on statelessness. Statelessness as a problem has been plaguing the United Nations High Commissioner for Refugees (UNHCR), its practitioner, human rights activists, jurists, social scientists and state parties for over half a century and yet no concrete solution seems to be in sight much to everyone's consternation. This volume is meant to contribute to that conversation further and also to add to it a post-colonial dimension. Needless to say that this volume, even while taking cognisance of the debates elsewhere, will give greater space and credence to the conversations on statelessness taking place in the global South, particularly in South Asia. This is a book on mapping statelessness in India, arguably the most important country in South Asia; and the literature on this subject in the global South is thin. This volume will, therefore, address a vacuum in global literature on the stateless.

The purpose of the book is to understand that citizenship and statelessness are part of the same grid. There are many people in South Asia who would fall within this grid. They would not be accepted as a citizen by 'competent authorities' within a state and neither will they be called stateless by legal experts on international law. International authorities might hope that these people be called citizens by a particular state; but the reality remains that they are completely unable to access most of the rights attributed to a citizen. Therefore, even if citizenship laws are made more accessible these people will seldom be able to access them. Thus, countries may refrain from defining these people and let them remain as 'in-between' people or people with indeterminate nationality/indeterminate status of statelessness, thereby adding to their vulnerability, rightlessness and the discrimination against them. This book is about the multiple layers of 'in-between' populations who are, for all practical purposes, stateless and yet who can seldom be termed 'stateless' in this age of politics of humanitarianism; nor would they be considered as citizens by any state. In fact for all that matters they remain the permanent exception to citizenship.

Any discussion on citizenship ultimately and necessarily implies a discussion on statelessness and vice versa. The history of statelessness is intimately related to the history of formation of State and citizenship. The problem probably begins from the juncture that there is no standard definition of what constitutes a state. Article 20 of the 2014 *Handbook on the Protection of Stateless Persons* defines it as: 'For an entity to be a 'State' for the purposes of Article 1(1) it is not necessary for it to have received universal or large-scale recognition of its statehood by other States or to have become a Member State of the United Nations. Nevertheless, recognition or admission will be strong evidence of statehood' (UNHCR 2014: 12). If countries were not called upon to define their respective citizen there would be no stateless people in the world. But because most political rights historically accrue from citizenship it becomes essential for a person to become recognised as a citizen by a state. Even when citizenship is so crucial today thousands are still deprived of their nationality in many different parts of the world and South Asia is no exception. 'In one recent global survey, 59.4 per cent of states responding reported that they have encountered problems of statelessness. However only 54.1 per cent of states surveyed indicated they have a procedure in place to identify cases of statelessness while only 44.6 per cent have general information available on the potential number of stateless persons in their country' (UNHCR 2004, quoted in Batchelor 1998: 156). This happens because as per international law it is the state that decides who are its citizens and who are not, as long as the state does not apply measures that conflict with international principles relating to acquisition and loss of citizenship as per principles enunciated in the 1930 Hague Convention, the 1997 European Convention, and the case law of both Permanent Court of International Justice and International Court of Justice (Batchelor 1998: 157). By January 2014, only 80 states became party to the 1954 Convention.

The social scientists and human rights activists privilege the lack in the notion of statelessness. The competent authorities anywhere on earth would not mark any individual stateless if they know that by doing so they lose out. In South Asia at least clarificatory exercises take place only when an individual stands before a court of law to find out his or her status of citizenship. The plight of the discriminated sections of world population show that human experiences most often are not or cannot be always divided into such neat categories. Often state parties refuse to clarify whether a person is a citizen or not; as a result such people can be deprived of rights that flow out of citizenship. The great irony is that in terms of international law the UN requires that state parties declare people they consider as not belonging to their citizenry as stateless so that the stateless can access the minimum of human rights. Yet, the state parties lose nothing by not doing so and by just ignoring the hapless population whom they consider less than citizens.

In historical moments when questions over citizenship assume great importance, the issue of statelessness emerges at the end of that same spectrum. But that does not mean statelessness just happens. The stateless or near-stateless people are dynamically created by sovereignties for their own interest and their marginality may be due to blood, ethnicity, nationality or even resource crunch, and often subject to vagaries of world economy. Otherwise, why is the presence of Roma people sometimes tolerated, albeit grudgingly, and at other times shunned with such a force that they become a global example of what happens to the alien or the unwanted? After all, the Roma people can never be described as enemy alien; so why is there so much rancour and hatred against them at certain historical moments? The states make conscious decisions about who to include and who to exclude. In this process of inclusion and exclusion, many are denied citizenship and, as a result, they become stateless.

Internationally, the first acute awareness of the presence of stateless people happened after the Second World War. Hence, Article 15 of the Universal Declaration of Human Rights (UDHR) of 1948 stated that all persons have the right to nationality (UN 1948). Very soon, the fallacy of this statement was revealed when the reconstructed states found thousands who were less than citizens. It was clear that this was a problem that cut across nations and the enormity of the problem showed that it needed an international intervention. In 1948, the Economic and Social Council of the UN requested the Secretary General to undertake a study and to make recommendations on the situation of stateless persons. The 1951 'Convention Relating to the Status of Refugees' could not accommodate all of these people but only the stateless refugees. It is true that there are many things in common between the life experiences of a refugee and those of a stateless person. In fact in terms of vulnerability all three groups of forced migrants—the stateless or those without nationality, the IDP who have been displaced but have not been able to cross an international border and the refugee who has taken refuge in another country—face similar conditions. Although the refugee, IDP and the stateless may be unable to get the protection of the state in which they are born or find themselves in and are often compelled to leave it, the refugees at least have the right to return. The stateless have no such rights. Further, those who have been accepted as refugees were fortunate due to the fact that a state pledged to provide them with some rights. Unless a stateless person becomes a refugee they do not have any state protecting their rights. Experiences from across the world has shown that protracted refugee experiences can be so debilitating that it may lead to conditions similar to statelessness. But that is the next stage of the problem.

Since none of the human rights conventions could encapsulate the experiences of the stateless until the middle of the last century, in 1954 the 'Convention Relating to Status of the Stateless Persons' was formulated explaining who the stateless were. A person was to be regarded as stateless when no competent authority within a state could vouch for the fact that they were the citizen of that state. Article 1.2 said that the 'Convention will not apply' to any persons 'who are recognized by the competent authorities of the country in which they have taken residence as having the rights and obligations which are attached to the possession of the nationality of that country'. It was thus assumed that for conferring statelessness the competent authorities had to deny the citizenship of the individual (Chapter 1, Article 1.2 [b], in Okoth-Obbo 2007: 68). With this background we need greater clarity on who the 'competent authorities' are. The *Handbook on Protection of Stateless Persons* (UNHCR 2014) says that competent authorities denote those that can confer or deny citizenship. There may be more than one competent authority and they may differ from state to state. This confuses more than it clarifies but is in no way a critique of the UN system beyond the fact that perforce this system is dependent on the states that are the problem in the first place. Further, in another clause, the state parties are prohibited from expelling stateless people except on grounds of national security or public disorder; but if the states did so, there are no mechanisms cited to audit or stop these states from taking such abusive actions against humans living within their own territorial jurisdiction.

From the beginning there were much opposition to this convention. The United States and Canada at the very beginning refused to ratify the convention as they were ostensibly overwhelmed by the refugee population after the Second World War and also because they did not want the displaced to use this convention to seek new nationalities for the sake of convenience. Little did the states realise that it was not the displaced who would emerge as the real problem but the state elites who for reasons of ethnicity, religion, poverty and other considerations might use the convention to wilfully deny citizenship to some groups and many others would fall through the cracks due to lack of clear perception of the legal mechanism. But it is a moot point to critique what the states did in the late 1930s and 1940s because the international community could then scarcely recognise what it would be by the end of the twentieth century and neither could it predict, for example, what form national security would take 50 years down the road in the twenty-first century when many nationalist polities would become obsessed with the 'war on terrorism' and displace thousands in the process (Kerber 2009: 86). They would have had no idea what the scenario of displacement would be when South Asia began its journey of liberation. This book is intended to deal with a particular group—the stateless in South Asia in the post-Independence period. As already stated, it includes people who became stateless due to partition; some were deprived of their nationality as a well-thought-out move when their nations emerged, and others became stateless simply by being unable to prove their nationality. Each of the cases addressed in this book is unique in its own way and adds to the corpus of our knowledge about the vulnerable population whose fight against the daily injustices they face forms so much of the history of South Asia. Statelessness as a phenomenon started with the State itself. The birth of South Asian states marked the birth of statelessness. This moment of birth would be the partition. Our first case will be from the late 1940s.

The global South became decolonised and a number of successor states emerged after India became independent in 1947. The question of statelessness appeared with a vengeance in most of the decolonised world as well as in South Asia. Normally statelessness emerges from a succession of states or territorial reorganisations. But it also emerges from partition, decolonisation and persecution of minorities, and a state's majoritarian bias. With the new citizenship laws in 1948–49 in Sri Lanka, in one stroke hundreds of thousands of plantation Tamils became stateless. It took years of inter-state diplomacy for many of them to get back their citizenship. The partition of South Asia in 1947 and the new borders between India and Pakistan occasioned one of the greatest mass movements of the displaced that the world had ever seen. Thousands of people were left in an indeterminate state, such as the Biharis in East Pakistan and subsequently Bangladesh, the Chakmas in the Chittagong Hill Tracts and then afterwards in Arunachal Pradesh and the plantation workers from the subcontinent. The case of plantation workers is particularly important. All through the early twentieth century, during the nationalist movement in the Indian subcontinent, the case of the plantation workers added fuel to the fire of hatred against colonial elites. These overseas plantation workers were portrayed graphically in nationalist discourses as Indian subjects who were being mistreated abroad by the rich, white plantation owners. Once independence was assured, the leaders of the nationalist movement did not spend their resources on bringing back the plantation workers no matter what the cost (Banerjee 2010: 69–105). Thus, those who were heretofore regarded as sons of the soil were wilfully made stateless and had to fight their own battles against near-bondage conditions and statelessness. It is true that Indians living abroad who could prove that their fathers and grandfathers had Indian citizenship could come back. But many plantation workers could not do so. It took some of the Sri Lankan plantation workers decades to get Indian citizenship. The Sirimavo–Shastri Pact helped confer Indian citizenship on many Tamil-Indian plantation workers but there were thousands who were not beneficiaries of this pact. During the ethnic conflict when they entered India they were marked as refugees, and in a protracted situation they slowly became stateless. Yet, consumed by the euphoria of the emergence of new citizens of brand new states, the world often forgot the plight of these stateless or near stateless people.

All through history with the reconstitution of states, the spectre of statelessness kept coming back to haunt the civilised world. In Eastern Europe, during the days of state socialism formal statelessness was not completely eradicated (Cahn 2012: 298). In the West, statelessness continued with sustained preference being given to people belonging to certain ethnic groups when conferring citizenship. This excluded all those who were considered aliens, such as the Roma people (Milton 1998: 35–48). The events of 1989 ushered in regime changes not only in Europe but across the world. In Europe, there were a number of successor states that tried to address the issue of citizenship. With the return of the question of citizenship, returned the issue of statelessness. Many minority groups lost their status of citizenship as they were considered as alien by successor states. Even the non-successor states severely guarded their rights to confer citizenship. Those who fell through the cracks of citizenship laws often became people with indeterminate status. Under the German Residence Act, for instance, such people came under the provision of 'Duldung' (toleration) which was defined by the German residence law (*Aufenthaltsrechts*) as *vorübergehende Aussetzung der Abschiebung* ('temporary suspension of deportation', of the obligation to leave of foreigners). This made such people mere 'tolerated' people. Their only right was that they would not be expelled by the state in which they lived. Many others became virtually stateless due to lack of proper documents. As Claude Cahn, belonging to the Office of the High Commissioner of Human Rights, has commented:

> Tens of thousands of persons throughout Europe are affected by a lack of documents, rendering them in essence administratively non-existent. Such persons are in principle the citizens of one or more states – they are rarely *de jure* stateless. However, their exclusion has been formalized in such a way that they are in danger of becoming stateless, or of bequeathing statelessness to their children. (Cahn 2012: 308)

Thus, in the post-Cold War period questions of *de jure* and *de facto* statelessness came back to torment the human rights community even further. However, even the UNHCR has confronted the difficulty of explaining these two terms recognising that they were never used in the 1954 Convention. The 2014

Handbook on Protection of Stateless Persons defines a *de jure* stateless as a person who fulfils the criteria presented in Article 1.1 in the 1954 Convention and who are not to be confused with the *de facto* stateless who may not be under UN protection (UNHCR 2014). In the context of India and South Asia it is the question of *de facto* statelessness that has tormented the rights-seeking communities. In this context let us clarify another issue, which is a mapping exercise of stateless persons in India that will inevitably bring in the context of South Asia not just because India is the largest country of South Asia but also because anything happening to India has spill-over effects in other countries of South Asia and vice versa.

In the post-Cold War period there were deep challenges to the nation form in South Asia as well. With the growth of a neo-liberal economy, obsession with national security and the borders escalated, thereby generating multiple conflicts between the states and the communities within them. This appeared to be marginalising more and more people who were now treated as aliens. Actually historically the Indian subcontinent, not unlike many other parts of the world, defined an alien much earlier than the citizen. The Foreigners Act of 1946 preceded the multiple citizenship acts. In fact, here there is no one marker of citizenship but many. One can refer to a passport as a marker of citizenship; another such marker could be the Electoral Photo-Identity Card (EPIC, that is, the voter's ID); a third could be the Permanent Account Number (PAN) Card; and a fourth the Below Poverty Line (BPL) card. The recently introduced Unique Identification Number (UID) or the AADHAAR card is not a marker of citizenship but only of residency in India. There are many who believe that the UID card is an instrument to control undocumented migrants, refugees, stateless and the other unwanted mobile population. Unless a person accesses a court of law, which a common person seldom does, it is very difficult to decipher the status of citizenship of any person in South Asia in the post-Cold War period. Therefore, a large group of people with indeterminate nationality surfaced who were further marginalised when most of their fundamental rights were denied. With marginalisation came massive displacements and more and more people lost their ability to access rights that came with citizenship. This included the people who, say, were forced to live in the *chhitmahal*s (Indo-Bangladesh enclaves in eastern India) or the Tamils of Jaffna or the Gorkhas in northeast India. New fissures and polarisations made newer groups politically vulnerable, with the states denying them access to the rights of citizenship and with the Geneva-based jurists denying them the right to call themselves stateless. This was also a fight between national and international legal regimes where one side said they were citizens who were not being able to access their rights and the other stoically denied that they had any rights to begin with other than the basic right to live. They were the South Asian counterparts of the 'tolerated' category in Europe. Many of the social scientists contributing in this volume would like to define them as *de facto* stateless but the question remains whether any competent state parties have clearly declared that they are not citizens? One can envisage a complicated legal problem here.

However, statelessness is not merely a legal problem; it is also a human problem. In an introductory note to the text of the 1954 Convention relating to the status of stateless persons, the office of the UNHCR reiterates its conviction to uphold the important minimum standards of treatment for those who qualify as stateless persons. It reminds us that stateless persons should have the same rights as citizens with respect to freedom of religion and education of their children. For a number of other rights—such as the right of association, the right to employment and to housing—the note reminds us that stateless persons are to enjoy, at a minimum, the same treatment as other non-nationals. In a world torn by strife and dislocation, historical dispossession and political repression, it is doubtful whether nation-states have advocated, let alone upheld, the noble intent of the 1954 Convention. In fact, talking about the human rights of the stateless appears ironical because Geneva-based legal regimes have made even that category exclusive. A lack is something that is not present; so, how can competent members of state comment on something that is not there? Yet, international legal regimes insist that for these people to access any rights competent authorities have to vouch that there is a lack. A given right can be vouched for; but, can a lack be vouched for? This is the critical question that the social scientists from the global South, who are closely working with the people with the lack at the grassroots level, ask. The other problem in vouching for the lack is that often people belonging to the same family find themselves in different positions in the grid of citizenship and statelessness as the cases of the Chakmas in Arunachal Pradesh and the Hindu migrants from Pakistan show us. The father can be a full citizen, the mother *de facto* stateless, a son *jus soli* citizen, a daughter *de jure* stateless.

In reality, failure to acquire status under the law can have adverse impact on the lives of individuals, including the right to vote, own property, have healthcare, work, send one's children to school and to travel to and from one's country of residence. As a consequence many complications may crop up for those who have no clear or stated and proven nationality including, for some asylum seekers, indefinite detention in a foreign state when that state cannot determine the individual's citizenship. As groups of stateless/near stateless/in-between persons continue to exist in conditions of abysmal disenfranchisement in South Asia and all over the world, this volume delves into certain concrete examples of such human-rights violations to understand the problems of statelessness and people living with the 'lack' in post-colonial South Asia.

In this volume social scientists, human rights activists, lawyers, journalists and jurists of South Asia are clearly in conversation with legal experts on statelessness in the international arena and the book needs to be looked at in this spirit. There are three clear sets of questions that they are grappling with:

- First, how are certain groups and communities rendered stateless or like/near stateless? In the ethnically heterogeneous successor states in South Asia, why are the minorities more vulnerable to statelessness or rightlessness emanating from situations of near statelessness than others? Does protracted refugeehood eventually result in statelessness or near statelessness conditions? Is the distinction between refugeehood and statelessness increasingly wearing thin?
- Second, is the existing legal regime adequate to deal with the problem of statelessness/near statelessness or

in-between people? What has been the experience with case laws in different situations related to statelessness or such lack in India and the subcontinent? Can judicial activism, as evident in some cases in recent years, serve as an effective guarantee?

- Third, do policymakers need to think beyond legal terms? Why does mere judicial activism prove ineffective? Does all this call for activating and strengthening the civil-society institutions and initiatives? But, how does one make the first move towards melting the ice of xenophobia against outsiders who remain in the host country as deprived populations?

This volume is exceptional in many ways. The authors have culled out experiences from seven different cases in South Asia. The research conducted in far-flung areas and among dissimilar groups presents its own particularities—even curiosities. No two experiences can ever be exactly the same. There are, as the case studies amply demonstrate, insidious currents that drive an overarching logic of statelessness, although for purposes of complete accuracy and to be in synchrony with international legal experts we may term it as near statelessness or experiences of people caught 'in between'. The pain of dispossession and non-belonging that scar the quotidian existence as well as the historical survival of near stateless persons, one could say, in not much unalike, despite the varied geographical coordinates or the various ethnic samples. In certain cases, the lesions are open. In others, they pull at the collective physiognomy like a surgically concealed scar. The points of coherence are not easily missed and the contributors of this volume working in various parts of South Asia discovered as much. What may be these ties that bind the stateless or near stateless groups in a terrifying history? This history takes the 1954 Convention not as the end product of dealing with statelessness in South Asia but as the starting point. Most of the authors after extensive conversations with jurists, UN practitioners, legal experts, rights-based activists and scholars realise that all are perturbed over the situation of the stateless in the region and are groping for better solutions.

The volume opens with a case study by Atig Ghosh (Chapter 1). This study of the people of the Indo-Bangladeshi enclaves brings to the fore the issue of legal liminality in what is essentially a fuzzy frontier in the place of an international border between India and Bangladesh. Here, concern for security fuelled by a porous border is coupled with a certain legal porosity that inscribes the life of the *de facto* stateless enclave-dwellers. The fieldwork has brought out the textures of survival strategies of people who literally inhabit the interstices of law and state on the one hand, and society and local economy on the other. It also questions the genuineness of the intention of the two states to resolve the issue of enclaves; history seems to militate against any affirmation of such a genuineness of intent.

The next chapter by Sahana Basavapatna deals with Hindu migrants from Pakistan (Chapter 2). Migrants from Pakistan came to India in three major waves—first, after the partition of India in 1947, then after the 1965 India–Pakistan War and then again after the 1971 War. Except those who came to Jammu and Kashmir, the refugees who came to India after Partition have full legal rights as citizens of the country. Those who came to Jammu and Kashmir are in a special category because of the special status of the state. No one was allowed to buy land in Kashmir without having state citizenship. Without that they ended up being near stateless, *de facto*. Migrants from Pakistan, however, continued to cross over to India even after 1971 and their numbers saw a spurt during the dictatorship of General Zia-ul-Haq and the numbers are believed to have increased after 2005 and then again between 2009 and 2012. After Partition, the Indian state treated Hindu migration from Pakistan as an internal matter of that state. Generally, they are not given the status of refugees. If they wish to become Indian citizens they have to prove their Pakistani citizenship, uninterrupted stay in India for over seven years, and also pay a hefty fee. Considering that these people are the poorest of the poor, the fee becomes a huge impediment for entire families to get Indian citizenship. Some, largely the male members who have to go out and work, apply for Indian citizenship but the women remain like stateless. Further, those who have escaped

Pakistan for reasons of state persecution find it extremely difficult to apply for Indian citizenship as they cannot give proof that they were living in Pakistan. They are then forced to become stateless. There are four different kinds of migration that have taken place from Pakistan to India: (*a*) those who crossed over to the rest of India (excluding Jammu and Kashmir) in large hordes during a calamitous event, like the wars of 1965 and 1971; (*b*) those who crossed over illegally post-1972 in an episodic manner to come and stay with their relatives in India hoping to stay on permanently—this has become increasingly difficult since the fencing of the border; (*c*) those who come legally on short-term visas granted on their Pakistani passports, get them converted to long-term visas in the hope of finally applying for Indian citizenship; (*d*) the migrants from West Pakistan and Pakistan Occupied Kashmir (PoK) who migrated to the Indian side of Jammu and Kashmir in 1947 and then again after the India–Pakistan wars of 1965 and 1971 from the villages in Chhamb and adjoining areas. The first three categories episodically get some legal status for their stay in India but, according to Sahana Basavapatna, those belonging to the fourth category find it impossible to get a legal status and become stateless. Here the issue of statelessness gets enmeshed in inter-state diplomacy. Pakistani migrants who are lucky are able to access citizenship when the situation between the two countries is really at its low point. However, with any signs of improvement of relations the situation for these people gets worse. Those coming from PoK are saddled with the added baggage of suspicion that they are connected with terrorism-related nefarious activities because it is impossible for them to prove otherwise. Accessing any claims to citizenship for them becomes impossible.

Anasua Basu Ray Chaudhury in Chapter 3 focuses on the up-country Tamils in Sri Lanka and India. Her study aptly tells us that the distinction between the stateless and citizens is dangerously thin—particularly for the erstwhile stateless persons who have been given citizenship by law. Surveys found little improvement in the life conditions of these newly made citizens. For them, becoming citizens has hardly made any difference. They continue to remain in a state of near statelessness even after the formal conferral of citizenship.

Suhit K. Sen (Chapter 4) focuses on the 'in-between' Chinese population in Calcutta. From the late 1950s leading up to the Sino-Indian conflict in 1962, the Chinese community in Calcutta and India began to face a number of disabilities imposed by the Union government and the state government of West Bengal. Getting Indian citizenship became difficult and Chinese residents were enjoined to acquire passports from Beijing which many were unwilling to do. Formosan (Taiwanese) passports were not recognised. As a result, many long-standing residents faced the prospect of statelessness. The situation of the Chinese was similar to the Japanese in United States during the Second World War when the American government ordered mass incarceration of the Japanese. According to one social scientist during the Second World War in the United States, 'internment was individual and presumably based on something the individual had done; the mass incarceration that took place was based simply on ethnic origin and geography. Each person interned had a right to an individual hearing, which, in some instances, resulted in release. There would be no such hearings for the incarcerated Japanese Americans; their "guilt" was their ancestry' (Daniels 1993: 27). Similar was the fate of the Chinese in India in the 1960s and until much later. It was only well into the 1990s that citizenship for the Chinese community became *de rigueur*, but that too after a lengthy process of litigation.

Samir Kumar Das and Anasua Basu Ray Chaudhury (Chapter 5) argue that the roots of stateless lay in the way the region was decolonised and partitioned. The case of the Chakmas is instructive in this context. The chapter outlines in brief the evolution of the problem over a little less than the past five decades. It dwells on the legal battle on the Chakma issue and the landmark verdict of the apex court delivered in 1996. Although a landmark judgment, not only could the verdict not bring about any significant improvement in the situation for the Chakmas—as their ethnographic study indicates—but it actually produced a stalemate. They describe the post-verdict stage as one of despair. The chapter reflects on the post-verdict scenario and also on the role of local media.

Atig Ghosh's second paper (Chapter 6), co-authored with Pravina Gurung, brings the case of the Lhotsampas (ethnic Nepali population of South Bhutan) to light. This chapter sets up a historical backdrop to understand the genesis of the problem. As for the Lhotsampas, the Bhutanese monarchy marked them as Nepali aliens and deprived them of their nationality. About 100,000 of them were living in UNHCR-run refugee camps in Jhapa. By 2012, many of them had got third-country resettlement. But those who remain dispersed in India and Nepal are in effect stateless. These southern Bhutanese refugees were deprived of their citizenship by the Citizenship Act of 1985 and then driven away from their homes from 1990 onwards. This happened in the wake of Drukpanisation of the Bhutanese people. The government devised various strategies to bring about a demographic balance that was favourable for a Drukpa/Ngalung nation by reducing the number of Lhotsampas to around 25 per cent of the population and to prevent the demand for democracy from southern Bhutan. It is to the credit of UNHCR that considering the fact that many of these people were forced across the border the UNHCR recognised them as refugees and quickly gave them recognition under the 1951 Refugee Convention. Against this backdrop, Ghosh and Gurung's chapter helps us understand the dynamics of *de facto* statelessness or near statelessness in a situation of protracted displacement and refugeehood.

Subhas Ranjan Chakraborty and Anup Sekhar Chakraborty, in Chapter 7, deal with the Nepali-speaking population in the northeastern states, who may have originated from Nepal during the colonial period but are now living like aliens in India. The authors deftly draw our attention to the wide range of variations that are possible between complete citizenship and complete statelessness. Statelessness, too, may be of many grades just as citizenship is. There is a vast gray area that no strictly legal definition of citizenship can actually capture. Similarly, the sliding of citizenship into statelessness turns citizenship into a sham.

The case studies included in this volume seem to indicate the following: Just as in other parts of the world the phenomenon of statelessness is invariably linked to the vagaries of citizenship and citizenship laws in India and all of South Asia. One reason for this is the way this country and the region has been decolonised. Statelessness in India cannot be described as one single clear category of legal existence; it consists of a range of what Hannah Arendt (1989) had called 'rightlessness', also of several levels of deprivation or enjoyment of rights. Though there is no uniform law on communities whose citizenship status is not clear—also no serious effort to clarify them—there are sometimes good practices of the State with regard to these communities from a humanitarian angle. There have been, for instance, a series of bilateral agreements, understandings and treaties between states—an issue that each of the case studies has demonstrated in meticulous detail and with great vigour. But everything falls short when one falls into the legal rigmarole of whether a certain group can be called stateless or not by international legal parlance. It is more important to define these people by their lack and then try to make enabling conditions for them.

To understand the precarious nature of these uncertain communities leading extremely perilous lives, both historical and legal approaches have been put to use. Additionally, efforts have been made to marshal exhaustive demographic data; albeit and admittedly groups which are deliberately denied nationality by states were found to be extremely difficult to account for statistically. The fieldwork conducted in the disparate geographies of the cases mentioned here has almost uniformly indicated a lack of dependable demographic information. Estimates vary, numbers disagree *inter se* and then the terminology itself becomes an impediment. How many are stateless, how many near stateless, how many indeterminate or in-between and who are tolerated or not? For indeterminate human geographies, this is only to be expected.

It has been emphatically suggested, that in many cases a dialogic route is better than a simple rights-oriented one based on legalities. Keeping in mind the well-meaning international legal framework, it is also important to take into account how people narrate their daily difficulties and how they wish to envisage their future. A solution to the scourge of statelessness can be found only by way of this kind of a fruitful and focused methodological dialogue. It is incontrovertible that South Asia needs clearer legal provisions and greater international commitment insofar as combating statelessness is concerned. In the final analysis, it seems that South Asia, with multitudinous stateless or near stateless groups living in it, needs a regional convention on statelessness in conformity with international norms but addressing the region's particular needs. After all it was the Organization of African Unity (OAU) Convention of 1969 and the Cartagena Convention of 1984 that pushed the margins of rights of refugees. If different groups of stateless people can hold a dialogue with the state governments, UNHCR and amongst themselves, can there be any hope of a solution? Without a dialogic approach and a will to look at the problem from the victim's perspective no hope of a solution can emerge.

In trying to figure a way out for these people, it is not only South Asian social scientists that are concerned but also members of the UN, particularly UNHCR on whose shoulders lies the heavy burden of determining the fate of these stateless people and/or 'in-between' people. Therefore, this volume intends to push the frontiers of rights and propose a path of legal pluralism where laws can reflect the realities of the ground and make the Convention on Statelessness effective in India if not South Asia. Most stateless people for their entire lives fall into the legal conundrum that has been highlighted in this volume and remain people of indeterminate nationality with no agencies campaigning for their rights and looking after their protection. The authors in this volume believe that the ultimate end is not to quibble over who is stateless and who is of indeterminate nationality but to improve the quality of the vulnerable sections of the population and make sure that they have the protection of either a state or an institution.

The editors of this volume take this opportunity to convey to the UNHCR their gratitude for unfailing support and advice and would particularly mention the names of Dominik Bartsch, Radha Govil, Hans F. Schroeder, Roberto Mignone and Kiran Rao for continuing the conversation even when opposed to some of the ideas expressed and also for supporting this study in this day of budget crunch for all humanitarian and human rights work. For Ranabir Samaddar and other members of CRG, the editors can only show their indebtedness for being able to call this wonderful team their own.

ONE

Words of Law, Worlds of Loss

The Stateless People of the Indo-Bangladeshi Enclaves

*ATIG GHOSH**

> Men are conditioned beings because everything they come in contact with turns immediately into a condition of their existence. The world in which the vita activa spends itself consists of things produced by human activities; but the things that owe their existence exclusively to men nevertheless constantly condition their human makers. In addition to the conditions under which life is given to man on earth, and partly out of them, men constantly create their own, self-made conditions, which, their human origins notwithstanding, possess the same conditioning power as natural things. Whatever touches or enters into a sustained relationship with human life immediately assumes the character of a condition of human existence. This is why men, no matter what they do, are always conditioned beings. Whatever enters the human world of its own accord or is drawn into it by human effort becomes part of the human condition. (Arendt 1989: 9)

An Introductory Anecdote

Who remembers Mayamana Khatun of Poaturkuthi in Cooch Behar? Not many; not many even in North Bengal, perhaps, where the district of Cooch Behar is situated. To refresh memory, Khatun, a 29-year-old mother of two, had filed her nomination papers from the Dinhata assembly constituency of Cooch Behar in 2011. She was contesting as a candidate of the Indian People's Forward Bloc (IPFB), or the Janabadi Forward Bloc in Bengali, which had emerged through a split in the All-India Forward Bloc (AIFB). Heavy-weight leaders of the AIFB had gone over to the new party. Among them were Jayanta Roy, the former AIFB Rajya Sabha member; Chhaya Ghosh, former West Bengal minister of agriculture; Amar Roy Pradhan, the AIFB Member of Parliament (MP) from the Cooch Behar parliamentary constituency who had won a record eight times between 1977 and 1999 (ECI n.d.-b); and Dipak Sengupta, the AIFB Member of Legislative Assembly (MLA) from the Sitai assembly constituency of Cooch Behar who had won four times between 1977 and 1991 (ECI n.d.-e). It would seem therefore that such a haemorrhage would affect the AIFB (and the Left Front of which it is a part) adversely electorally in North Bengal, especially when we consider the fact that, ahead of the 2006 legislative election, IPFB had reached an alliance with the Congress, the other major player in the district.

However, that was never the case. The Left Front, along with the AIFB, continued to hold sway in the district, particularly in the four assembly constituencies—Mekliganj, Sitalkuchi, Sitai and Dinhata—which share the border with Bangladesh and, as such, are critically important for the purposes of the present chapter. In fact, in Mekliganj—a constituency which will be given particular importance in this chapter—the AIFB has never been defeated since 1962, barring the single term of the Congress MLA Madhu Sudan Roy between 1972 and 1977 (ECI n.d.-d).[1] Even in the historic 2011 assembly elections, which resulted in a landslide victory for the Congress–Trinamool Congress alliance and the end of the 34-year-long Left Front rule in the state, the Left Front did considerably well in these constituencies. The Congress–Trinamool Congress candidates won in Sitalkuchi and Sitai, but only by a whisker, while Dinhata elected the AIFB candidate by a huge margin.[2]

Mayamana Khatun's chances of winning from Dinhata were non-existent. She was pitted against veritable political titans. The frontrunner was Udayan Guha of the AIFB whose father Kamal Guha, while he lived, was the undefeatable AIFB MLA from Dinhata, elected in 1962 and 1967 and then continuously from 1977 till 2001, no matter which party he represented (in 1996 he represented the break-away group, Forward Bloc [Socialist]) or whom he contested against.[3] The AIFB MLA of Sitai, Dipak Sen Gupta, was brought over to Dinhata to fight against Guha in 1996 and was defeated. Sen Gupta again took his chances in 2001, this time as a Trinamool candidate, and lost yet again, after which he went over to the IPFB.

Udayan Guha's chief opponent was Muhammad Fazle Haque, contesting as an independent candidate. He had been the Congress MLA from Sitai for four consecutive terms between 1967 and 1972 and then got re-elected to the seat again as an independent candidate in 1996 and as a Congress candidate in 2006.[4] In this marathon of mammoths, Khatun should not have even got a mention in the media. Yet, she succeeded in grabbing not inconsiderable media attention (see, for instance, Chakraborty 2011). The novelty factor that got her media coverage at the hustings was the fact that she was the only electoral candidate of post-colonial South-Asian history who hailed from one of the Indo-Bangladeshi enclaves or *chhit*s, as they are called in Bengali. Khatun's case deserves closer attention; therefore, we will have to return to her later. As of now, let us begin by considering the categories of critical concern involved in a discussion of the Indo-Bangladeshi enclaves.

Chhitmahal

The numerous Indo-Bangladeshi enclaves, which are sprinkled along the international border of Bangladesh and India, are collectively known as *chhitmahal* and constitute a bizarre political geography. Most of these enclaves are in the Cooch Behar and Jalpaiguri districts of West Bengal, India, and in the

Kurigram, Nilphamari, Lalmonirhaat and Pachagarh districts of Bangladesh. In his magisterial study of the enclaves of India and Bangladesh, Brendan R. Whyte tells us there are exactly 198 enclaves in total—106 Indian enclaves in Bangladesh and 92 Bangladeshi enclaves in India. These totals, for Whyte, include three Indian and 21 Bangladeshi counter-enclaves inside the exclaves of the other country and one Indian counter-counter-enclave inside a Bangladeshi counter-enclave (Whyte 2004: 194).[5] In an article that has now attained the status of a standard reference, Willem van Schendel mentions 197 enclaves which '[look] like a group of islands of unequal size', and produces a map to substantiate his claim (2002: 117). The map hardly lives up to any standard of cartographic clarity and van Schendel, perhaps realising this lacuna, quickly adds, '[P]ositions and sizes [of the enclaves] are approximate since no map of the enclaves has ever been published' (ibid.: 117n9). All claims to contemporary accuracy are thereby candidly abandoned.

Arindam Kumar Sen confidently asserts that 'there are, at present, 130 Indian enclaves in Bangladesh (20,957.07 acres in total); likewise, there are 95 Bangladeshi enclaves in India (12,289.37 acres in total)' (2003: 4).[6] In Sen's estimate, then, there are no less than 225 enclaves covering an area of 33,246.44 acres. If the estimates of Whyte and van Schendel differ in number by one enclave, Sen's estimate exceeds theirs by more than 25 enclaves. What further complicates the exercise is the fact that the Indian government and its Bangladeshi counterpart will concede no more than 162 enclaves in total—although there is no clarity on how and why this number has been fixed upon—and the Indian news media at large has accepted this (*Bengal Post* 2012; Dasgupta 2011; Dholabhai 2011; Mandal 2011; Nagchoudhury 2011).[7]

Knottier is the problem of calculating the number of enclave-dwellers. Van Schendel does not attempt a methodical headcount. Whyte is cautious:

> With no census conducted in the enclaves since 1951, the population of the enclaves has been the subject of increasingly exaggerated

> estimates, but this study [Whyte's book] has shown that figures for Indian and Bangladeshi exclaves of about 12,000 and 10,000 respectively in 1951 are likely to have risen to no more than 30,000 and 25,000 by 1991, and are still certainly less than 100,000 in total today. (Whyte 2004: 194)

Combining the approximate estimates of population given by those who had come to settle on the Indian mainland from Indian enclaves in Bangladesh, the number of subjects who paid land revenue to the king of Cooch Behar and the partial data that the enclave-dwellers produced by conducting amateurish micro-censuses of their areas of residence in 1996–97, Sen provides the guesstimate that more than 100,000 people lives in the enclaves (2003: 5). Therefore, Sen, writing in 2003, and Whyte, writing in 2004, arrive at contradictory—almost opposite—conclusions.

However, the situation has changed since. In July 2011, India and Bangladesh started conducting a joint census of the enclaves (Mandal 2011). In the process, the Joint Boundary Working Group counted 51,590 people in enclaves on both sides of the border and claimed to have given house numbers to all residents (Dasgupta 2011). This figure completely belies what would now seem to be the over-exaggerated academic estimates. However, the census figures have not been universally accepted, least of all by the Bharat-Bangladesh Enclave Exchange Coordination Committee (BBEECC), an organisation fighting for the rights of enclave-dwellers.[8] BBEECC Assistant Secretary Diptiman Sen Gupta declared: 'In the 37 enclaves in the Dinhata subdivision alone, the headcount is 23,552, according to our report dated June 28, 2010, that we submitted to the government. It is absurd to believe that the total is 51,000 across all enclaves' (reported in Dasgupta 2011). In BBEECC's estimation, around 113,000 people reside in the Bangladeshi enclaves in India and around 186,000 live in those in Bangladesh. It is clear, then, that none of the parties involved in the effort to count heads know with certainty how many people live in the enclaves; we may not be even close to an accurate estimate. About 17 years back, on 20 March 1995, the then Union External Affairs Minister Pranab

Mukherjee (who is now the president) had said on the floor of parliament by way of answering Question no. 809 that '[T]he [Indian] government has no dependable data on the population of the enclaves' (Pradhan 1995: 2). Mukherjee's confession in 1995 seems to still hold true.

From the point of view of human-rights violation, the number of enclaves or the dwellers therein should not matter. However, an exercise in enumeration is never useless, simply because states have a pervasive tendency to think in terms of numbers. Perhaps, the framers of law and makers of policy are shaken out of their paralytic complacency only when huge numbers are forced upon them: this might explain why the BBEECC must insist on almost 300,000 enclave-dwellers, in sharp contrast to the official number of 51,000. Further, at least in this particular case, the number game is important, if for nothing else, then to iterate the already axiomatic: the fecklessness with which the two states of India and Bangladesh have dealt with the lives of the enclave-dwellers. But, what was it that brought things to such a pass?

On the Tracks of a History of Disenfranchisement

The word *chhit* ordinarily invokes a number of senses in Bengali. It may mean a fragment, a piece or portion (as of a cloth); it may mean a drop or a blob (as of ink); alternately, when used to describe a person, it suggests eccentricity—that the person thus described is dotty (Biswas et al. 1988). The appositeness of the first two senses of the word in describing the enclaves is self-evident. However, the third sense is also not wide of the mark. It is rumoured that the enclaves came into being when the king of Cooch Behar and the Mughal *faujdar* of Rangpur used land in high-stake chess games in the seventeenth century—an eccentric origination, surely. Even if one considers the claim made in such a fantastic story to be misleading, it has to be admitted that the enclaves represent a markedly unusual example of political and human geography.

The elusive—almost illusive—nature of the enclaves as seen in the accounts detailed here has ceaselessly invoked another metaphor among commentators: the metaphor of the sea. The *chhitmahal* is a landlocked *archipelago* which strives to create *isthmuses* with the mainland to allow the episodic, tide-like *flows* of the enclave-dwellers going about their quotidian business, failing which, it is feared, *waves* of people fleeing the enclaves may crash upon the mainland.

That the *chhits* paid taxes to one state but were surrounded by the territory of another, however, did not render them intractable to the revenue collectors of pre-colonial and colonial South Asia. Then, as van Schendel correctly says, '[s]overeignty was expressed not so much in terms of territorial contiguity as in terms of jurisdiction and tax flows' (2002: 119). In other words, the overarching anxiety, so to speak, about territorial contiguity comes with decolonisation and what can be described as the birth of the modern nation-state.

When the British withdrew in 1947, they left behind the princely state of Cooch Behar wedged between India and East Pakistan. Two years later, Maharaja Jagaddipendra Narayan merged his state with India. The first section of the 'Cooch Behar Merger Agreement' of 28 August 1949 stated that all land under the jurisdiction of the king of Cooch Behar would become part of the Indian nation.[9] As a result, the pieces of land belonging to Cooch Behar but surrounded by East Pakistan technically became Indian territory and the people residing therein, at least in theory, became Indian citizens. The land belonging to the Rangpur zamindar but surrounded by Cooch Behar, similarly, became Pakistani territory and the residents therein, Pakistani citizens. However, in reality, history followed a more dubious trajectory.

The ambition of the modern nation-state to produce gaunt, clear-cut borders was belied in the fastnesses of North Bengal. The Boundary Commission somewhat hurriedly 'drew' the border between India and East Pakistan, basing itself on district maps rather than field surveys (Chatterji 1999: 185–242). The presence of patchwork jurisdiction further complicated, and ultimately scrambled, the border-drawing exercise in the north. The patchy and amorphous 'border' that emerged therefore was more in the nature of a 'frontier'. Attempts to tame this obstreperous frontier were at the root of the production of a stateless population in North Bengal.

The first such attempt came only in August 1950.[10] It was agreed that district officials would be allowed to visit enclaves if they had a photograph identity card and if their visit was announced no less than a fortnight in advance by telegram. They would then be escorted back and forth across foreign soil. Police officials could also visit the enclaves, provided they wore uniforms and went unarmed. Only mustard oil, kerosene oil, sugar, matches, cloth, medicine and medical appliances could be moved between mainland and enclaves. This meant that commodities could be imported to the enclaves but local produce—especially jute, paddy and tobacco—could not be exported to the mainland.[11] What this in effect meant was that the government continued to control, in however tenuous a manner, the enclaves for the purposes of revenue farming and administration while the people were cut off from their livelihoods. Yet, paradoxically, they were expected to cough up the taxes. The precariousness notwithstanding, one can argue that the enclave-dwellers continued to be citizens of either India or Pakistan—even though the bureaucratic and administrative traffic turned out to be slow, intermittent, and often in the teeth of non-cooperation of the host state (see van Schendel 2002: 124). At this time, citizens of East Pakistan needed no travel documents to visit India, and vice versa.

This changed in 1952 when the two governments agreed to introduce passports and visa controls (Ministry of Foreign Affairs and Commonwealth Relations 1952). The agreement, as if in a fit of forgetfulness, failed to mention the inhabitants of the enclaves. This was the apical moment of territorial closure. That is, if a person of, say, an Indian enclave in Bangladesh wanted to obtain passport and visa for free movement, he/she had to illegally trespass into Bangladeshi territory; if the person managed to reach a border outpost undetected he/she had to be admitted illegally into Indian territory for he/she carried no identification proof, and then travel hundreds of kilometres to the nearest consulate. If all this resulted in the issuance of a passport and a visa, then the person could return to the enclave only till the visa expired. Then he/she had to repeat the illegal procedure all over again. Marooned in their enclaves, sometimes only a few hundred metres away from their mother countries, the people could not leave without infringing the laws of both countries. For the people in the counter-enclaves, the infringement of law and the consequent criminalisation was fourfold. For state officials wishing to visit their enclaves, visas were now required. This created a new obstacle in the enclave hurdle race. By the mid-1950s, both states had largely given up trying to establish their authority and to collect taxes in enclaves. On paper, the enclave-dwellers remained citizens of one or the other country; but in fact they were rendered stateless.[12]

Stateless in Law

It is a curious coincidence that mid-1950s onwards was also the time when international bodies were busy forging and implementing laws to deal with the figure of the stateless person. The two milestone international conventions that have attempted to define the status and rights of stateless individuals and groups, sometimes, though not necessarily, in contradistinction to the refugee, in fact, took place in this period: the 1954 Convention relating to the Status of Stateless Persons[13] and the 1961 Convention on the Reduction of Statelessness.[14] As of 8 December 2013, there were 79 state parties to the Convention of 1954 ('Convention Relating to the Status of Stateless Persons', Chapter V, in UN [n.d.]) and 55 state parties to the 1961 Convention ('Convention on the Reduction of Statelessness' [ibid.]). India and Bangladesh are party to neither. Yet, the conventions, insofar as they provide a working frame for identifying and addressing statelessness, provide us an important legal *entrée* into the problem of the enclave-dwellers. Further, they help us engage with and interrogate the activism of Indian and Bangladeshi governments, or the lack of it, in comparison to how other states in the world have gone about addressing statelessness.

To begin with, however, one needs to establish if, from the legal point of view, the people of the *chhitmahal* qualify as stateless. The International Law Commission observes that the definition of a stateless person contained in Article 1(1) of the 1954 Convention is now an integral part of customary international law. Both the 1954 and 1961 conventions exclusively deal with the issue of statelessness. Both these legal instruments explain statelessness predominantly in two ways: *de jure* and *de facto*.[15] While defining a stateless person as a person who is not considered a national by any state under the operation of its law, Article 1 of the 1954 Convention generally equates the term with *de jure* statelessness. The issue at stake in Article 1 is not whether the individual has a nationality that is effective or not, but whether the individual has a nationality or not in the first place. Although the line between being recognised by law as a national but not being treated as such, on the one hand, and not being recognised as a national at all, on the other, may be fine, the two problems are nevertheless conceptually distinct: the former is connected to the rights that are attached to nationality, whereas the latter problem is connected with the right to nationality itself.

De facto stateless persons, in contrast, are persons who are outside the country of their nationality and hence are unable—or, for valid reasons, are unwilling—to avail of the protection of that country. Protection in this sense refers to the right of diplomatic protection, exercised by the state of nationality in order to remedy an internationally wrongful act against one of its nationals, as well as diplomatic and consular protection and assistance generally, including repatriation. This situation may be evidenced in practice by, for instance, the refusal of the country of nationality to allow him or her to return home, even though it still recognises the individual as a national. In such a situation, the person may also fall under the definition of a 'refugee', depending on the circumstances, and refugees are indeed the numerically most important category of *de facto* stateless persons.

As we have seen, the two legal instruments made to address statelessness—the 1954 and 1961 conventions—have an inherent limitation. In spite of increasing encouragement from international humanitarian organisations to accede to these conventions, the number of state parties remains low and India and Bangladesh are among the non-signatories. However, these two documents are not the only sources of international norms relating to statelessness. The Hague Convention of 1930, the Universal Declaration of Human Rights of 1948, the Convention on the Elimination of All Forms of Discrimination Against Women in 1979, the Convention on the Rights of Child in 1989 and the European Convention on Nationality in 1997 are some of the major attempts at reducing statelessness. Although it may be important to plead for accession to both the instruments of 1954 and 1961, this is not a necessary precondition for action against statelessness and it is important to develop an understanding of the other legal tools that are available. Such is the case because, conceptually, the idea of the state—and by that logic, 'nationality' and 'citizenship'—cannot be dissociated from the idea of statelessness. 'Nationality' and 'citizenship' are two words most commonly used to describe the same phenomenon: the legal bond of membership between an individual and a state. Nationality is an attribute that can be given only by a sovereign entity or the state and states are responsible for protecting the fundamental rights of everybody on their territory including those of stateless persons. Thus, for all activities relating to statelessness, the states are indispensable actors. If a person is stateless, then by the same token he/she is without nationality and citizenship.[16]

Viewed in the light of this elaboration, the residents of the Indo-Bangladeshi *chhit*s are victims of *de facto* statelessness. It is true that in terms of legal straitjackets and definitional imperatives, it may seem that the enclaves are still part of the territory of the mainland state and, as such, the prerequisite for *de facto* statelessness (being outside one's country of nationality) is not met. In theory and in terms of public opinion, they are citizens or nationals of either India or Bangladesh (previously East Pakistan). However, due to the gradual tightening of national territoriality in the early 1950s, they have in practice been rendered *de facto* stateless. Having said this, it must also be mentioned that the enclave-dwellers belong to the somewhat rare group of *de facto* stateless people who are not, at the same time, refugees: for, they live in little 'islets' of land that legally belong to the mother country but are completely cut off from it and surrounded by a foreign country. No benefits of citizenship, of belonging to a state, are available to these people at all.

What about the Nation's Responsibility Towards its People?

We have seen that in the incunabula of nationhood, India and East Pakistan had tried to maintain *status quo* by ensuring the 'right' of passage between the enclaves and the mother countries. Such attempts came to grief due to the disingenuousness at the grassroots level, and misdirected and haphazard policy decisions at the apex. They resulted in *de facto* statelessness. However, while maintaining *status quo* remained the predominant mood in government circles in the late 1940s and early 1950s, the realisation that such an endeavour may prove unworkable was crystallising. In 1950, the chief secretaries of East Bengal and West Bengal:

> agreed to recommend to their respective Governments that in the interest of administrative convenience the question of exchange of these enclaves should be considered at a very early date. For this purpose the two Governments should exchange their preliminary suggestions with a view to a detailed joint examination and possibly also a joint local inspection at a later date.[17]

However, three years passed and concrete steps were yet to be taken (*Amrita Bazar Patrika* 1953). This in a way set the mood for statist activism vis-à-vis the enclaves for good, a mood that has ever since been marked by procrastination and vacillation.

After much deliberation, Indian Prime Minister Jawaharlal Nehru and his Pakistani counterpart Malik Sir Feroz Khan Noon ultimately agreed, for the first time, 'to an exchange of enclaves of the former Cooch Behar State in Pakistan and Pakistan enclaves in India' in 1958. Known as the Indo-Pakistan Agreement of 10 September 1958 (together with the Joint Communiqué or the Nehru–Noon Agreement of 12 September 1958), it also stated in Section 2 Clause 10 that 'exchange of old Cooch Behar enclaves in Pakistan and Pakistan enclaves in India [will be made] without claim to compensation for extra area going to Pakistan' (see Ministry of External Affairs 1958b; also see Appadorai 1982: 96–103; Sreedhar and Kaniyalil 1993: 6–9, 149). In other words, India would not receive compensation for the extra area going to Pakistan. However, the agreement was never implemented. The alleged pro-Pakistan bias of the agreement polarised public opinion in India, and the oppositional parties seized the opportunity to brand it an unconstitutional act. An appeal case was fought up to the Supreme Court of India, stalling any exchange for years. By the time the apex court decided to dismiss the appeal, India and Pakistan were on the brink of the 1965 War. Relations between the two countries did not thaw after this till the break-up of Pakistan in 1971 and the birth of Bangladesh. As such, the exchange of the enclaves was also put on the backburner.

With the birth of Bangladesh (and India's aggressive midwifery, so to speak, in the process), the possibility of an amicable exchange once again presented itself. Prime Ministers Indira Gandhi and Sheikh Mujibur Rahman of India and Bangladesh, respectively, met in New Delhi over 12–16 May 1974, and agreed to exchange the enclaves as soon as possible. An agreement was signed on 16 May 1974, which came to be variously known as the Indira–Mujib Pact, the Land Boundary Agreement, or the Delhi Treaty.[18] It was specified how the remaining sectors of the boundary were to be demarcated. After demarcation, strip maps were to be prepared and signed by plenipotentiaries, so that transferral of adversely held areas could take place by a target date of 31 December 1975, and six months after signature of remaining areas. Apart from setting a deadline (although one which was never met), Article 3 of the Agreement also specified that the residents of the transferred territory were to have the right to remain *in situ* as the nationals of the country obtaining their land—a component that became a standard detail of all bilateral agreements that followed.

This agreement was ratified by the Bangladeshi parliament but was not tabled in the Indian parliament. Like its controversial precursor, the Nehru–Noon Agreement, the Indira–Mujib Pact, too, failed to take off. Ever since, the prompt and amicable exchange of the enclaves has been a standard item on the agenda—almost a ritual talking point—between the two countries, a high-profile avatar of which was the meeting at Dacca of the then prime ministers of India and Bangladesh—Manmohan Singh and Sheikh Hasina respectively—in September 2011. Once again, the commitment to speedily exchange the enclaves following the blueprint laid down in 1974 was reaffirmed, but no definite deadline was specified in the 'Protocol to the Agreement between India and Bangladesh concerning the demarcation of the land boundary between India and Bangladesh' (Ministry of External Affairs 2011). As such, it seems likely that this agreement too, like its illustrious predecessors, will remain a dead letter.

This likelihood may seem too pessimistic to some observers in the light of the developments—political and diplomatic—at the time of writing this chapter in 2015. The possibility of an exchange of the enclaves held adversely by the two countries have again got a shot in the arm following West Bengal Chief Minister Mamata Banerjee's visit to Dhaka and her meeting with Bangladesh Prime Minister Sheikh Hasina on 21 February 2015. Her visit has 'raised hopes' about the 'ratification of the land boundary agreement' which entails exchange of enclaves by both countries (*NDTV* 2015). Banerjee had so far been the fly in the ointment of Indo-Bangladeshi diplomatic *démarches*. Her agreeable disposition in Dhaka therefore has reinvigorated many a crusader and Facebook has been flooded by the enthusiastic declamations of activists and stakeholders. This, they have declared in one voice, is a definitive step forward. Hopes have been further emboldened by the Union Cabinet's clearance of a bill to operationalise the land boundary agreement with Bangladesh (*FirstPost* 2015). The Narendra Modi government's 'capitulation' is somewhat surprising as it has been the Bharatiya Janata Party (BJP), along with other right-wing parties, that have been vehemently opposed to any exchange. However, Manan Kumar in the *DNA* had, some time back, offered a 'change-of-heart' argument in favour of Modi. He wrote in December 2014:

> Modi understands the merits of the LBA [Land Boundary Agreement]. He knows how it can help check illegal immigration by Bangladeshis to a large extent and at the same time help boost the ratings of Sheikh Hasina's Awami League government in Bangladesh. The moderate Awami League government is best bet for India to contain growing Jihadi threat. (Kumar 2014)

The argument seems somewhat forced; however, the cabinet level passage of the Bill cannot be overlooked, whatever be its underlying rationale. Be it as it may, these developments do not dislodge the vexed question why the exchange of enclaves, in spite of highest-level agreements, has never been implemented so far.

Is it a matter of simple administrative fecklessness or is there a deep and deliberate rationale guiding action or the lack of it? Since Bangladesh actually ratified the 1974 Agreement in parliament, it is only justified that one looks more critically at India's sincerity. And, perhaps, it is possible to find an explanation for the decades-long stasis by way of understanding India's somewhat 'oversensitive national ego'. The fact that any exchange of the enclaves will necessarily mean that Bangladesh gains more land from India than the other way round, given that Indian enclaves are more numerous than Bangladeshi enclaves, has rankled the jingoistic pride of certain political groups in India, especially those of the religious right. Further vitiating the mood of the oppositional parties, of which the religious right has over time become a key component, are two major issues, one old and one relatively new. Curiously enough, the geographical foci of both the issues are located in the hook of Cooch Behar comprising the assembly constituency of Mekliganj, which is bifurcated into the two administrative blocks of Haldibari and Mekliganj by the river Tista.

The older issue of acrimony may be termed the 'Berubari affair'. Berubari is not an enclave but a small area of disputed land held by India on its border some kilometres away from the right bank of Tista in the Haldibari block of Cooch Behar. The Agreement relating to Border Disputes (East Pakistan), 10 September 1958, decided to divide Berubari 'to give half the area to Pakistan, the other half adjacent to India being retained by India'. The southern half of Berubari was to 'be exchanged along with the general exchange of enclaves and [would] go to Pakistan'.[19] This decision was met with extreme resistance from the oppositional parties in India, which saw this as an attempt by the government to give away what they considered lawfully Indian territory. The reason for the delay in exchange in the first phase was at least partly because the exchange was linked to the Berubari affair (*Statesman* 1960, 1965g; Jha 1972: 170–74; Chakrabarty 1974: 402–04, 470–73).

The more recent bone of contention that has partly held up exchange and poisoned ground-level relations between the two countries relates to the *chhit* Dahagram-Angorpota, located on the left bank of Tista in the Mekliganj block. Though the controversy regarding this enclave is being described here as one of recent provenance, it too goes back in a way to the first years of independence. Dahagram-Angorpota is the largest Bangladeshi enclave in India, almost touching its mainland. To the east it has the natural boundary of the immense and treacherous Tista River and almost cuts off a portion of Indian territory (Kuchlibari of the Mekliganj block) from the rest of India. Pakistan (before the formation of Bangladesh) had initially and publicly claimed that this *chhit* was connected to it, but in 1953 found out that it had based its claim on a faulty map.[20]

In fact, Dahagram-Angorpota was separated from the Pakistan mainland by about 85 metres of Indian territory that later came to be known as the Tin-Bigha (One-Acre) corridor. What made this enclave's situation somewhat unique is that from the beginning, the state was present in it. Pakistani policemen were stationed there with the permission of the Indian authorities, and without permission when no 'route permit' was given. As a result, whenever the relation between the two countries became tense, its effect was immediately felt in Dahagram-Angorpota. For example, during the Rann of Kutch dispute in 1965 on the other side of India (Jha 1972), Pakistan alleged that Indian troops were being amassed around Dahagram, and that they had entered the enclave and occupied it. India denied these charges, complained about the heavy concentration of Pakistani troops along the border facing Dahagram and accused Pakistan of expelling Hindus from the enclave (*Statesman* 1965a). Soon fighting broke out in the area, resulting in heavy casualties on both sides and the evacuation of border villages. Jingoistic claims were made on both sides: Pakistan decried deliberate Indian aggression while the Indian government assured parliament that 'not an inch of our territory' would be allowed to fall into Pakistani hands (*Statesman* 1965b, 1965c). However, ceasefire was negotiated two weeks later; India issued permits to Pakistani officials to visit Dahagram and some 4,000 enclave people returned to their heavily damaged homes (*Statesman* 1965d, 1965f, 1965e).

After Bangladesh was formed, it seemed that the precarious situation of Dahagram-Angorpota was on the verge of being resolved: a faith that was emboldened by the Indira–Mujib Pact of 1974. In an attempt to achieve two goals by a single stroke of diplomacy, Bangladesh agreed to give up its claim to half of Berubari and four *chhit*s, a total of 18.13 square kilometres, in return for being allowed to retain Dahagram-Angorpota, a total of 18.68 square kilometres. India agreed to lease Bangladesh an access corridor, 178 x 85 metres, through uninhabited paddy fields at the narrowest point between Dahagram and Bangladesh—that is, the famous Tin-Bigha Corridor. What seemed to be a possible amicable settlement on paper, however, turned out to be a much-contested issue around which muscular claims of Hindu nationalism congealed in India. Precisely which side proposed this arrangement remains obscure, although it seems most likely to have been an Indian offer. The Indian White Paper on Tin Bigha said that India proposed it to Bangladesh (High Commission of India 1992), while Bharatiya Janata Party (BJP) broadsheets (that is, the religious right) attacking the Tin Bigha transfer suggest Bangladesh initiated the idea (BJP 1992a, 1992b).

Be that as it may, when nothing transpired in terms of of exchange post-1974, separate negotiations were commenced, whereby a curious arrangement was arrived at in 1982[21] but not enforced till 1992.[22] India and Bangladesh agreed to open the Tin-Bigha corridor intermittently during the day (it was to remain open every alternate hour), while it would stay closed during the night. This arrangement, once implemented, conferred upon Dahagram-Angorpota the dubious honour of being the only part-time enclave in the world. However, the Singh–Hasina Agreement in 2011 did away with this elaborate, and hence somewhat cumbersome, arrangement and opened the corridor permanently, thereby making the enclave a curious form of pene-enclave or 'proruption', which is now connected to the mainland by an 'isthmus' of permanently accessible foreign land. The enforcement of the arrangement did not go unopposed by the religious right. In 1992, inflammatory speeches were made by the BJP against the enforcement of intermittent passage, which was portrayed as a measure that would undermine security and cut off Kuchlibari (see Whyte 2004: 135–59). The opposition of the BJP has continued down the years up to the permanent opening of the corridor last year and thereafter. It may be argued, then, that the controversy about Dahagram-Angorpota, linked to the question of the overall transfer of enclaves as it is, has in the recent years impeded the process of peaceful exchange.

In 2015, however, as has been noted earlier, the position of the BJP has softened under the stewardship of Prime Minister Narendra Modi and it has, at least going by its public stand, agreed to the exchange. However, as anxious commentators in the media are quick to point out, Modi and Minister of External Affairs Sushma Swaraj (another recently emerged strong advocate of the exchange) have to do considerable fire-fighting within the party ranks and fringe right-extremist hangers-on to push this agenda through. Hence, in a milieu of heightened expectations in the borders, all we have had still and again are speeches at the time of writing.

However, merely apportioning blame to the Berubari affair in the initial decades and the Dahagram-Angorpota controversy in the later ones may not fully explain why the two states have failed to implement the exchange of enclaves, despite successive commitments to do so over the years. To understand the full implication of this failure, one will have to delve into the human dynamics of the region.

The World of the Enclaves: The Case of Kuchlibari in Particular

In van Schendel's opinion:

> Although there is a small literature on enclaves, it has no connections to the new literature on nations and nationalism. Most writings on enclaves treat these as geographical curiosities, or as problems of state sovereignty, international law, and efficient administration . . . The literature on enclaves is highly statist. It contains very little information on how social life in enclaves evolves, what identities are created by enclave people, or their ways of coping with ideologies of the nation and citizenship. (2002: 116)

While admitting the value of such an argument, it has also to be emphasised that nothing in the nature of a pure statist narrative exists; it is invariably shot through—is shaped—by the narratives from below, that is, the narratives of the people at large. The state may be mostly an abstraction that plans, legislates, governs, even oppresses, from faraway centres of power, especially when viewed from the perspective of the borders. Yet, it is run by governments that have to seek mandates when their terms end. Mayamana Khatun of the Poaturkuthi enclave, with whom our deliberations had commenced, assumes importance in this context. Khatun was not born in an enclave. It was only through marriage that she came to reside in one and gained first-hand experience of the disenfranchisement faced by the people of the *chhits*. She had to, for instance, give birth to both her children at home 'because the doctors at a hospital in official India refused to admit us. They said they could not treat us because we are not Indians' (Chakraborty 2011). This may have caused her enough grief and anger to contest the 2011 assembly polls as a candidate from the Dinhata seat.[23]

However, the backing she received from the BBEECC had also mattered. Now, BBEECC has been fighting for the rights of the enclave dwellers for some time. It has primarily been insisting that the rapid and effective exchange of enclaves be implemented; while such an exchange is underway, the committee demands that the state government grant 'housing, food, water and nationality' to 'those living in the Indian enclaves situated in Bangladesh' (Diptiman Sen Gupta, quoted in *Bengal Post* 2012). The BBEECC is not a voice in the wilderness. Under the capable leadership of its assistant secretary, Diptiman Sen Gupta, it has been able to mobilise the enclave dwellers and has been organising a number of hunger strikes in the enclaves as well as in Dinhata town to put pressure on the powers that be (*Bengal Post* 2012; CoochBehar Calling 2011). Further, Sen Gupta is not a person without considerable political traction in the area. He is the son of the famous Dipak Sen Gupta, the politician we have already discussed, and this explains why Khatun chose to be a candidate of IPFB. It also explains why a political heavy-weight like Muhammad Fazle Haque had been troubled by a person who was, after all, a candidate representing approximately 300,000 people spread over four assembly constituencies in Cooch Behar, many of them without voting rights (that is, if we accept the BBEECC's estimates). Haque had initially objected to her candidature, saying she was a resident of an enclave in Bangladesh. However, her papers were found to be valid. Khatun's decision to participate in the electoral process to alleviate the life conditions of the enclave-dwellers—

and the insecurity, however inconsequential in degree it may be, it caused the high and mighty—typically demonstrates how discourses of the state get crosshatched with experiences of daily disenfranchisement. Statist activity cannot be delinked from a telling of these experiences.

As we have seen in some detail, the two governments of India and Pakistan/Bangladesh came to a series of understandings to effect the exchange of enclaves. But none ever got beyond paperwork and diplomatic pleasantries. In the meanwhile, the people had to survive—make sense of their survival, devise strategies of survival. In the process, the people in the enclaves were confronted with a slew of identitary options; none of them felicific, but such were the choices. Van Schendel (2002) has identified at least three such self-reckoning strategies of the *de facto* stateless people of the enclaves. Two of them, he argues, are transterritorial: the enclave-dweller could think of himself/herself as a citizen of the patron state. Conversely, a Bangladeshi Hindu could identify with India and an Indian Muslim could identify with Bangladesh. This he calls 'proxy citizenship', which was often induced by the ideological goading of the mainland nation-states. This latter claim, however, does not fit neatly with the evidence collected over time. In fact, van Schendel himself finds a Muslim interviewee residing in an Indian enclave, Md Bokhtaruddin, who describes how Pakistan had disowned him and his community after 1947. Suspended in this void, the third available identitary option was, of course, one of belonging to the enclaves. This is not transterritorial but locally rooted, and one that forms the ideological anchor for bodies such as the BBEECC (ibid.). However, identity as a claim-making device can only be effective when it has numerical, economic and political teeth. The residents of the enclaves, separated by swathes of foreign, often hostile, territory, with no health, education, civic and administrative guarantees, could hardly make such identity claims effectively.

Add to this the atmosphere of coiled tension that often erupts into violent engagements. It is inarguable that the quantum of violence has dwindled since Bangladesh came into being.

However, it has hardly disappeared. The examples are legion. Resisting the ghoulish temptation to inventory the macabre, I would limit myself to one example from either side. In May 2000, a Hindu girl from India eloped with a Muslim youth from South Moshaldanga, a Bangladeshi enclave in India. On 11 May, a crowd of Indians entered the enclave and looted five houses. A week later, the enclave was once more invaded by hundreds of Indians who set fire to 55 houses, wounded 10 people and abducted four, and looted cattle and valuables. Jitendra Nath Roy, 65, of Balapara Khagrabari, the largest Indian enclave in Bangladesh, reports: 'They [Bangladeshis] used to loot our grain silos and rob our cattle by day. When night fell, we would all go and hide in the forests. When they came to rob us during night, they beat up the men and tortured the women.'[24]

From the interviews by van Schendel (2002) and Sen Gupta (quoted in *Bengal Post* 2012) Mentioned previously, another recurrent source of conflict seems to be the attempt of enclave-dwellers to visit nearby markets or avail of other basic facilities. It has to be borne in mind that the predominant occupation of these people is agriculture. Only six or seven out of every 100 people here are landless. In every enclave there are a number of santhals or mundas. They comprise the bulk of the landless population. Most others are middle peasants. Many of them lease land from big peasants to cultivate it under the *barga* system. Up till the 1940s, tobacco was an important crop in this region. However, the lack of modern tobacco-processing technology in this part—especially in East Pakistan—led to the decline in the cultivation of this crop. This has not been a major setback, for the soil here is extremely fertile. Sen's respondents told him they had never seen urea with their own eyes, yet the per-acre yield of *aman* paddy in this region is 18 quintals (Sen 2003: 6).[25] If one compares this with the fact that the average per-acre yield of *aman* paddy in West Bengal, facilitated by advanced farming technology, at 12.67 quintal, then we get a grasp of how fertile this region must be.[26]

If the yield is bounteous, then the enclave-dwellers must participate in the local markets regularly to earn a decent livelihood. However, their political situation turns such an economic logic on its head: what should have proven profitable for them turns out to be a source of great distress and harassment. For an enclave resident, it is a daily ordeal to eke out a living. 'Going to the marketplace to sell anything is a difficult job,' says Syed Ali, 41, from the Mashaldanga enclave. 'The customers know us by face and force us to charge less as we are outsiders. Besides, extortionists threaten to get us arrested as Bangladeshis under the Foreigners' Act, 1946,' he says (reported in Dasgupta 2011).

Many of the Muslim respondents also spy a communal pattern to the arrests. Mohammad Mansur Ali Mian, 76, of Poaturkuthi enclave, is convinced there is a communal angle to the arrests and the extortion. He is seconded by Ahamed Ali Mian, 67, a retired primary school teacher. 'Most extortionists are Hindus. Also, since 1947, there has not been a single case of a Hindu being arrested,' says Ahamed (ibid.). Rana Mukherjee, the Deputy Superintendent of Police (Crime), Cooch Behar district, however, refuses to take such a charge seriously. He argues that if such is indeed the case, then it 'is because the enclaves have a 92 per cent Muslim population.' Even if this were true, one cannot write off the possibility of communal targeting in an area which has seen intense activity of the religious right at least since 1982. Mukherjee, however, does not deny that the enclaves, which are beyond the jurisdiction of the local police, may have become safe havens for cross-border smugglers. 'Even if we have information on opium cultivation and livestock smuggling in these areas, we will not be able to crack the cases,' says Mukherjee (quoted in ibid.).

It is Mukherjee's identification of livestock smuggling as a critical problem that may particularly give us a lead into the nature of communal mobilisation in the area. When I took the road to Kuchlibari, across the Tin-Bigha Corridor, what struck me was the long lines of cows marching languidly, as only herbivores can, along the entire length of the journey—literally hundreds of cows. The city slicker that I am, I put it down to a general picture of rural India and as a historian of nineteenth-century Jalpaiguri, I further tried to intellectualise my observation by reading into it an affinity to cows continuing as a cultural vestige of the *moishal*s in the area.[27] Of course, I was being inane, as I soon discovered while talking to the members of the Farmers' Club at Dhaprahat.[28] The heads of the club told me over cups of syrupy slush that passed as tea that the sight was in no way common. It was specific to the area where livestock smuggling was rampant. Cows were illegally taken across the border to Bangladesh to be slaughtered, especially during Islamic festivals when the demand for the animal peaked. I was not taken in that easily. How could smuggling be carried out in broad daylight under the nose of the Border Security Force-Bangladesh Rifles (BSF-BDR) personnel? They carried forged documents, I was told. This was still more unconvincing. If such a forgery was an open secret, then the security personnel surely would have done something about it. Or else, there could be two possibilities: the government/ security personnel actively colluded with smugglers, or the herders were plying an honest trade. The former, I was told emphatically, was not the case; but all the same, these were smugglers. A little peeved, I decided to address the elephant in the room: What if it was proven beyond all conceivable doubts that this was a perfectly legal trade, would the Farmers' Club still oppose it? A pregnant silence followed. When at last the secretary of the club spoke, he answered in the affirmative. They could not after all allow *cows* to be slaughtered. I had overstayed my welcome. I left.

Returning to the issue of violence, it should be said that, from all accounts, it seems that the quotient of violence perpetrated against the residents of the enclaves was evenly matched in both countries. However, some very perceptive fieldworkers have told me that their extensive travels in the enclaves on both sides have convinced them that the Bangladeshis are harsher in their treatment of the enclave population than their Indian counterparts. Now, this is a very dangerous argument to make: fuel for the hate politics of extremist groups. But one sees why otherwise perceptive researchers would draw such conclusions. When I reached Kuchlibari in Mekliganj block, Cooch Behar, for my fieldwork, *prima facie* what struck me was the ease and comfort the people of the enclaves radiated. They were very happy in India, they said unanimously.

Shambhunath Chowdhury, 44, a resident of the Dhabalsuti Chhit Mirgipur of Bangladesh, declared that if the exchange of enclaves took place following the Singh–Hasina Agreement, he would not leave for Bangladesh. He is a shop-owner and I was buying cigarettes from him. Changing tack, I insisted that they could not be that happy after all, what with statelessness and disenfranchisement. But he would not be budged. 'All of us have Electoral Photo-Identity Cards and ration cards. We are happy here', he argued. But, my importunate inquiry continued, till the irritated Chowdhury told me that there was no longer a way to find out which part was Bangladesh and which India in the Dhabalsuti Chhit Mirgipur area. 'You are standing in Bangladesh, for instance, and my shop is in India', he shot back.[29] Startled, I handed him a five-rupee note in Bhutanese currency that the bus conductor had given me, reaching out over the counter and across an international border. Muhammad Belal Hussain, 51, who has all his land in a Bangladeshi enclave, too, echoed Chowdhury. He would not leave. My insistence on the woes of statelessness, in fact, made me the target of friendly jibes. A few of us—residents of *chhit* and mainland alike—were playing football on the grounds of Upanchowki High School. The ball went over the hedge into the adjoining paddy fields. As I moved to retrieve the ball, my comrades shouted: 'That's Bangladesh. Don't go in without having sought Sheikh Hasina's permission. You might end up stateless'.

The examples of xenophobic violence detailed here militate against such jolly instances of belonging. Accepted *prima facie* and outside their historical context, they may be misguiding. In the case of Dhabalsuti Chhit Mirgipur, for instance, a violent history of forcible expulsion in 1955, one could suggest, may have left only those who wanted to remain, to belong unconditionally. A horde of mainland Hindus had, in 1955, demanded 'the blood of Muslims' and driven almost all dissenters into Bangladesh or the Bangladeshi enclave of Dahagram-Angorpota nearby (van Schendel 2002: 131). But for other Bangladeshi enclaves in the region, the tenor is similar and they do not necessarily have the same historical background. Conducting his interviews sometime before September 2011, Partha Dasgupta found that feelings of insecurity were not strong enough for residents of enclaves in India to want to be part of Bangladesh if given a choice during the proposed swap. Mohammad Ali, 75, of Batrigachha enclave told him, 'We have lived here for generations and will never be part of Bangladesh.' Mansur Ali Mian, who has never resorted to using a fake identity, echoed Ali: 'We consider ourselves Indian and will never leave the country. We are an integral part of India.' The septuagenarian added, 'I only hope I become an Indian again before I die.'

In these cases, one feels a careful audition of what the respondents say holds the key. Gobinda Chandra Das, Kailash Roy, Ashwini Roy, Pramathesh Chandra Roy and Muhammad Jaleel of the Khamcharhat *chhit* had agreed to talk to me. They were repeating the same saga of belonging and happiness: they would not leave for Bangladesh when the exchange happened. However, as dusk gathered in eldritch anticipation, they were all of a sudden speaking of their collective insecurity. 'We will not go. But, those in the Indian enclaves in Bangladesh would come. The government has promised to settle them. Where will the government settle them? There is no land but that of ours.'[30] The Heimlich pleasures of the hearth had slipped surreptitiously into the Unheimlich fear of the Other. The tenuous belonging and wilful oblivion was slipping in the face of the proximate possibility of dislocation. The Indians may come to claim their 'rightful place'; what would the Bangladeshis do? The Stockholm Syndrome, so to speak, was imploding, when suddenly the group, as if collectively, snapped back into confidence. 'But these governments will never reach an agreement; they never have,' they chuckled in self-assurance.[31]

One needs to turn their confident statement into a question: Will these governments actually never reach an exchange agreement? Not even after the Singh–Hasina Agreement of September 2011? Not in spite of the relentless demand and growing clout of the BBEECC in the Dinhata block of Cooch Behar? Going by historical track record, they would not—not India more than Bangladesh. The historical jingoism of the right-wing apart, recently another factor has cropped up to collude against an amicable exchange: the growth of tea gardens in the area. The enclaves, and their attendant instability in national space, have meant that land has been sold dirt cheap here, sometimes at as little as Rs 8,000 per acre, as most of my respondents told me. Major big-business players have bought land and started plantations. More of their ilk is on its way. An eco-tourism resort of the GBC Enterprises Limited has come up a stone's throw away from the Tin-Bigha Corridor, which offers leisure walks through tea gardens, a modern saloon and massage parlour. If one provisionally accepts Giorgio Agamben's contention that attributes a determined character to the state and a determining power to the economic forces of capitalism that conditions particular forms of the state then the neo-liberal Indian state is unlikely to rip through the tightening tangles of big investment.[32] In fact, post-liberalisation, it never has. But, I offer this only as a possible outcome. Who knows, the nation-state may still surprise us and Agamben.

Conclusion

The states of India and Bangladesh cannot grasp the everyday experience of living in an enclave—its textures and tangles—if they keep their noses buried resolutely in the ever-accumulating paper trail of bilateral agreements that fail. The letter of the law creates categories that are engaged with and transformed creatively as part of the people's lived world. Such quotidian negotiations have produced in Cooch Behar a vast array of experiences of territorial belonging that range from what the legislators understand as an enclave, to what is described as mainland. In the process, both have been reworked and redefined, at least in terms of how people have coped over the years with such abstract legal categories. A simple rendition of the *chhitmahal* as a landlocked archipelago of enclaves obfuscates these myriad spatial configurations and strategies that have emerged in the area over 60-odd years since Partition.

Not every bit of non-enclave border territory is settled in terms of belonging to a country: the case of Berubari demonstrates this. Then there are, as we have seen, counter-enclaves, that is, enclaves completely enclosed by another enclave. Shalbari, the second largest Indian enclave, for instance, encloses four Bangladeshi exclaves. There is also a globally-unique counter-counter enclave; the largest Indian exclave, Balapara Khagrabari, embodies one Bangladeshi exclave, Upanchowki Bhajni, which itself embodies an Indian exclave called Dahala Khagrabari, thus making the last one a counter-counter enclave. Then, there existed until very recently arguably the world's only part-time enclave, Dahagram-Angorpota, which after September 2011 has assumed the dubious character of a pene-enclave or proruption. Pene-enclaves are, however, not unknown to the residents of the area, though they have curiously escaped academic as well as journalistic scrutiny. One example of a pene-enclave that immediately comes to mind is Kalsi para (or simply Kalsi), the Muslim-majority Indian proruption into Bangladesh located in Kuchlibari (a bulbous Indian landmass that projects into Bangladesh, north of the Jikabari Border Outpost or BoP1). Though all my respondents pointed out that it is not a *chhit* technically, they unanimously concurred that the life conditions there best represent what is normally considered the life conditions in an enclave: it has no electricity; no healthcare; it is cut off from the mainland by a towering barbed-wire fence—its heavily guarded, solitary gate opens only during the day; a BSF camp is located within it, which keeps a close watch on activities of its residents. When I went to speak to the residents of Kalsi, a BSF *jawan* was deputed to follow me around.

Then there are the elusive enclaves. My respondents were mostly at a loss to point out where exactly a *chhit* commenced and where it ended. They continuously bickered over the coordinates of enclaves. If someone declared a particular hedge as the beginning of a *chhit*, then the next person contradicted him and pointed out a windbreak of trees in the distance as the place where it really began. My plucky companion Shyamal, 21, who drove me around the area for 10 days, would then tell me in private on our way back that 'these villagers' knew nothing. Actually the *chhit* in question began where the cows were grazing. Which cows, I wondered to myself? There are cows all around. In this sense, the cartographic bickering that has gone on between the state governments are not very unlike what the people do on the ground. All this is not to say the *chhit*—the reality of it as a territorial entity and issue of international dispute—is a myth, but that the conduct of everyday life at the border will be rendered impossible if one were to be continuously acutely conscious of its impedimental existence; hence, perhaps, the subconscious suppression of its solidity.

That is to say, there are borders in the mud that may prove elusive and there are borders in the mind that are terrifying. The *chhit*, in this latter sense too, exists. There is always the fear of imminent foreignness: the scary prospect of being prosecuted as trespassers by the national selfish giants. Between the polarities of law and crime, we know, there is the immense range of quasi-legality, compromise, necessary illegality, malfeasance, petty crimes and so on, and obviously the people of the enclaves have liberally made use of these strategies to survive. In doing so, if these people have normalised their state of precariousness, then it amounts to a psychopathological condition that is best avoided. In this sense, the BBEECC is correct in demanding an immediate and effective exchange of the enclaves. But, in the process of achieving such an exchange—if, that is, the states in question are at all serious about it—they would do well to take into account the way people have recreated their *modus vivendi* in the trackless and patchy border-frontier of India and Bangladesh. It remains to be seen what kind of an impact the new developments of 2015 will have on the people of the enclaves.

Notes

* This chapter includes content drawn from various Calcutta Research Group publications, which have been used with permission.

1. For 1962, 1967, 1969, 1971 and 1972, see the 'Statistical Reports of Assembly Elections' on the relevant years for West Bengal (ECI n.d.-a).

2. At Dinhata, Udayan Guha of AIFB defeated the independent candidate, Muhammad Fazle Haque, by 30,026 votes. At Sitalkuchi, Hiten Barman of Trinamool Congress defeated Communist Party of India

(Marxist)'s (CPI[M]'s) Biswanath Pramanik by a slender margin of 257 votes, even though Barman had for decades been a front-line AIFB leader who, sensing the impending change in political dispensation, had shifted loyalty at an opportune time. At Sitai, Congress's Keshab Chandra Ray fared no better than Barman and defeated AIFB's Dipak Kumar Roy by 1,577 votes. For Dinhata, see Empowering India (n.d.-a); for Sitalkuchi, see Empowering India (n.d.-c); for Sitai, see Empowering India (n.d.-b) .

3. For 1962 and 1967, see the 'Statistical Reports of Assembly Elections' on the relevant years for West Bengal in ECI (n.d.-a, n.d.-c).

4 For 1967, 1969, 1971 and 1972, see the 'Statistical Reports of Assembly Elections' on the relevant years for West Bengal in ECI (n.d.-a, n.d.-c).

5. Whyte's book is particularly useful for its exhaustive annexure; almost all official and semi-official documents as well as the propaganda pamphlets of political parties that have originated after 1947 are represented here. They are the unabridged reproduction of the original documents and I have often referred to them without acknowledging my debt to Whyte. As such, I take the opportunity here to apologise for the lapse. Fortunately, Whyte's book can be accessed at: http://dtl.unimelb.edu.au/R/RMLYH2U45FV5PF1U6XV5I3D1FPLQGG3JGJG6MGGSFSL8K16NDH-01756?func=dbin-jump-full&object_id=66438&pds_handle=GUEST (accessed on 17 October 2011).

6. Since Sen gives no citation to corroborate his claim, one assumes that his estimate is based on the fieldwork he conducted between 1998 and December 2002, in the course of which he interviewed 9,755 displaced families scattered over North Bengal. See, 'Bhumika' [Introduction] to Sen (2003). An English version (though not an exact translation) of this article was published a year later as Sen (2004).

7. A rare exception is Arpita Chakraborty's article 'She's the Reason' (2011) in *The Indian Express*, which gives the number of enclaves as 198; journalists in the early years after Independence, too, had a figure of around 197 in mind. Niranjan Majumder, for instance, writing for *The Statesman* on 1 May 1965, famously wrote: 'Surgeons have been known absent-mindedly to leave behind in the belly they had cut open for an appendix or an ulcer, an old swab or a towel. Sir Cyril Radcliffe, Chairman of the Boundary Commission in 1947, left a mere 123 Indian enclaves in East Pakistan and 74 Pakistani enclaves in India, which have in recent weeks been the cause of some belligerency'.

8. We will have the opportunity to return to the BBEECC in greater detail when we take up Mayamana Khatun's case later in the chapter.

9. For the text of the 'Cooch Behar Merger Agreement', see Majumdar (1977: 40–42).

10. *Decisions taken at the 17th Chief Secretaries' Conference held at Dacca on the 29 and 30 August, 1950*; in Government of East Bengal, Home [Political], Confidential Records, B. Proceedings (hereafter abbreviated as

CR; these records, available at the National Archives of Bangladesh, are quoted from van Schendel [2002], unless specified otherwise). Overtures to facilitate communication between the enclaves and their mother countries had started in 1947, but had come to nought. See, for example, *Decisions taken at the Chief Secretaries' Conference held at Calcutta on the 7–9 April, 1949, Sixth Conference*, p. 5; in: CR 3C1-4/50 (September 1961).
11. *Decisions taken at the 17th Chief Secretaries' Conference held at Dacca on the 29 and 30 August, 1950*, p. 4, in CR 3C2-5/50 (2237-55, March 1953).
12. Jurists may question the basis of this assertion. The test of being stateless, they may argue, is whether the mainland state considers inhabitants of the enclaves to be. There does not appear to be evidence that Indian or Bangladesh did not consider inhabitants of their respective enclaves not to be their citizens; not the difficulty of such inhabitants to procure nationality documentation. However, in the introduction to this volume, it has been already argued that statelessness is not merely a legal problem; it is most importantly a human problem.
13. The Convention was adopted by the United Nations Conference on the Status of Stateless Persons, held at the Headquarters of the United Nations in New York during 13–23 September 1954. The Conference was convened pursuant to Resolution 526A (XVII) of 26 April 1954 of the Economic and Social Council of the United Nations. For the Final Act, recommendation and resolution adopted by the Conference, see UN (1960a: 117); also see UNHCR (1954).
14. The Convention was adopted and opened for signature by the United Nations Conference on the Elimination or Reduction of Future Statelessness, convened by the Secretary-General of the UN pursuant to General Assembly Resolution 896 (IX) of 4 December 1954. The Conference met at the European Office of the United Nations at Geneva from 24 March to 18 April 1959, and reconvened at the Headquarters of the UN at New York during 15–28 August 1961; C.N.472.2011. TREATIES-2 of 19 July 2011 (proposal of corrections to the original text of the Convention [Spanish version] and to the certified true copies). Also see UNHCR (1961).
15. It is important to note that *de facto* statelessness is not referred to in the 1961 Convention nor in the 1954 Convention, but in the Final Act of the 1961 Convention. In this chapter, *de facto* statelessness is legally referred to in accordance with the working definition of the term as set out in the UNHCR's guidelines. However, it is never discussed as completely divorced of its lived, human dimension.
16. I am greatly indebted to Samir Kumar Das and Anasua Basu Ray Chaudhury for helping me understand the basic structure of international law on statelessness and its applications.
17. *Decisions taken at the Chief Secretaries' Conference held at Calcutta on the 21 and 22 April 1950, Fourteenth Conference*, p. 4, in CR 26A-1/50 (1050-69, December 1952); cf. CR 31-68/52 (102-6, January 1954).

18. For the text of the agreement, see Whyte (2004: 378–80).

19. See Section 2, Clause 3 of the 1958 Agreement, in Ministry of External Affairs (1958b).

20. CR 1B2-28/52 (85–89, July 1955), cf. CR 1B2-3/53 (2057–84, January 1955).

21. *Tin Bigha Lease Terms Agreement*, 7 October 1982; for the text see Whyte (2004: 382–83).

22. 'Tin Bigha Lease Modalities', 26 March 1992; for the text see Whyte (2004: 384).

23. Again to preempt juristic nitpicking, it may be argued that the doctors are not the competent authority from the perspective of determining how each state recognises those residing in their enclaves under the operation of their respective laws. The rebuttal to this question is commonsensical: the 'competent authorities', whichever these may be, do not live in the enclaves and share the lived horror of the people therein.

24. The cases have been quoted from van Schendel (2002); Sen (2003).

25. A quintal is a unit of weight equal to 100 kilogrammes.

26. Report of the Director of Agriculture, Evaluation Wing, quoted in Sen (2003: 6).

27. *Moishal*s were pre-colonial cow- and buffalo-herd keepers whose annual pastoral migratory patterns encompassed the full northern swathe of Bengal Proper until its disruption by colonial state-making.

28. The nonprobability sampling strategy deployed in conducting the interviews at Mekliganj is one of purposive sampling. However, it has to be admitted that given the gender of the interviewer and the nature of society and religion in the enclave area, the interviewer found it difficult to interact with women. Almost always, the men stepped forward to answer the questions I put to women, or to participate in conversations I attempted to initiate with women, and the women gladly allowed this. Does such a male bias of the interviews camouflage the reality of existence in the *chhit*s? It surely does: at least in the sense that it dilutes, or renders comparatively mild, the experience of statelessness. Given the persisting patriarchal nature of our society, the enclave women are at least doubly marginalised—in terms of being stateless, of course, but also in terms of being 'a woman' in a male-normative society. Mayamana Khatun's case therefore assumes even greater significance in this context.

29. Interview with Shambhunath Chowdhury, Dhabalsuti Chhit Mirgipur, September 2013.

30. Interview, Kuchlibari, September 2013.

31. Ibid.

32. For an elaboration of the proper role of politics in contemporary life, see Agamben (1993, 2000).

TWO

The Remains of Partition?

The Citizenship Question of Stateless Hindus in India

SAHANA BASAVAPATNA

India's asylum policy is better understood as a constantly changing set of rules that are dictated by political considerations. One can discern a clear 'policy' on managing its refugee population only in the case of those who migrated to India in the wake of Partition. Confronted with an estimated 14 million people who, by circumstances, were variously called displaced, oustees or refugees, the Government of India found itself in the unenviable position of having to deal with a large number of people and unexpected events on a continuing basis in the years following Partition (1947–57). For the newly elected government, the responsibility to rehabilitate and resettle refugees was part of its 'nation-building' project (Samaddar 2003: 151). Most Hindus (it may be incorrect to suggest that all Muslims left India or decided not to leave the newly created state of Pakistan) were cared for, given all possible support to start their lives afresh and settled.

Sixty years into, and an independent India presents an entirely new scenario. Even while the legacy of Partition continues to touch the everyday lives in Pakistan, Bangladesh and India, the lens through which the migrant or citizen living in either of these countries can be viewed has changed radically over the decades. A number of examples may be noted in passing. The

Urdu-speaking Muslims in Bangladesh fought a bitter political battle before they were considered formal citizens in the country. Muslims in India are constantly challenged about their nationalistic credentials, in what is projected as a 'Hindu' India. The Jummas of the Chittagong Hill Tracts (CHT) continue to live a life of limbo in Arunachal Pradesh and have been seeking Indian citizenship, driven as they were by projects in CHT. The Islamicisation project in Pakistan in the decades since Zia's rule has left not only the minority Hindus and Christians persecuted, but also fellow Muslims, such as Shias and Ahmadias, who are considered *kafirs* (Naqvi 2012; Samantaray 2012).

These developments are at once the cause and consequence of the dilemma of confronting the idea of citizenship in each of the South Asian countries because of what Samaddar calls 'reflexive nationalism', with the result that 'supression and sufferings due to forced migration' is made 'tolerable to the ethics of a nation' (2003: 28). The patterns of migration are also a veritable mirror, indicating how various communities are at once the victim and the perpetrator. It is this additional aspect that makes the question of citizenship in the South Asian subcontinent a highly contested affair. Sharing similarities with the examples noted here are the Hindus of Pakistan, who form the vantage point with which to analyse the asylum policy in India.

This chapter focuses on two groups of people, a majority of whom are Dalits/adivasis who migrated not only to different parts of the country, but also at different points in time from Pakistan. One of the groups is the lower-caste population from Sindh that has been migrating to India in recent years. The second group consists of the approximately 500 families[1] who decided to travel to Jammu from Punjab at the time of Partition in 1947. Their population today is approximated to be about a lakh (100,000). While they are considered citizens of India, they remain illegal migrants in Jammu mainly due to the constitutional status of the state. This community can be said to occupy the margins of the debate on citizenship and rights in the politics of Jammu and Kashmir. The West Pakistani refugees fled to Jammu because of the social ties but remain stranded even after 60 years of India's Independence. What complicates the issue of citizenship for this group is not so much the citizenship in India, but citizenship of India as *residents* of the state of Jammu and Kashmir.

In keeping with the larger project on statelessness conceived by the CRG, this chapter is concerned with understanding the processes by which the migrating population become stateless in the subcontinent. I hope to understand whether these two groups of Hindus can be understood as the remains of Partition, indicating that Partition refugees may have been perceived as an asset in the nation-building enterprise in the years and decades following the event, but are no longer considered so. Assuming that this is how one may understand the circumstances of these groups of refugees, this chapter proceeds to understand why.

The research for this study was carried out for little over two weeks in Jammu and Jodhpur in October and August–September 2012 respectively. The research in Jodhpur was conducted in loose collaboration with Seemant Lok Sanghatan (SLS), an organisation that works throughout Rajasthan providing assistance to refugees and campaigning for cross-border peace initiatives. In Jodhpur, interviews were conducted with refugees in a temporary/transit camp called the Al Kausar camp located in the city's outskirts near the famous Dali Bai Temple. The population of this camp at the time of interviews was a total of 371, which included women, men, children and the very old. Due to time constraints and availability of volunteers, interviews were restricted to this camp alone, although the researcher was able to visit the Kali Beri colony, set up by the Rajasthan government in around 2003. Interviews were also conducted with volunteers Govardhan and Prem Chand as well as Hindu Singh Sodha, the head of the Pak Visthapit Sangh/SLS.

In the case of West Pakistani refugees, the researcher travelled to Kathua, about an hour's drive from Jammu, where a number of families live. In Kathua, a monthly meeting of West Pakistani refugees in the locality is held on the 15th of each month. Interviews with refugees were conducted in one such meeting held on 15 October 2012. In addition, interviews were held with journalists such as Ved Bhasin of *Kashmir Times*; Krishan Dev Sethi, former General Secretary of the National Conference and later associated with the communist movement in Jammu; Professor Rekha Choudhury of the University of Jammu; and Labha Ram Gandhi, who heads the West Pakistani Refugees Action Committee, based in Jammu.[2]

This chapter is divided into two substantive parts. Apart from the introduction and the conclusion, the section titled 'Migration Narratives from Sindh and Jammu' consists of personal accounts by refugees. Going back and forth through contemporary political history, this section is intended to also map events that are intimately connected with histories and politics of India and Pakistan. Thereafter, the section titled 'Citizenship and Statelessness' considers the process by which a community is rendered stateless. It also looks at the operation of law vis-à-vis these two groups of Hindus and whether in law, they may be termed as stateless.

Migration Narratives from Sindh and Jammu

What distinguishes the lower-caste refugees of Sindh and Punjab from asylum seekers from other regions of the world living in India is that irrespective of what labels are given to explain their legal state of being—migrant, refugee, stateless, displaced—their singular aspiration and claim is to be considered citizens and allowed to live in India with all rights and entitlements that flow from citizenship. The similarity therefore ends with the fact that such claim-making—of citizenship—is possible because, in the words of Ritu Menon, the Hindus, like the ones that arrived during Partition, were never considered aliens. They were the 'natives returning home' (quoted in Samaddar 2003: 156). The lower-caste Hindus from Sindh, those who have arrived in the last decade and those who have lived in Jammu for the last 60 years, have shown different trajectories of legal existence in India. The reasons why such claims to citizenship are easily made are that these two groups of people *belong* in South Asia; the wealthier class that preceded this group have made quiet entries and settled in various parts of the country.

Hindu Refugees in Jammu

Most of the Hindu families, an estimated 18,428[3] according to recent estimates of the West Pakistan Refugees Action Committee, 1947, belong to the lower castes (and include Ravidas, Megh); they are landless agricultural labourers who left little behind in the areas that went to the territory of Pakistan. According to Joginder Pal Singh,[4] the Tehsil President of West Pakistani Refugee Action Committee, these families have lived in Jammu, Kathua and Rajouri for the last 60 years unrecognised in law by the State of Jammu and Kashmir. Some families reportedly have moved out of the state but most others came because of family ties.[5] The latest census of 2011 does not count population on the basis of place of origin or community. It appears that it was only in around 2012 that the West Pakistani Refugee Action Committee began to take stock of the population of West Pakistani refugees in Jammu. The organisation began to mobilise people in a more serious way in around 2004.

The West Pakistani refugees are considered citizens of India, but not of Jammu and Kashmir. To make claims against the state and be entitled to basic services, a Permanent Residence Certificate under Article 6 of the Jammu and Kashmir Constitution is mandatory. Joginder Pal Singh explains that the localities do not have provision for water, land or other monetary assistance; children are unable to enrol in schools; BPL cards are not issued; and some efforts to provide employment in state services that was formulated by way of recruitment in the Indian Reserve Battalion was never implemented.[6] Most people live in huts/jhuggis and make a living as wage labourers,[7] domestic helpers[8] and beggars.[9]

The Hindus from Sindh

The lower-caste refugees from Sindh are the Bhils, Meghwals and Mali, who make up the community that is fast dwindling in Pakistan. Journalist Bharat Bhushan (2013) notes that as per the 1951 census, the population of Hindus was reported to be 22 per cent (which included East Pakistan); much later in 1998, which is the last available census, it was said to be 1.6 per cent (Government of Pakistan n.d.).[10] The lower castes make up 0.25 per cent of the total population of Pakistan. Further, Tharparkar district in the southern part of Sindh accounted for high Hindu concentration until 1970 after which the Hindu population reportedly reduced to 30 per cent (Bhushan 2013; Sikand 2009).[11]

A majority of the refugees interviewed have lived in Sanghar (Tando Adam village) and Mathihari districts (Rana Bhugiyo village) of Sindh and do not intend to return. All those who spoke to this researcher noted that they had been planning to leave Sindh for over several years but were unable to travel sooner.[12] Most refugees staying in the camp are landless labourers, earning Pakistani Rs 50 per day, who have worked as bonded labourers on agricultural lands owned by Sindhi Muslims. Some also worked as daily wage labourers during the non-agricultural season or as drivers.[13] Most come from an extremely poor economic background and therefore it took anywhere between a few years to about a decade before they were able to save money for the passport and the visa.

The reasons for leaving Pakistan included systematic discrimination against the Hindus, with no avenues for redress.[14] Many reported that they were personally aware of young girls being abducted and forcibly converted to Islam.[15] There was a general feeling of a lack of safety and insecurity amongst most refugees. Men in particular stated that they did not feel that their families were safe[16] and had to live with the constant fear of abduction or any other kind of violence. While some hear about abductions, some others report their own close women relatives being abducted[17] and huge sums of money extorted in return. It was also reported that Hindus in general and the younger lot in particular are called *kafirs*.

Rewaram, who has lived in India for about a decade, says the Hindu–Muslim relations were amicable until about 30 years ago.[18] He says that unlike the older zamindars, who did not indulge in name calling, their sons started calling him *kafir*. Bharat Bhushan (2013: 107), writing about Tharparkar, in particular, shares a similar narrative. He states,

> In the past, Tharparkar never witnessed inter-community or communal strife—not even in 1947 when the northern parts of India and Pakistan were burning. The relations between the Hindus and the Muslims have traditionally been one of tolerance . . . [where people of both communities shared] a common culture and worship[ped] common deities, although by different names. The Hindu Meghwals of Rajasthan and Sindh, for example, worship Baba Ramdevji, believed by some to be a fourteenth-century Tanwar Rajput King, while the Muslims of the region worship him as Baba Ramsaa, Ramaa Peer or Ram Shah Peer. The area is influenced by Sufi traditions and there has never been any major anti-Hindu violence in Sindh.

Despite this, Bhushan (ibid.) notes that Hindus have continued to flee. This is because,

> Each time there is a war or communal development in India such as the Babri Masjid demolition in 1992 or major communal violence such as the one in 2002 in Gujarat, the inter-community strife between the Muslim majority and the insecure Hindu minority of Pakistan increases and becomes more apparent . . . The destruction of the Babri Masjid, for example, led to the burning of Hindu temples in Sindh and Southern Punjab. The backlash against the Hindu minority in Pakistan even saw some killings which again resulted in a fresh spurt of migration to India.

The contemporary social and political picture, however, has changed. The causes outlined by Bhushan remain while others may also be noticed. Interviewees reported, for instance, that there is a constant fear of conversions[19] under duress. Discrimination on the basis of religion appears to take on different forms. Chetan, who fled Mathihari zilla along with his family, reports that Hindus are unable to complete the last rites of their loved ones.[20] Men also complained that as labourers, there is constant fear of insecurity, violence and the refusal of the landlord to pay wages. Harichand, for instance, stated that women can work in the fields only in the presence of a male escort. As far as their earnings are concerned, labourers are promised 50 per cent of the produce (most work on cotton, sugarcane and wheat farms) but are never given their share. Most work as bonded labourers. In addition, there is little security of work since they are likely to be asked to leave.

Rewaram is among the first people from the Bhil community to come to India in the late 1990s. He left for Sindh again and returned around 2005. When asked why his family migrated to India, he says, *hukumat ka koi sahara nahin tha* ('we did not feel supported or secure in Pakistan'). His family has never been directly attacked or discriminated, but he says that he saw other Hindus being targeted and facing violence. He felt that if other Hindus could face such insecurities, it could happen to his family too. In Sindh, Rewaram lived in Tindo Sumro village, in Tando Allayar tehsil and district (this was part of the Hyderabad district earlier). Rewaram's father worked as an agricultural labourer in Bhaddi (in Shiv Tehsil, Jaisalmer) and migrated seasonally to Sindh province of undivided India. During the drought in the 1940s, which a number of individuals recollected,[21] water was a problem in Rajasthan. As a result, in 1947, his father decided to stay back in Sindh. Rewaram also started working as an agricultural labourer. They cultivated wheat, sugarcane and cotton. Earlier, half of the wheat would be given to the labourer. They also had animals, including goats and cows. His family, which includes five children, were unable to come to India all at once. He says that the Indian government does not want Sindhis like him to migrate to India permanently. Rewaram can apply for citizenship, he says, but he does not have the money.[22]

Citizenship and Statelessness

Stateless in Jammu and Kashmir

The State of Jammu and Kashmir has 'special status' under the Indian Constitution. Under Article 370, which is 'a special provision for amending the Constitution [of India] to the State of Jammu and Kashmir' (Anand 2011: 111), limited autonomy is granted to the state, curtailing the powers of the Parliament. In view of its special status, the State of Jammu and Kashmir is regulated by its own constitution; the Constitution of India has no application, except under certain circumstances.

The Constitution of Jammu and Kashmir defines the rights, duties and privileges of its 'citizens' who under Article 6 are termed 'permanent residents'. It may also be noted that:

> Part II of the Constitution of India dealing with Citizenship was *not* made applicable to Jammu and Kashmir State. Even Entry 17 of the Union List, which empowers the Union Parliament to make laws for the State on matters of '*Citizenship naturalisation and aliens*' was modified to read '*naturalisation and aliens*' in its application to Jammu and Kashmir State; the omission of '*citizenship*' from this entry in its application to Jammu and Kashmir, in fact, meant that in the State the old State Citizenship law prevailed. Thus, the people of Jammu and Kashmir State were 'protected subjects' in the rest of India and not 'Indian citizens' even after India became a Republic in 1950. (ibid.: 197, 199–201; emphasis added)

The Partition refugees from Punjab who migrated to Jammu have been expressly denied the status of permanent residents (Bashir 2012). However, they are considered citizens of India in all other respects. The most common example given is that while they can vote in the parliamentary elections, they do not have the right to vote in the Jammu and Kashmir Assembly elections. The West Pakistani Refugees Action Committee, however, argues that this class of refugees were deliberately excluded. It says,

> J & K Constitution was implemented in 1957 after ten years of migration [of the lower caste Hindus from Punjab to Jammu] but while determining the citizenship of the State under Part III, Section 6 of the J & K Constitution we people were ignored by the constitution makers. (West Pakistan Refugees Action Committee 2012)

The barriers to their legal status in the Constitution of Jammu and Kashmir were raised in a petition filed before the Supreme Court late in 1980.[23] Bachan Lal Kalgotra, who at the time coordinated the work of the Action Committee of West Pakistani Refugees, argued that they should at least be given the same rights as are given to those who voluntarily migrated to West Pakistan at the time of Partition. The petition initially challenged the constitutional validity of the Jammu and Kashmir Resettlement Act, 1982, under which all these rights are given to erstwhile residents of Jammu and Kashmir who had voluntarily migrated to West Pakistan at the time of the partition of the country in 1947, and to their children, and who may now choose to return to Jammu and Kashmir. The Court recognised that the Hindus were not 'permanent residents' of Jammu and Kashmir as per Section 6 of the Jammu and Kashmir Constitution. It also pointed out that this provision cannot be called into question in a court of law as violative of Part III of the Constitution because of the Constitution (Application to Jammu and Kashmir) Order, 1954 issued by the President of India under Article 370(1)(d) of the Constitution, by which Article 35(A) was added to the Constitution in relation to the state of Jammu and Kashmir. Thus, it observed:

> The net result is that persons in the position of the petitioner, though citizens of India and entitled to the various Fundamental Rights guaranteed by the Constitution, are not in a position to enjoy many of those rights within the State of Jammu & Kashmir though they are domiciled in that State for nearly 40 years.[24]

The Supreme Court held that in view of the special status of the state of Jammu and Kashmir, there is little that it can do, although it expressly stated that 'the petitioners have a justifiable grievance'.[25] It left it to the state legislature to amend the concerned laws so as to make it possible in law for those who migrated from West Pakistan to India in 1947 to enjoy and exercise their right to vote, to acquire land and to stand for local body elections. We are told that they constitute nearly 7–8 per cent of the population of the state of Jammu and Kashmir. It went on to note that:

> they are entitled to expect to be protected by the State of Jammu & Kashmir. In the peculiar context of the State of Jammu & Kashmir, the Union of India also owes an obligation to make some provision for the advancement of the cultural, economic and educational rights of these persons. We do hope that the claims of persons like the petitioner and others to exercise greater rights of citizenship will receive due consideration from the Union of India and the State of Jammu & Kashmir. We are, however, unable to give any relief to the petitioners.[26]

About two decades later, in around 2006, the Government of Jammu and Kashmir constituted a committee under G.D. Wadhwa, the then Financial Commissioner (Revenue) in the Ghulam Nabi Azad government 'to look into the problems of PoK and West Pakistan refugees in Jammu and Kashmir' (*Greater Kashmir* 2007). In November 2007, the Committee submitted its report to the Government (*One India News* 2007). Eight years later, the recommendations, which have never been made public, are reportedly under consideration by the state government (*DNA* 2014).

This category of refugees, who are now citizens of India (with the right to vote and the subjects of fundamental rights guaranteed by Part III of the Constitution of India), cannot by definition be termed stateless. But the case of Hindu refugees in Jammu gets complicated owing to the fact that they reside in Jammu and Kashmir, which under India's Constitution, has a special status. The Bachan Lal Kalgotra case, in this respect case, is instructive and clearly highlights the inability of the

Supreme Court to pass a judgement even while it observes that the petitioner's grievance was valid. The internationally accepted definition of statelessness (both *de jure* and *de facto*) may not appreciate such complications. Questions of whether the conditions of nationality, including 'whether the State in question considers a person to be its national', 'whether an individual actually is a national of a State under the operation of its law' as assessed from the point of view of that State, whether the nationality legislation accepts them as citizens, the question whether such persons are considered nationals of that State 'at the time the case is examined', the factual situation, all of which guide the determination of whether a person is stateless (UNHCR 2010), would be answered in the affirmative in the case of the Hindus of Jammu. They are recognised as citizens of India; their fundamental rights are guaranteed by the Constitution of India; they are, as the Supreme Court has recognised, considered nationals of India, and therefore, under international law, are citizens of India. Yet, the case of Hindus in Jammu gets complicated in the context of the constitutional status of the state in India's federal setup. Under the existing law, therefore, the Hindu refugees who migrated to Jammu may not qualify as stateless. In an ironic twist of events, they, however, constitute a class to whom neither Pakistan nor India is able to guarantee the rights, privileges and entitlements that a citizenship would otherwise enjoy.

The Hindus in Jammu are often called *de facto* stateless, or refugees, while those living in Rajasthan are addressed as 'oustees', 'displaced', 'migrants', 'refugees'. How would one classify this class of people under existing definitions under international law?

The Dalit Migration from Sindh

The statelessness question of the lower caste or Dalits from Sindh is not easily answered. The Sindh migration has been a continuous process, but specific events have led to a larger influx. The more recent ones, which this chapter is concerned with, began in the 1990s and have continued since then. As the previous section noted, most families had to save up for passports and visa, which, in some cases, has taken a lifetime. One of the milestones in case of the Sindhis living in Rajasthan has been the decision of the central government to grant them citizenship, a demand that SLS has been making since 1998. In order to appreciate why this is considered a milestone, it may be relevant to consider the procedure for applying for citizenship in India.

Sketch of Citizenship Law in India

The Citizenship Act, 1955 provides for acquisition (by birth under Section 3, by descent under Section 4, by registration under Section 5, by naturalisation under Section 6, by incorporation of territory under Section 7), renunciation (Section 8), termination (Section 9) and deprivation (under Section 10) of Indian citizenship. The Sindhi migrants acquire citizenship under Section 5(1)(a).[27] The Ministry of Home Affairs clarifies that a person 'shall be deemed to be a Person of Indian origin if he, or either of his parents, was born in undivided India or in such other territory which became part of India after the 15th day of August, 1947' (Ministry of Home Affairs 1955).

The application, along with an oath of allegiance (in the form of an affidavit), has to be submitted to the Collector/Deputy Commissioner/District Magistrate within whose jurisdiction the applicant is ordinarily resident. This application is forwarded through the concerned office to the central government. The application has to be supported by a copy of the valid foreign passport, valid long-term visa/residential permit, evidence of the date of birth of the parents, viz., a copy of the passport or birth certificate or domicile certificate issued by the competent authority clearly stating that he/she is a citizen of India, and a copy of a bank challan in original amounting to Rs 500 in the manner prescribed under the law. A fee of Rs 5,000 is mandated for each application for citizenship under Section 5(1)(a); a fee of Rs 500 is mandatory for every instance of witnessing the signing of an application or declaration mentioned in Rule 28 of the

Citizenship Rules, 1956,[28] administering the oath of allegiance and supplying a certified true copy of any notice, certificate, order, declaration or entry given, granted or made by or under the Citizenship Act (Ministry of Home Affairs 1955).

Sindhi refugees first arrive on a pilgrim visa, which is valid for 33 days. On the basis of this visa, a residence permit is issued first for a period of three months and subsequently renewed in Jaipur (a first renewal is valid for one year and subsequent extensions of the permit are given for two years). Their visas allow them little mobility, for most get visas with restrictions not to travel out of Jodhpur. Since most of the families have social ties in other parts of the state, the SLS has sought the non-application of this rule to Sindhi refugees.

Some instances of how the process of applying for citizenship in Rajasthan works is discernible if one looks at the cases of Gaji, who is a citizen himself, but four of whose children born in Sindh have been unable to get citizenship because of the high visa fee; or Govardhan, who, in his view, has completed all steps to apply for citizenship; or Ajitha Ram, who also aspires for Indian citizenship.

Gaji came from Tando Allayar in around the mid-1990s. He has six children, two of whom were born in India. His parents migrated from Bawadi village, Chotan tehsil, Barmer to Sindh where Gaji was born. His other siblings were born in India. Gaji is a poster boy for how the experience of applying for citizenship can be different for one's own family members. He and his wife became citizens in 2005,[29] but other members of his family were not as lucky. The children born in India are citizens by virtue of Section 3(c)(i) (both Gaji and his wife became citizens under Section 5). However, for four of his children born in Sindh, he was unable to pay Rs 1,800 per child. He says:

> I could not afford to pay for my children's application for citizenship. I asked the District Collector to reduce the fee but he said that he did not have the powers to do so.The problem came when they asked for domicile and citizenship certificate for kids in school. The kids did not apply for a passport as they were minors.

> Now it is impossible for me to get them Indian citizenship. My children are unable to study because they do not have identity documents.[30]

In Jodhpur, Gaji works as a scrap dealer; he says, 'my wife sells vegetables in the market. Laddi bai [his daughter] studies but I am not sure how long this will go on. The problem is that when she has to write board exams she has to give evidence of her Indian citizenship'. He adds, going back to the citizenship application process, 'I feel tied down because of this. The scrap dealing hardly pays. I earn Rs 200/day, and my wife earns Rs 150/day'.[31]

Govardhan came to India on 18 May 2001 because of religious discrimination and applied for citizenship in 2009. In view of the seven-year domicile rule, he could have applied earlier but had to save up enough money.[32] Govardhan did not have a valid passport but held a residence permit valid until 2013. He explained the citizenship procedure:

> The application form, which costs Rs 400, was submitted at the Collector's office. I got a letter of acknowledgement from the Collector after about a year and a half of applying. At the time of application, I also had to get a letter from a guarantor that he has no objection if I was made a citizen. This is required under the current rules. Next, I had to get a letter stating that there is no case pending against me and I have not gone to Pakistan since I came to India or left Jodhpur. All this takes 10–11 months. The CID also conducts its enquiry. They ask questions such as where have I travelled, whether I am in debt, they also called my guarantor. I was asked to give a letter of guarantee in 2011. In 2010, I received a letter from Jaipur which said that my Long-Term Visa (LTV) (issued by the MHA in Delhi) had not reached their office but I had never applied for one.[33]

In 2012, a second Crime Investigation Department (CID) enquiry with respect to Govardhan was reportedly undertaken, to know what he does and where he has travelled to in the past five years. In September 2012 he received a letter asking where he went to in Pakistan.

As the law now stands, they are required to have a valid passport, a copy of which has to be submitted along with the citizenship application form. Govardhan says it has become increasingly difficult for the refugees in Rajasthan to get this passport once it expires. Pakistan authorities ask for national ID cards, the new version of which was introduced in 2004 when Pervez Musharraf came to power. Reportedly, there is no standard renewal period for these cards.

Ajitha Ram came to Jodhpur on 16 November 2004. His family includes six girls, four boys and his wife. Not all family members could come to India together. His eldest son came before the Kargil War. He says the family could not contact their son for three years. The Samjhauta train service was suspended in 2002 after the Parliament attack, and resumed in January 2004. Ajitha Ram first sent his children; his wife then followed and about seven months later, he too landed in Jodhpur for good.

Two of his children, who arrived much earlier, have been granted citizenship, but the rest of the family live on long-term visas. It has been eight years now but he has no citizenship. He has been unable to pay the citizenship fee. Ajitha Ram stated that there is no application form and in his case, he made an application on a stamp paper with the help of a typist. This document then passes through the Additional Superintendent of Police of the city, who signs it and forwards it to the District Magistrate's office. This is followed by an enquiry by Intelligence which, in his case, was completed in eight days. During the enquiry, Ajitha Ram was asked whether his relatives live in Jodhpur, details of all their relatives and close family members, and questions that to Ajitha Ram seemed as if he was suspected of being a terrorist. He says he had to bribe the Intelligence officers; that the entire process was maddening and he felt harassed. He had faced three enquiries at the time of interview. The District Magistrate's office forwards this letter/application to the Collector, who acknowledges the receipt of the letter to the applicant. Ajitha Ram received this letter from the Collector's office after about 45 days. Following this letter, the applicant has to submit a copy of the challan of payment of Rs 500 made in favour of the Collector or the District Magistrate. These documents (the application, the enquiry report, the Collector's report) are then sent to the Home Department in Jaipur.[34]

In September 2001, following a representation, the Government of Rajasthan constituted a Review Committee to oversee and resolve the issues of citizenship and rehabilitation of 'the oustees.'[35] Some of these demands included grant of citizenship to the Hindus migrating from Sindh, reduction in the citizenship application fee and reduction in the time for processing the citizenship application. Thus, as Bhushan (2013) also concludes in his research, 'the migrants from Pakistan have sometimes been treated as refugees and sometimes as illegal aliens.'

The Committee recommended the following:

- 24.11.01: Renewal (of the passport), Renunciation (of Pakistani nationality) and penalty payments mandatory in the process of applying for Indian nationality to be waived off. Exempting the oustees from applicable fee of Rs 1,680 payable to the Pakistani Embassy.
- 24.11.01: Creation of a cell within the Colonisation Department of Bikaner to deal with issues of land allotments in the canal area.
- 24.02.02: The powers to grant citizenship delegated from the Centre to the District Magistrate, Rajasthan.
- 24.02.02: Creation of a cell in Jodhpur to address issues of land and citizenship.
- 24.02.02: The existing order—of the Union Home Ministry—by which oustees' movement was restricted to their respective localities—Amended to the effect that oustees residing in India for 5 years or more could move freely across given border districts.
- 24.02.02: To review the Centre's rehabilitation package in which Rs 9 crores [90 million] was given to the State Government for land allotments to the oustees.

- 24.02.02: Reservations for oustees in educational institutions, employment and welfare schemes. (Aman Trust 2005)

On the one hand, an application for citizenship of India by a Pakistani national is a long drawn and expensive process (or tedious, as some would term it), which looks upon applicants with suspicion, and has made the citizenship process effectively out of bounds for the Sindhi migrants. One question that emerges out of the situation, such as that of Ajitha Ram noted here, is whether he does not remain a Pakistani citizen even if he is not formally naturalised as an Indian citizen. An answer to this question is based on a number of factors that have to do with the citizenship acquisition, renunciation and deprivation process under the Pakistan Citizenship Act, 1951. Under this law, a Pakistani citizen can lose his citizenship if:

> he has been ordinarily resident in a country outside Pakistan for a continuous period of seven years beginning not earlier than the commencement of this Act and during [this] period has neither (i) been at any time in the service of any Government in Pakistan or of an International Organization of which Pakistan has, at any time during that period been a member; or (ii) registered annually in the prescribed manner at a Pakistan Consulate or Mission or in a country where [there] is no Pakistan Consulate or Mission at the Prescribed Consulate or Mission or at a Pakistan Consulate or Mission in a country to the country of his residence his intention to retain Pakistan citizenship (Sections 16[4][i] and [ii], Pakistan Citizenship Act, 1951; see Government of Pakistan 1951).

Under this provision, the application for deprivation can be made either by the holder of citizenship or by the State on its own motion. Safeguards are built into this provision, which provide the person concerned an opportunity to state his/her case before an order depriving citizenship is passed (UN 2009: 10–13). Thus, whether a Pakistani citizen becomes *de facto* stateless is dependent on each fact situation. Be that as it may, Hindus from Pakistan are technically foreigners and are regulated by the Foreigners Act, 1946.

Residence permits are granted to them to make their stay legal while their application for citizenship under the Citizenship Act is processed. It may be argued that even if the Government of India stops issuing residence permits to Pakistani Hindus, they are unlikely to be considered stateless in the absence of an order depriving them of their Pakistani citizenship. Nonetheless, it is inconceivable that the political histories of the two countries of India and Pakistan would allow India to stop granting them residence permits, which is a veritable surveillance document. On the other hand, the inability of Pakistani citizens to successfully navigate the naturalisation process under the Indian Citizenship Act, 1955, would, if not make them stateless, consign them to being discards of the politics of the two states.

Hindu 'Refugees' and India's Asylum Policy

The only common thread running through the political experiences and history of the lower-caste refugees from Sindh and Punjab who migrated to Rajasthan and Jammu, respectively, is their connection with Partition, admittedly more so for the latter group. However, the experience in both these cases suggest that announcing one's 'return' in a South Asian country that has lived 60 years as an independent nation has not been easy. What is striking about the case of both Rajasthan and Jammu is they have challenged the state, unlike other refugee groups. Both groups assert their right to return and their right to claim what they believe is their share in the country they believe is for all Hindus returning home. Both the SLS and the West Pakistani Refugee Action Committee seek and receive the support of political parties, particularly the BJP. In informal interactions in both Jammu and Rajasthan, it was striking that support for the refugees was the result of common religious beliefs.

In the case of Rajasthan, the demands of groups such as SLS therefore need to be viewed against the backdrop of effective advocacy and strategy as well as the support for 'our people'. In Jammu, the deliberate forgetting of the Partition refugees is a factor of the complex nature of politics of the state.

Rekha Chaudhury from the Department of Political Science, University of Jammu, says the Partition refugees were 'denied history' like others who are caught in the conflict zones of Jammu and Kashmir but that history in the state 'has been appropriated by ideology'. She argues, keeping the specific patterns of displacement and migration, especially in the Line of Control in mind, that 'for the rest of India, Partition was a finished process. Kashmir, on the other hand had not resolved the dispute'. When I asked what can possibly explain that the West Pakistani refugees have been consistently ignored over the last six decades, she says that the 'leadership does not want to annoy the Kashmiri constituency'.[36]

Conclusion

That states like India and Pakistan communalise politics and events is not new. Both organisations in Rajasthan and Jammu are part of the system that has capitalised on the communal ideology. Refugees from Sindh unanimously stated that India is their land, and that they love the country more than perhaps Indians themselves. In Jammu too, it is impossible to understand the Partition refugees and their legal status without factoring in the local politics of the state. Separatist groups like the Hurriyat (Geelani) have in the past voiced their concerns regarding the efforts to change the demography of the state. The Hindu population, on the other hand, believe that implementation of the Armed Forces (Special Powers) Act, the symbol of repression, is the only way to contain militancy. Thus, political developments over the course of the last 60 years impact how refugees are perceived and what policies dictate their existence as members of our society.

Notes

1. Interview with Joginder Pal Singh, District President, West Pakistani Refugees Action Committee, Kathua, 15 October 2012.

2. In Jodhpur, I wish to particularly thank volunteers Prem Chand and Govardhan for identifying interviewees and assisting me in translation and other logistical support; and Hindu Singh Sodha, without whose assistance, this research would have been impossible. In Jammu, I wish to acknowledge the assistance of Anuradha Bhasin, researcher and journalist with the *Kashmir Times*. Thanks also go to Dilip Simeon and Jamal Kidwai in New Delhi for assistance in accessing documents and use of the Aman Trust library.

3. Memorandum, 'Charter of Demands of West Pakistani Refugee of 1947', 22 July 2012. On file with the author.

4. Interview with Joginder Pal Singh, Tehsil President, West Pakistan Refugees Action Committee, Kathua, 15 October 2012.

5. Interview with Beruram of Jirahi village, Kathua, 15 October 2012. Translation assistance from Joginder Pal Singh from Dogri to Hindi. Beruram left his village Musadgarh in Sakargarh tehsil in Narowal district of Punjab in Pakistan as an eight-year-old boy. He says seven families came together. He did not elaborate on the journey from Musadgarh to Jammu but talks about how Muslims they met on their way had promised to feed them but they had found out that the food was poisoned. In Jammu, he remembers that empty houses were occupied by them. He also talks about stories he heard about Sheikh Abdullah travelling to Lakhimpur and asking people to return to Jammu.

6. Interview with Joginder Pal Singh of Keerian village, near Kathua, 15 October 2012.

7. Interview with Sumitri, Kathua, 15 October 2012; Interview with Somnath, Kathua, 15 October 2012.

8. Interview with Dharmodevi, Kathua, 15 October 2012.

9. Interview with Purodevi, Kathua, 15 October 2012. Purodevi was about 25 years old when she left Punjab, India. She came from Halla village, Shakargarh tehsil, Gurdaspur district. She says there were about 2,000 people accompanying her at the time of leaving. They had nothing with them when they left except for the clothes they were wearing. The Muslims, she says, stopped them on their way. 'They had knives on them', she said. They arrived in Kathua through a border village called Pansar. She says she is considered a Pakistani.

10. Bhushan also notes in his work that there are no definitive estimates of the Hindu population of Pakistan until 1998. According to the Pakistan Hindu Council (n.d.), they are an estimated 5.5 per cent of the total population of Pakistan. Others, such as Mariana Baabar (2006) claim that Hindus constitute about 2.5 per cent. For population figures by the Pakistan Hindu Council, see Pakistan Hindu Council (n.d.). See also Internet FAQ Archives (n.d.).

11. Mirpur Khas, Sanghar and Umarkot are the other districts of Sindh with a sizeable Hindu population. Bhushan also adds Hyderabad, Ghotki, Khairpur, Dadu, Badin, Sukkur and Karachi to this list.

12. Interview with Surmi and Harichand, Al Kausar temporary camp, Jodhpur, 28 September 2012.
13. Interview with Krishan, Al Kausar temporary camp, Jodhpur, 29 September 2012.
14. Interview with Chetan, Al Kausar temporary camp, Jodhpur, 28 September 2012.
15. Interview with Surmi, Al Kausar temporary camp, Jodhpur, 28 September 2012.
16. Interview with Devji, Al Kausar temporary camp, Jodhpur, 28 September 2012.
17. Interview with Harichand, Al Kausar camp, Jodhpur, 28 September 2012.
18. Interview with Rewaram, Jodhpur, 28 September 2012.
19. Interview with Krishan at his residence in Ramdev Nagar, Chopasni, Jodhpur, 28 September 2012.
20. Interview with Chetan, Al Kausar temporary camp, Jodhpur, 28 September 2012.
21. I interviewed another man, easily in his 80s, who did not wish to be named. A resident of Ala tehsil, Matiari district (in Sindh), he was only visiting India and making arrangements for the migration of his immediate family. He said it would take about six months for all of them to get a visa. At the time of this visit, he travelled to his village near Kawas (in Barmer district, Rajasthan) and asked for the lands that belonged to his ancestors to be given to his family. This village is about 3 kilometres from the Kawas railway station. He says people recognise him. People in the village know that the land belongs to his grandfather.
He also gives an account of migration in the 1940s. He says, in 1940, Barmer (they lived in village Kawas) was hit by drought. It was following this drought that the entire family (parents and five brothers) left for Pakistan. The hunger was intense, he says. He was around 20 years old then. Some time later, he returned to Kawas, on foot, with three brothers and five others, to get married and after a fortnight, returned to Sindh to find that his village continued to reel under drought. The districts of Barmer, Jaisalmer and half of Bikaner and Jodhpur were affected. He remembers that they ate gruel made of *bajra* (millet) because there was nothing else to eat. Before drought hit, they grew *jawar* (sorghum), *moong* (green gram lentil), *mot* (grass grown mostly for fodder) and *bajra*.
In his opinion, the Indian government should allow people to come to India because there are problems in Sindh. As an agricultural labourer, he earned 50 per cent of the produce. He states, 'At the time, the zamindars and we had good relationship, they looked after us well, gave us shelter. During the time of Ayub Khan, it is said that the goat and tiger both drank water together. He was considered a good ruler. Farmers got the land but after Bhutto died, the situation reverted to the original state. Lands owned by the Hindus were forcibly taken by the Muslims. This

is when forcible conversions began, girls began to be abducted. Now Muslims don't give us work. Even when I got married, I borrowed my wedding dress, the poverty was so bad then'.
His family did not stay in one village for too long. He says he did not even know who the prime minister or the president was then. Interview with Anonymous, Al Kausar transit camp, Jodhpur, 2 October 2012.
After his marriage, he has come to India about five times and twice without a visa. He says, 'We have to live here'.
22. See the section on 'Sketch of Citizenship Law in India' in this chapter for an account of the law and procedures applying to persons like Rewaram.
23. *Bachan Lal Kalgotra v. The State of Jammu & Kashmir and Ors*, AIR 1987 SC 1169.
24. *Bachan Lal Kalgotra v. The State of Jammu & Kashmir and Ors*, AIR 1987 SC 1169 at ¶ 3.
25. Ibid.
26. *Bachan Lal Kalgotra v. The State of Jammu & Kashmir and Ors*, AIR 1987 SC 1169 at ¶ 5.
27. According to Section 5(1)(a), Citizenship Act, 1955, an application is made by a person for acquisition of citizenship if he/she is 'a person of Indian origin who are ordinarily resident in India for seven years before making an application for registration' (Ministry of Home Affairs 1955).
28. Rule 28 of the Citizenship Rules, 1956 requires that an oath of allegiance administered or a person before whom an application or a declaration is made will not be accepted or registered or the oath of allegiance required under Section 5(2) will have no effect unless it is administered by or signed in the presence of the Collector, the Deputy Commissioner or the District Magistrate (Rule 28[i], Ministry of Home Affairs 1956).
29. Certificate of Registration under Section 5(1)(a), Citizenship Act, 1955 read with Rule 10, Citizenship Rules, 1956 issued by District Collector, Jodhpur on 1 February 2005. On file with the author.
30. Interview with Gaji, Jodhpur, 28 September 2012. The communication in Hindi by the Pakistan-displaced Public Cell, dated 21 February 2008, to Gaji stated that the authority to reduce the fee lies with the Government of India and that the domicile certificate in the name of his children can only be issued after they become citizens. Author's translation. Document on file with the author.
31. Interview with Gaji, Jodhpur, 28 September 2012.
32. Govardhan is a full-time volunteer with SLS and is based in Jodhpur. At the time he left Sindh, Govardhan was studying in eleventh standard. When asked about discrimination, he said, 'I could not get admission because I could not pay fees. My wife's brother-in-law's son was working in a dispensary. I started working with him. I worked there for about 4–5 years. I got trained as a Non-Medical Assistant (NMA) in a government

hospital and qualified as a medical technician. Thereafter, I set up my own clinic in Tando Allayar in Hyderabad [now in Sindh]'. Interview with Govardhan, Al Kausar camp, Jodhpur, 1 October 2012.

33. Interview with Govardhan, Al Kausar camp, Jodhpur, 1 October 2012.

34. Interview with Ajitha Ram, Jodhpur, 2 October 2012.

35. The Review Committee was headed by the Home Secretary, Government of Rajasthan; the Revenue Secretary; the Rehabilitation Secretary; the Divisional Commissioner of Jodhpur; the Deputy Home Secretary; and Hindu Singh Sodha of SLS. The Report of the Review Committee was submitted in 2004.

36. Interview with Professor Rekha Chaudhury, Department of Political Science, University of Jammu, 12 October 2012.

THREE

Ordeal of Citizenship

The Up-Country Tamils in Sri Lanka and India

*ANASUA BASU RAY CHAUDHURY**

It has been estimated that as many as 28,500[1] up-country Tamils (popularly known as Indian Tamils/estate workers), who now live in 112 refugee camps (including two special camps)[2] of Tamil Nadu, are regarded as stateless (Ramakrishnan 2012). They fled to India from Sri Lanka to escape the civil war between the majority Buddhist Sinhalese and the minority Tamils. The survey report says these people are 'unable to return to Sri Lanka due to the uncertain conditions prevailing in the neighbouring country' (ibid.). The report reveals that:

> [T]hey were originally from the hilly region of Sri Lanka. Having faced the ethnic violence of 1977, a large section of people in the hilly region migrated to areas in the Northern Province such as Vavuniya, Killinochchi and Mullaitivu, and when the 1983 conflict broke out, they had fled to India. (ibid.)

Being doubly displaced, most of these people were forced to take refuge in different camps of Tamil Nadu.

The ancestors of these up-country Tamils were brought from India to work in the expanding plantations of Sri Lanka by the British more than two centuries ago. They became permanent settlers in the island for generations and enjoyed all rights (including political rights) at par with the Sinhalese during the British period. Though they initially worked as slaves, by the 1930s, Indian Tamils unionised and became the country's largest proletarian force. Political solidarity of the Indian Tamils was considered a potential threat by the Sinhala politicians. To prevent this burgeoning solidarity from gaining political power, the Sinhala politicians strategically enacted the Citizenship Act in 1948 soon after Independence. A group of experts argue that the new and predominantly Sinhalese-dominated government used the Ceylon Citizenship Act of 1948 and the Indian and Pakistani Resident Act, No. 3 of 1949 to render the up-country Tamils stateless. However, another group indicates that this is not quite correct—instead this had a complementary effect as it required a seven- or 10-year period of uninterrupted residence as a condition for citizenship, whereas most estate Tamils had visited India in that time. It also imposed an income threshold requirement which disqualified most Hill Tamils. As a matter of fact, since then, these Indian Tamils have been inducted as bonded labourers into tea estates and, by all accounts, were never integrated into the political and cultural life of Sri Lanka. Thus, statelessness deprived them of their political power. They had been denied the most basic rights—such as the right to own property, state employment, hold a national identity card, obtain a passport and travel abroad, and vote. In 1986, Sri Lanka passed the Grant of Citizenship to Stateless Persons Act, No. 5 which, however, did not change the situation.

Against this backdrop, the enactment of the Grant of Citizenship to Persons of Indian Origin Bill in 2003 by the Sri Lankan government has become a landmark event for the stateless Tamils. The Bill gives citizenship to any person of Indian origin who has permanently resided in Sri Lanka since 30 October 1964, or descended from someone who had permanently resided in Sri Lanka since that date. This bill grants citizenship to approximately 168,141 stateless plantation Tamils. In January 2004, it was predicted that 145,000 Sri Lankan citizens of Indian origin would receive their National Identity Cards (NICs) within three months. However, the up-country Tamils living in the refugee camps of India are not covered by the new law because they have been living in the camps in India since 1983, and some have children who were born in India. Their refugee status caused a break in their continuous residence in Sri Lanka. Moreover, at the time of their journey to India many lost their documents. They fear that they may not be given citizenship once they return to Sri Lanka and will never receive any legal status in India either since they came to this country as refugees. In Sri Lanka, they were regarded as stateless; however, on their arrival in India, they got their new identity as refugees.[3] Has their identity as stateless people become subdued by their existence of protracted refugeehood? Does protracted refugeehood eventually result in statelessness? Is the distinction between refugeehood and statelessness increasingly wearing thin? These are a few questions our study seeks to find suitable answers to.

In order to solve the problem of statelessness legally in Sri Lanka, the act has been amended again in 2009 as Grant of Citizenship to Stateless Persons (Special Provisions) Amendment Act, No. 5.[4] Since then, it has been claimed at the popular level that Sri Lanka has legally solved its age-old problem of statelessness with regard to the up-country Tamils. Against this backdrop, one of the objectives of this study is to understand the estate workers' general perception of their newly found recognition of citizenship. Are they really aware of the importance of citizenship certificates?

To understand the dynamics of the ordeal of citizenship and the multilayered nature of statelessness in the post-colonial states like Sri Lanka and India, the researchers paid visits to Hatton, Sri Lanka, the place with a large concentration of Indian-origin Tamils in the district of Nuwara Eliya; Coonoor of the Nilgiris district of Tamil Nadu, India, the place where a large number of Indian Tamil repatriates were resettled; and also to the camps in Thiruvannamalai at Tamil Nadu[5] to capture the voices of Indian Tamils in order to get their perspective on statelessness. These three apparently different cases, somewhere linked together, will help us understand the nature of post-colonial citizenship and the dynamics of statelessness in post-colonial states like India and Sri Lanka.

A Brief History

Favourable climatic conditions for growing coffee and tea enthused British plantocrats in Sri Lanka, and the acute demand for labour-intensive ventures in these plantations made them look for cheap labour in the populous neighbouring Tamil-speaking region of India. The first group of Tamil emigrants from India moved to Sri Lanka (then Ceylon) in 1837, which was 'followed by successive batches until 1939, when the Government of India banned the movement of unskilled labour to Ceylon' (Ladduwahetty n.d.). No disagreement existed regarding the status of persons of Indian origin in the beginning because 'at that time, India and Ceylon were parts of the British Empire, and consequently, persons born and living in the territory of India and Ceylon had identical status, namely "British subjects"' (Jain 1963: 66).

The Donoughmore Commission was set up in 1927 to examine and report on the reforms to the Constitution. The Commission made far-reaching proposals, the chief of which was the introduction of adult franchise. It is important to note in this context that political representation along ethnic lines prevailed in Sri Lanka from the time of the unification of 1833.[6] Altering this arrangement, the commission recommended territorial representation in the Legislature. The Commission recommended the creation of the State Council comprising a majority of members elected by the people. It proposed that suffrage should be extended to all men over 21 years of age and to all women over 30 who had resided in the island for a minimum period of five years. Income, property and literacy qualifications were to be abolished. With regard to the Indian Tamils, the Commission wanted the abolition of two Indian seats in the Legislative Council and proposed a wider franchise, which would lead to some degree of democratic representation of the interests of plantation workers in the legislature (*Donoughmore Commission Report*, 1928, cited in Ladduwahetty 2010: 34–57). According to its report, the total number of registered voters in Sri Lanka in 1924 'was 204,997 or four per cent of the total population of five million' mainly due to 'property qualifications' (Donoughmore Commission Report, 1928, cited in Ladduwahetty 2010: 34–57).

Neville Ladduwahetty (n.d.) writes, '[t]he political leadership in Sri Lanka was very apprehensive about giving large numbers of Indian Tamils voting rights as recommended by the Donoughmore Commission.' They were fearful that the Kandyan Sinhalese would lose political traction in most of the constituencies in the Kandyan areas (see Kumar 1977: 14). Their fear further increased when the Commission stated in 1931 that the number of Indian Tamils registered as voters was about 100,000 in comparison to the earlier number of registered Indian voters (12,438) under the old Constitution. The number further increased to 145,000 in 1936 and by 1938, out of a total population of 670,000 Indian estate workers and their dependents, more than 170,000 had been registered as electors. In 1939 this figure exceeded 225,000.[7]

Until 1930, the Indian plantation workers in Sri Lanka were treated as slaves. Universal franchise and unionisation helped them emerge as the largest proletarian force of the country, and it brought substantial improvement in their previously exploited working lives. By the 1940s, the Ceylon Indian Congress (CIC) became the representative trade union and political wing of the Indian Tamil estate workers. As a result of unionisation, these estate workers elected their own representatives wherever they were in majority since the general elections for State Council from 1931 to 1947.

However, the situation became worse after the first parliamentary election held under the Soulbury Constitution in 1947. The result of that election confirmed the misgivings of the Sinhalese. The Indian Tamils were able to secure seven seats in the House of Representatives in the Kandyan districts and influence the results of another 12 constituencies. The outcome of this election revealed that the five-year residency qualification for franchise that had existed since 1931 worked to the advantage of the Indian Tamils at the expense of the Sinhalese.

Statelessness of the Estate Workers

At the time of decolonisation, the Soulbury Commission had left the question of citizenship within the jurisdiction of independent Sri Lanka somewhat open. After Sri Lanka attained independence on 4 February 1948, the Parliament of Sri Lanka passed the following laws related to citizenship: The Ceylon Citizenship Act, No. 18 of 1948, which came into operation on 15 November 1948; the Indian and Pakistani Residents (Citizenship) Act, No. 3 of 1949, which came into operation on 5 August 1949; and the Ceylon (Parliamentary Elections) Amendment Act, No. 48 of 1949.

Under the provisions of the Ceylon Citizenship Act 1948, a person shall be or become entitled to the status of a citizen of Ceylon either by right of descent or by virtue of registration. According to it,

> A person born in Ceylon before the appointed date of November 15, 1948, shall have the status of a citizen of Ceylon by descent if his father was born in Ceylon or both his paternal grandfather and paternal great grandfather were born in Ceylon. A person born outside Ceylon before the appointed date is a citizen by descent if both his father and parental grandfather were born in the country or his paternal grandfather and paternal great grandfather were born in Ceylon. A person born in Ceylon after the appointed date is a citizen by descent if his father was then a citizen of Ceylon while if he was born outside the country his birth should have been registered with the appropriate official. (*Legislative Enactments of Ceylon* [Revised], 1956, volume 2, Chapter 349, cited in Nadesan 1993: 152)

On the basis of these provisions, the Citizenship Act conferred citizenship by descent on the Sinhalese, Ceylon Tamils, Muslims, Malaya and Burghers, but, in effect, denied citizenship to the people of recent Indian origin (Nadesan 1993: 154).[8]

On the other hand, the Indian and Pakistani Residents (Citizenship) Act, No. 3 of 1949 though described as 'an

Act to make provision for granting the status of a citizen of Ceylon by registration to Indians and Pakistanis who have the qualification of past residence in Ceylon for a certain minimum period' (Indian and Pakistani Residents [Citizenship] Act), was no less restrictive than the Citizenship Act of 1948. The act came into force on 5 August 1949, and all applications were required to be submitted within two years from that date to a Commissioner appointed for that purpose. After investigation, the Commissioner had the discretion to allow or reject an application. In case of rejection under Section 16 of the Act, the applicant was entitled to appeal to the Supreme Court. Even if the Commissioner made an order allowing the application, it could be objected to by any member of the public, and this member was entitled to appeal to the Supreme Court against the Commissioner's order.

Even before the fate of a million Indian-origin Tamils could be decided under the citizenship acts, the Ceylon (Parliamentary Elections) Amendment Act, No. 48 was passed in 1949, which 'in one stroke disenfranchised the entire people of Indian Origin' (Nadesan 1993: 160). Taking into consideration the complicated procedures to obtain Ceylon citizenship under the 1948 Act, the CIC decided to boycott the act at its annual session held in 1949. It is interesting to note in this context that the application forms were in English and it was difficult for the Indian Tamils, especially the plantation workers, to fill them out without assistance. This notwithstanding, altogether 237,034 applications were submitted.

In March 1952, Don Stephen Senanayake, the first prime minister of independent Ceylon, passed away, and his son Dudley Shelton Senanayake succeeded him as prime minister. Soon, there followed general elections in May 1952. The ruling party, the United National Party (UNP), called it 'a fight for democracy against the threat of totalitarianism' (Nadesan 1993: 161). This was the first general election to be held after the Citizenship Act had been enacted. Although the Indian Tamils constituted one-tenth of the total population of Ceylon, a mere 8,000 of them were eligible to exercise their franchise, representing only about one-twentieth of the number who enjoyed franchise rights in the 1947 general elections. No member was elected from among the Indian Tamils in the 1952 election and thereafter till 1977.[9]

Experts argue that during those days the Sri Lankan government thought that whoever was not a Sri Lankan citizen was to be treated as an Indian citizen. India was not in a position to accept this as it had already established its own qualifications for citizenship under constitutional provisions. These made it difficult for Indian residents outside India to qualify for Indian citizenship. This situation was made even more difficult by the enactment of a separate citizenship law by the Government of India in 1955.[10] The result of these prevailing legal complexities of citizenship in Sri Lanka was the creation of 'Stateless Indian Tamils'. These were the Indian Tamils who did not qualify to be either Sri Lankan or Indian citizens.

Issue of Statelessness: India and Sri Lanka

Statelessness of the Indian Tamils in Sri Lanka has become one of the key issues of tension between India and Sri Lanka in the past few decades. Since the 1940s, both the countries made attempts to solve the problem related to citizenship of the Indian Tamils of Sri Lanka; however, they failed to do so till 1964. Two conferences took place between India and Sri Lanka, namely the Indo-Ceylon Relations Exploratory Conference of November 1940 and the Indo-Ceylon Relations Conference of September 1941. At the end of the second conference, both the countries signed a Joint Report on various issues, including the Immigration Bill and the question of franchise (Bains 1962: 89). Although it was a joint report, it was rejected by India later on.

In June 1954, there were discussions between Jawaharlal Nehru, the then prime minister of India, and Dudley Senanayake, the then prime minister of Ceylon, on the question of the Indian Tamils of Ceylon. Unfortunately, no positive conclusion came out of it. These discussions were followed by the Nehru–Kotelawala Agreement in which, for the first time, the question of 'illicit-immigrants' was recognised as a part of the Indian Tamil problem. As a result of this, the Government of Ceylon proposed to prepare the electoral register comprising all unregistered adult residents. In this context, it was stated that, 'when this registration is completed, any person not so registered will, if his mother-tongue is an Indian language, be presumed to be an illicit immigrant from India and liable to deportation and the Indian High Commissioner will extend all facilities for implementation of such deportation' (Ministry of External Affairs 1958a). It was also stated in the agreement that:

> [T]he registration of citizens under the Indian and Pakistani (Citizenship) Act will be expedited and every endeavour will be made to complete the disposal of pending applications within two years . . . All persons registered under this act may be placed by the Government of Ceylon on a separate electoral register, particularly in view of the fact that the bulk of the citizens do not speak the language of the area in which they reside. This arrangement will last for a period of only 10 years. (ibid.)

The Agreement further indicated that it was open to the persons who were not registered thus 'to register themselves as Indian citizens, if they so choose, at the office of the Indian High Commissioner in accordance with the provisions of Article 8 of the Constitution of India' (ibid.). Ceylon proposed to 'offer special inducements to encourage such registration and [said] that these inducements will be announced from time to time'. The Government of India stated that they would 'offer administrative and similar facilities to all persons of Indian origin to register themselves as Indian citizens under the Constitution of India, if they so choose, and would also give publicity to the availability of such facilities' (ibid.).

The Ceylonese press was generally favourable to the Agreement. However, the critics argued that the Agreement had given undue prominence to the menace of illicit immigration from across Palk Strait. The main problem of citizenship for Ceylon Indians related to the second part of the Agreement (Nadesan 1993: 166). In the process of implementation, the aforesaid agreed proposals started facing problems, as on 1 March 1954 the Government of Ceylon suspended the Temporary Residence Permits (TRPs) and the issuing of Identity Certificates to Indian Tamils. In May, it proposed a ban on the employment of non-citizens. While the Indian High Commission registered applicants for citizenship in the spirit of the Nehru–Kotelawala Agreement, the Ceylon government adopted a policy of rejecting thousands of applications for Ceylon citizenship merely on technical grounds. By early 1956, it became clear that the Nehru–Kotelawala Agreement had reached a stalemate.

Finally, negotiations between the two prime ministers, Sirimavo Bandaranaike of Sri Lanka and Lal Bahadur Shastri of India, brought this matter to a conclusion. As a result of a series of talks between the two countries, in October 1964, Shastri and Bandaranaike signed an agreement on the status and future of persons of Indian origin in Ceylon, which was popularly known as the Sirimavo–Shastri Pact. It divided the stateless people on a ratio of seven to four between India and Sri Lanka, respectively. The Agreement said:

1. The declared objective of this agreement is that all persons of Indian origin in Ceylon who have not been recognised either as citizens of Ceylon or as citizens of India should become citizens either of Ceylon or of India.
2. The number of such persons is approximately 975,000 as of date. This figure does not include illicit immigrants and Indian passport holders.
3. 300,000 of these persons together with the natural increase in that number will be granted Ceylon citizenship by the Government of Ceylon; the Government of India will accept repatriation to India of 525,000 of these persons together with the natural increase in that number. The Government of India will confer citizenship on these persons.

4. The status and future of the remaining 150,000 of these persons will be the subject matter of a separate agreement between the two governments.
5. The Government of India will accept repatriation of the persons to be repatriated within a period of 15 years from the date of this Agreement according to a programme as evenly phased as possible. (Ministry of External Affairs 1964)

In 1974, Prime Minister Bandaranaike and the Indian Prime Minister Indira Gandhi signed another accord, which divided these stateless people equally—75,000 each between the two countries.

According to the Indo-Sri Lanka Agreements of 1964 and 1974, India and Sri Lanka agreed to issue citizenship to about 6 lakh (0.6 million) and 3.75 lakh (0.375 million) persons, respectively. Though the Tamils had faced ethnic disturbance before 1983, they never opted to come back to India. Usually, during such events of ethnic violence, they moved to villages (within Sri Lanka) for a short while and returned home once conditions went back to normal. However, in the 1983 Pogrom a large section of Tamils of Indian origin were attacked by a Sinhala mob, and those who escaped and moved to the villages were killed by the military troops. This caused heightened security dilemmas and forced the people to migrate to India. Considering the security issues, the repatriation of the people of Indian origin from Sri Lanka has been temporarily suspended since October 1984. A large section of Indian Tamils, having applied for Indian citizenship, waited in the queue. Their turn never came.

Taking these facts into consideration, in the next three sections we shall try to portray the situation of up-country Indian Tamils in Sri Lanka and India on the basis of the collected narratives from our field visits. For clarity of analysis, we shall divide them into three categories: up-country Tamils staying in the refugee camps of Tamil Nadu; repatriated up-country Tamils staying in Coonoor; and the estate workers of Hatton, Sri Lanka.

Unheard Voices: Refugee Camps of Tamil Nadu

He was born in Nagamachi village in Devakkottai district on 2 March 1938. He went to Sri Lanka in 1943 to join his father, who was working in a tea estate in the island. He was granted Indian citizenship under the Sirimavo–Shastri Pact,[11] but could not get repatriated to India. During the communal violence in July 1983, his family lost all its belongings; so he came to India with his family members as a refugee. He arrived at Rameshwaram in 1984. In spite of several attempts to convince the officials of the Repatriation Department of the Government of Tamil Nadu about his Indian citizenship, he failed. Twenty-nine years have passed since he came to India. Given his prolonged refugee status, now he considers himself as 'a refugee in his own motherland'. A refugee in the Kottapattu camp, Tiruchirapally, has expressed his agony and anguish in this manner.[12]

The most articulate among these refugees in Kottapattu camp was Ranganathan (name changed). According to him, without citizenship papers, they are non-entities. They cannot avail of the benefits earmarked for the Scheduled Castes and the Backward Classes. Though their children are qualified, they cannot apply for government jobs. Their children are not entitled to scholarships either.

While Ranganathan was very vocal about issues of identity, Rupabardhana (name changed), a middle-aged refugee woman, initially narrated with pride the achievements of a bright boy living in the same refugee camp, Adisheshan. Despite all hardships faced by the refugees, Adisheshan studied well, and scored 1,105 out of 1,200 marks in the plus-two examinations in 2009. If he were an Indian citizen, he could have easily got admission in any good medical college with scholarship. His parents, with considerable difficulty, raised some money and got him admitted into an engineering college. He cannot even apply for an educational loan from a bank because his parents have not been given citizenship papers (Suryanarayan 2010).

These are not the only cases, as a total of 61 families living in the Kottapattu refugee camp near Tiruchirapally were conferred Indian citizenship under the Sirimavo–Shastri Pact of 1964. However, their turn did not come for repatriation to India before 1983. As the process came to an end in July 1983, these families were not repatriated legally. They were affected very badly during the riots and, having faced the violence, they decided to migrate to India as refugees. As a result, they could not avail of the facilities provided to the repatriates by the government. Most of them came illegally to India by the Eelam Shipping Service in 1984. They sold whatever property or business they had and brought their savings to India. They have lost their links with Sri Lanka today. Their children were born here; their sons and daughters married into local families.[13] Their representations to concerned authorities, both at the state and central levels, have not elicited any favourable response so far.

Kottapattu is not the only camp. The researchers visited Kondam and Thenpallipattu refugee camps situated in Thiruvannamalai to capture the voices of the Tamil stateless people. These camps were specifically chosen because they have a significant Indian Tamil population as refugees. The respondents were chosen using the purposive sampling technique. Qualitative interviews were conducted to capture the experience of security issues of the stateless Tamil people, and to understand why they do not want to go back to Sri Lanka.

The official record shows that the Tamil refugees entered India in phases;[14] during the first phase, 134,053 Tamil refugees sought asylum in Tamil Nadu. In the second phase, 122,078[15] Tamils entered India. The Tamils from Sri Lanka sought refuge as a result of the ongoing conflict in Sri Lanka between the government-led forces and the rebel Tamil group called the Liberation Tigers of Tamil Eelam (LTTE). Most of the Tamil refugees were housed in various government-managed camps in Tamil Nadu. The registered refugees were allowed to reside in camps, and the 'unregistered' Tamil refugees took up residence with relations and friends in Tamil Nadu.[16] The third wave of refugee flow began in 1995, in which 22,418 Sri Lankan Tamils fled Sri Lanka.[17] During a recent phase between 2006 and 2011, the record shows us that 25,711 Sri Lankan refugees came to India.[18] The number of non-camp refugees is not accurate because not all of them have registered themselves—the actual number could vary between 35,000 and 45,000. Neither the Government of India nor the state government of Tamil Nadu thought of identifying the Indian-origin Tamils separately in those days due to the magnitude of the influx.

In India, various reception centres were established by the Government of Tamil Nadu in Mandapam (the closest point of entry from Rameshwaram) to receive Tamil refugees. The refugees arrived from Sri Lanka by ferry across the Indian Ocean in small boats, fishing vessels, and the like, from the northern and eastern parts of Sri Lanka. At the point of entry into India, the Rameshwaram registration process was held by officials after an intense session of interrogation; refugees were then sent temporarily to Mandapam camp. Each refugee family received a settling-in allowance from the Government of Tamil Nadu, and some basic utensils, etc. Often, the allowance consisted of food items (rice, oil, salt, lentils, dry chillies and dried fish on some occasions), clothing items (during festivals), and in some cases, cash. In the initial days, refugees living in these camps were relatively comfortable. They had frequent visits from officials (of the Government of Tamil Nadu) and some non-governmental workers.

The system of power hierarchy was quite effective in the day-to-day functioning of the camps. Each camp had a refugee leader who was responsible for bringing grievances from the refugees to the notice of the camp officials. Each camp's staff comprised the camp officer, camp supervisor, accountant, storekeeper, block-in-charge and other contingent staff. The leader (camp officer) was responsible for maintaining the 'black board' that indicated the exact number of refugees present in the camps. This camp-in-charge was assisted by other officials in the distribution of rations, etc. Each camp had a small medical centre, with one doctor and two nurses, and a small nursery. The nursery provided adequate nutrition and other medical necessities to new mothers and their infants.[19]

The camp officials were responsible for managing refugees within the camps as well as distributing rations, clothing, etc., to the refugee families. To do their jobs efficiently, officials often undertook regular 'roll-calls' twice a day, once in the morning and again after sunset, to determine the exact number of refugees.[20] This made the refugees feel more like prisoners within the camps. Although they could go out after acquiring special permission from the officials, it was mandatory to return before the curfew that was assigned to each of them. Essentially, this meant that refugees were denied and discouraged any opportunities to mingle with the local population. Since the officials in the camps had absolute authority over the day-to-day administration of camps, the involvement of local officials was limited to crisis management. The *tehsildar* was the highest official at the local level of administration, and the district magistrate was the highest at the district level.

Our respondents in the camps in Thiruvannamalai talked about corruption and the 'chain of bribery' among some officials who register names in birth certificates. Each household (family) in the camp comprised family members related by blood. When children were born in the camps, officials had the tough task of including their names in the existing list, which was mostly a ration card. Each individual living in the camp had his or her name included on a ration card belonging to the head of the family. Often, it was necessary either to include or exclude names, depending on births and deaths. In the interviews, respondents mentioned that since their quota of rations (dole) depended on the exact number of members in each household, it seemed imperative that the inclusion of names regarding births was more crucial than the exclusion of names upon death. The officials were quite reluctant to add new names to the card of an existing ration-card holder.

Ethnic affinity was one of the factors that influenced the Sri Lankan Tamil refugees to seek asylum in Tamil Nadu, since they shared a common language and ethnicity with those living there, and since the Government of Tamil Nadu empathised with the plight of the Tamils in Sri Lanka. The domestic politics in Tamil Nadu were effective in encouraging the central government to adopt a proactive role in the ethnic conflict in Sri Lanka. Thus, the central government was persuaded to take an active role in the plight of the displaced people from Sri Lanka.

With the onset of ethnic violence, Tamils of Indian origin were badly affected in Sri Lanka. On the one hand, the Sinhala mob attacked the Tamils to destroy their social identity; so properties were systematically looted to break down their economic growth and temples were demolished to destroy their religious identity. On the other hand, the army, the state institution which was supposed to protect them, engaged in activities that were equally bad in terms of destroying lives and livelihood. As such, Tamil civilians were repeatedly forced to flee just ahead of shelling and bombing, resulting in repeated displacement. When they returned home, many found their homes and land methodically looted and destroyed. The fear that anything can happen at any time was persistent. Their lives oscillated between the military and the militant group, the former in the name of security and the latter in the name of liberty. Both were perceived to be equally dangerous in terms of causing destruction to their lives. The people lived under constant threat. The trauma they went through was so intense that even the sound of fire crackers reminded them of getting bombed by the army. Even after the many years since they had left Sri Lanka, great fear is still alive among the Tamils of Indian origin.

As a result of this, even those refugees of Indian origin who have become Sri Lankan citizens would like to renounce their Sri Lankan citizenship and take up Indian citizenship. It has been reported that in the Kottapattu camp, there are families that were conferred Sri Lankan citizenship under the Indian and Pakistani Residents Act No. 3 of 1949. Having stayed in India for many years, they now want to acquire Indian citizenship. Thomas George (name changed) came to India in the early 1990s with his family, and is currently the administrative officer in a non-governmental organisation (NGO). His wife teaches in a local school and his children, having finished higher education, are employed in good organisations. Thomas George repeatedly said that they would not like to go back to Sri Lanka.[21]

In this context, it is worth mentioning that when the repatriation of Sri Lankan refugees from India to Sri Lanka began after the conclusion of the India–Sri Lanka Accord in July 1987 and subsequently in 2002 under UNHCR assistance, these refugees chose to stay on in India. Most of them prefer to remain in the camps now so that they at least have legal protection as refugees. It may be recalled that a section of the refugees filed a writ petition before the Madras High Court, expressing their unwillingness to return to Sri Lanka. The court disposed of the petition after an undertaking made by the Government of India to the effect that the refugees will not be sent back to Sri Lanka unless they agree to the same, and there will be no compulsion in that process, which reflects the spirit of the principle of *non-refoulement*. Thus, status quo was preserved in their case.

It is pertinent to note that in 2003, several regional meets were organised for the representatives of the refugee camps by the Organisation for Eelam Refugee Rehabilitation (OfERR), an NGO, to identify their issues and needs. As a result of the consultations, the '*Nallayan* Declaration', consisting of 41 demands, was made; conferring citizenship rights to the stateless Indian-origin Tamils before getting repatriated to Sri Lanka was also mentioned.[22] OfERR organised camp visits, where out of 102 refugee camps, they received permission to visit 96. They could not visit four camps, namely, Thiruvarur, Uchapatti, Annaiyur and Koodalur. Two-day meetings were organised in the 96 camps that were visited to discuss the history and consequences of statelessness and to collect information on stateless refugees. They identified 28,500 refugees as stateless, who did not fulfil the criteria for continuity of domicile in Sri Lanka.[23] Thereafter, they met many political leaders in Sri Lanka and put forth the request for bringing an amendment to the 2003 Bill to confer citizenship on the stateless refugee. Most of the leaders said they would look into the matter and raise the issue in Parliament, but nothing really came of it subsequently.

In 2007, a group of Janatha Vimukthi Peramuna (JVP) leaders came to India from Sri Lanka to participate in a meeting at Kolkata via Chennai, Tamil Nadu. OfERR took the initiative to meet them and arranged a meeting with the representatives of the refugee camps at Chennai. The refugees expressed their dual plight of being a refugee as well as a stateless person. They also spoke about how their prolonged stay as refugees within the camps has subdued their stateless status. Neither Sri Lanka nor India was bothered about their citizenship. Moved by the plight of the Tamils, the JVP promised to raise the issue in Parliament.[24] As they had 40 seats in Parliament at the time, the efforts made by them resulted in the Amendment Bill of 2009.

Indian Tamil Repatriates at Coonoor[25]

Coonoor, one of the prominent hill stations of the Nilgiris in Tamil Nadu, is 'located at the head of the Hulikal ravine at an altitude of 1,800 metres above sea level and is 19 kilometres away from Ooty (Ootacamund), another famous hill station of south India. Coonoor is not only famous for its verdant environs but also its tea plantations' (Coonoor.com n.d.). It is also home to a large section of the Indian repatriates from Sri Lanka who were granted Indian citizenship by way of the Sirimavo–Shastri Pact. The CRG team of researchers paid a field visit to Coonoor in December 2011 and had the opportunity to meet few Tamil repatriates resettled there. The following is a brief ethnographic account of the journey of these repatriates from Sri Lanka and their struggle for existence in their homeland, India.

Remembering his past, Ramakrishnan (name changed on request), a resident of Palathottam of Coonoor, revealed that as violence broke out, they decided to return to India. Many other families in their estate were waiting for their travel papers. They were from Badulla district and belonged to the Uri group. In their area, a very small number of families opted for Sri Lankan citizenship. The situation became worse as days passed. He said,

> We were suffering from discrimination perpetrated by the Sinhalese *gramaniladari* [village headman]. We were facing scarcity of work [like only working twice a week] within the estate, low wages, scarcity of food grains, insufficient rations. Our 'lines' [one-room tenements] had become dilapidated and lacked basic

> amenities. We travelled all the way to Kandy, a place where we had never been to. After our head of family was interviewed, we were given a family card that contained our detailed family profile. With these documents we started our journey by train to Talai Mannar, the boarding point for the ferry to India. However, the journey in between was not without difficulties.[26]

Although repatriation of Indian Tamils was expected to commence in 1965, it started only in 1968 and moved slowly throughout the 1970s. Following the communal violence of July 1983, when the trickle of Sri Lankan refugees into India became a flood, the arrival of repatriates by ferry service was stopped from October 1984. However, after that very few repatriates have arrived in India by air of their own accord. According to government statistics, till October 1984, the number of repatriates who arrived from Sri Lanka was registered as 461,631 (see Department Of Rehabilitation n.d.: 11). As on July 1983, the number of Indian passport holders[27] yet to be repatriated to India was 84,141, plus their natural increase (Vamadevan 1989: 5–6).

The repatriates, on their arrival from Sri Lanka, were given free meals at the reception centre at Rameshwaram and sent to the three transit camps at Mandapam in Ramanathapuram district, Kottapattu in Tiruchirapalli district and Gummidipundy in Tiruvallur district. In the transit camps, the repatriates were paid cash doles, and supplied rice at subsidised rates with free accommodation, electricity and medical facilities. They were provided with rehabilitation assistance and sent to the place of their choice for settlement. However, there were many and varied problems in the transit camps. Some of the repatriates exhausted their financial resources and were forced to sell their possessions for food. Some had to wait in the camp for several months to get placements. Some were not willing to proceed to destinations outside Tamil Nadu because they did not feel safe enough to travel to places where they were 'strangers' in terms of language and customs. Some were anxious about the Provident Fund (PF), which they could not collect before their departure. It may be noted here that the PF scheme came into operation in Sri Lanka since 1958. To finalise the arrangements to obtain the PF was part of the whole process of repatriation. If a repatriate stayed in one estate, it became easier to get his/her dues in time. If he/she changed his/her estates then the process of withdrawing money became more complicated as the applications passed through the estate officials.

Almost all our respondents complained about the high prices of essential commodities and the uncertainties and slow pace of working of the machinery for rehabilitation at the initial phase of repatriation. Some complained about the fact that they could not get *ad hoc* cash grants. Sometimes they felt cheated and misled. Many of the repatriates had arrived in India penniless. On reaching the transit camp, the largely illiterate labourers, who had given the best part of their lives on the plantations making Sri Lanka one of the world's leading tea exporters, came to understand their grim plight. They were supposed to receive a cash dole depending on the size of the family, varying from Rs 35 per month with a family consisting of one member to Rs 115 for a family with seven members. But to get this help, they had to often wait for two weeks or more, and during this period, no additional financial assistance was provided for their maintenance (Nadesan 1993: 160).

> The place of the repatriates' resettlement in India was decided by the Indian High Commission in Kandy, Sri Lanka. The repatriates were often ignorant, or were misled, about their eventual destinations. Usually, only the largest families were selected for and deployed to the comparatively well-organized government-colony schemes. Alternatively (for smaller families, or if a designated scheme was not ready), the government supplied Rs 1,000 as a business loan. But obtaining such a loan involved the bureaucratic delays. (South Asian Politics and Governments 2013)

Further, due to lack of business experiences, many repatriates failed to utilise the money in an efficient or economic manner. Due to this, many became disillusioned as their hopes of obtaining land and financial assistance were dashed.

Ramakrishnan said:

> We got shelter at the Mandapam Camp. This was a transit camp for repatriates from Sri Lanka. It was a well-planned housing estate, supplied with running water and electricity. In one way we got excited realizing the fact that we were in India. We were enthusiastic to resettle ourselves. But in another way, we were also a bit anxious about our future, which was still uncertain.[28]

Over 95 per cent of the families were settled in Tamil Nadu and the rest were accommodated in other southern states like Kerala, Karnataka and Andhra Pradesh. As they were mostly plantation labourers, these repatriates wanted to opt for hilly areas like the Nilgiris of Tamil Nadu. The official records reveal that a large section was also resettled in Tiruchi, Salem, Pudukottai and Madurai. Rehabilitation assistance was a package mainly consisting of resettlement schemes, housing loans, and education and training facilities. However, the major thrust of this programme was on the first two. Resettlement schemes were of three types: loan scheme, employment and land colonisation scheme. Under the employment scheme, Tamil Nadu government took the initiative to give jobs to poor estate repatriates.

In 1968, the Government of Tamil Nadu started implementing the government tea project in the Nilgiris. It was managed by the Forest department as a scheme to rehabilitate the Tamil repatriates. In 1975, the project was brought under corporate management in the name of the Tamil Nadu Tea Plantation Corporation Limited (TANTEA). Official records show that, till date, the TANTEA has rehabilitated 2,445 Indian Tamil repatriate families, and has on its roll 6,700 permanent workers. About 4,500 casual workers (mostly dependents of permanent workers) have also been employed in TANTEA during the high-cropping periods (TANTEA n.d.).

Chandramohan (name changed), a worker of the Tiger Hill tea estate in Coonoor, started narrating his story almost in the same manner as Ramakrishnan had.

> We are from Hatton area of Nuwara Eliya district of Sri Lanka. Our family migrated to Sri Lanka long time back. I was born and brought up at Hatton. Our family also faced the same problems as stated by Ramakrishnan. In 1979, our family came to India. Some of our family members left Sri Lanka before our departure and they suggested that we too come to the Nilgiris. After coming here, we saw that like our family, many chose the Nilgiris for resettlement. We also got information that the Tamil Nadu government established tea estates to rehabilitate us.[29]

However, not all repatriates came to the Nilgiris and got jobs in TANTEA estates. According to our respondents, the total number of Tamil repatriates (including the natural increase) living in the Nilgiris is around 250,000. Many of them started working as day labourers with very low wages in small private holdings by the Badagas, the local landowning (but otherwise backward tribal) community. The main challenge before the estate Tamils from Sri Lanka seeking refuge in these hills was negotiating with the two distinct non-Tamil speaking people dominating in the area. Out of four *taluk*s in this district—Ooty, Coonoor, Kotagiri and Gudalur—the first three are in the plateau, while the last one is situated on the slopes of the Western Ghats. While the Badagas, speaking a dialect derived from Kannada, dominated the plateau, Gudalur was under the domination of the Malayalis. Besides, Kannadigas also lived there though they kept a relatively low profile.

Our respondents spoke about the way they were humiliated by the Badagas. Chandramohan, one of our respondents, said,

> We were treated as *agadhi* [refugees]. What an irony! We became refugees in our own homeland! When we came here, the place was sparsely populated and was under the control of the Badagas. They were not ready to welcome us and did not want to make a distinction between refugees and repatriates. Those who got jobs at TANTEA were lucky. For getting a job at TANTEA estates, each worker had to surrender his/her passport [issued under the rules

> of the 1964 Pact]. But many had to work under the Badagas like bonded labourers. The situation was not at all congenial. We were discriminated against and harassed by the Sinhala *gramaṇiladaris* in Sri Lanka; after coming here, we faced almost the same harassment perpetrated by the Badagas. We were unwanted in Sri Lanka and unwelcome here.[30]

In Gudalur, the problem was related to land acquisition. In this *taluk*, vast stretches of forest land were occupied by Kannadigas and Malayalis without proper *patta*s and they started cultivating the land. During the initial stage of their survival, the repatriates also joined that process. Soon, it created large-scale tension between Malayalis and the repatriates. The general impression that these repatriates had created among the locals was that they would be competitors for the existing scarce resources. In the majority of the cases, the rehabilitation assistance provided did not help to resettle them fully, and therefore their impoverishment continued.

Our respondents highlighted the role of the Malayaka Makkal Maru Vazhvu Manram (popularly known as Manram), a forum for the rehabilitation of the hill people from Sri Lanka, based in Kotagiri, 30 kilometres away from Ooty, as the only glimmer of hope on their otherwise bleak horizon. It was due to Manram's constant and active initiative that many repatriates got *patta*s from the government. They also cherished the leadership of R.R. Sivalingam and his trusted lieutenant S. Tiruchendooran, and mentioned that their leaders had enabled the organisation to chalk out a long-term vision for their development. They also spoke about the United Front Federation for Repatriates (UFFR), the United Front for Repatriate Workers (UNIFRONT), and the Ceylon Repatriates Association, Kodaikanal (CERAK), which served the repatriates in those days. But, it was the Indo-Sri Lanka Development (ISLAND) Trust that tried to form a platform for people's movement through organising this Manram in 1984–85 at Kotagiri. Manram helped them become aware of their rights as full-fledged citizens of India and was able to mobilise the masses politically (see in this context, Gopalan 1995; Sivalingam 1984, 1995).

All our respondents emphasised that Coonoor has always been regarded as the stronghold of the Dravida Munnetra Kazhagam (DMK). DMK's anti-Malayali stand and pro-Tamil rhetoric helped it gain loyalty of the repatriates. Moreover, the opening of the TANTEA during the regime of the then Chief Minister Karunanidhi strengthened its political base in the Nilgiris. Not that the DMK has really placed any repatriate in important positions, but given the Badaga-Malayali factor, they tend to feel more comfortable with the DMK than the All-India Anna Dravida Munnetra Kazhagam (AIADMK). Insofar as the Communist Party is concerned, it is active in the trade unions and is very sympathetic towards the repatriates. But it is too small a party to make a big difference in their lives.

Our interviews with the plantation workers living in Coonoor helped us understand the fact that though the state government started tea plantations to provide employment to the Tamil repatriates, the Tamil repatriates unfortunately remain an extremely disadvantaged group, who often live in poverty with very little means to support themselves. Their living conditions frequently lack clean drinking water, electricity and proper sanitary facilities, which, combined with an inadequate diet, often result in severe health issues. Repatriate youths have a poor record of education, with children dropping out of school early and experiencing a wide array of social problems. It is true that NGOs are working with this community and forming women's groups and self-help groups to empower people, provide education and healthcare, and encourage means of income generation but the result is far from satisfactory.

Tamil repatriates have urged the Tamil Nadu government to lend a helping hand to uplift their economic and social conditions (*Hindu* 2007). They argued that India had promised jobs for one member per family, besides business and housing loans. However, after the influx of refugees from the island nation following the violence in 1983, the focus of the government turned only towards rehabilitating the refugees. Since then, they have not got any concession from the government. Hundreds of repatriates who were employed in cooperative spinning mills had lost their jobs after their closure. The Repatriates Cooperative Finance and

Development Bank (REPCO Bank), which was primarily meant for the welfare of repatriates, had stopped employing them. They opined that it had become yet another commercial bank and they also wanted the government to revive the Rehabilitation Department for Repatriates to look into their welfare.

Voices from Hatton

To understand the dynamics of the benefit of citizenship and to capture the voices of the up-country Tamils about their own situation after the enactment of the new citizenship law of 2009, the CRG researcher visited Hatton, in Nuwara Eliya district, in the heart of Sri Lanka's tea industry, which is home to 50.57 per cent of the Indian Tamils (Department of Census and Statistics 2009: 61). It is the centre of up-country tea-growing regions such as Maskeliya, Talawakelle, Bogawantalawa and Dickoya. P.P. Sivapragasam states that the new citizenship law of 2009 is comparatively simpler in nature than the earlier one. According to this new legislation, individuals need not to apply to state authorities for citizenship; rather he/she can obtain a 'general declaration' which is to be countersigned by a 'justice of peace' and serves as proof of citizenship. 'Yet, the issue has not been resolved for thousands of individuals and discrimination against the plantation Tamils continues' (Sivapragasam 2009: 71).

The researcher interviewed individuals on plantations in Hatton in March 2011 and got mixed reactions about their new status as Sri Lankans. The researcher visited Strathdon Estate, located east of Hatton, and the Battalgala Estate. A few respondents were very happy to be recognised as Sri Lankan citizens, while the majority was not very sure about their future. One of the respondents identified a number of positive effects of obtaining citizenship: 'After getting citizenship we shall be treated as human beings. We hope to enjoy the freedom to participate in our country's politics in terms of right to vote and to stand as a candidate for local elections.'[31] They opined that they are happy that their nationality and national identification has been ensured. Their children, members of the younger generation, have the right to basic documents. They thought that once their political rights are recognised, people from the younger generation can engage themselves in political processes in a meaningful way.

The respondents also highlighted the fact that younger workers are more likely to benefit from the citizenship campaigns. There is evidence of migration from the estates to large cities like Colombo and Kandy. In addition to age, obtaining an NIC is considered essential to be able to leave the plantation area. Many plantation youth have migrated to Colombo or Kandy for jobs as they do not wish to work on the estates like slaves. Getting an NIC is easier for some with the citizenship certificate. However, many workers are being arrested by the police in its absence. Sometimes, due to lack of proper documentation, allegations of terrorism are also slapped on them. Although it has been stated that the Tamils of up-country can travel to Colombo and other areas in the south without any restriction (TamilNet 2009), the restriction prevails.

According to our respondents, formal documentation appears to be a major factor for personal and social development. Many of those who obtained citizenship have been registered as voters. They feel that they have been politically strengthened and their political rights guaranteed. Though this is a progressive step, their economic conditions have not yet improved. Several participants in our discussion reported that those who have applied through some NGOs after the enactment of the 2003 Act were able to receive citizenship certificates. Others who applied through trade unions were less successful. Considering the influence that the tea and rubber estates wield in the region, it is possible that the authorities are not favourable to applications that come via trade unions and are more inclined to support applications for citizenship sent to them by NGOs.

Our respondents also argued that they are still facing difficulties in getting their names enlisted as registered voters. Wages have not been increased, and indebtedness is growing. They said that their day-to-day life is tough as they depend on the estate work alone without other options. They do not have their own land to cultivate. *Gramaniladaris* are not always informed of legal developments, and this has negatively affected their rights to participate in political and other activities. This lack of awareness has resulted in people approaching certain officers, in the hope of being registered on the voter's list, only to encounter problems. The right to citizenship has not yet addressed the high degree of poverty. Generally, poor living conditions have not changed for the plantation Tamils.

It also appears that little improvement has occurred with regard to educational development of the population. The drop-out rate is very high in the secondary schools in the estate areas. In fact, in spite of educational reforms, there is a particular problem among parents who refuse to regularise the status of their children. In her writing, Sulakshani Perera recounts one teacher explaining that:

> We try and educate the students about the need for national identity cards and proper documentation. . . . But when they tell their parents, the children's comments are simply brushed aside. Some parents also question why national identity cards and birth certificates are important, because they themselves have managed perfectly fine without them. So these children grow up with absolutely no evidence of their parentage, except a piece of paper issued by the estate management. (2007: 20–23)

While most residents of Sri Lanka obtain citizenship by descent, the plantation Tamils are required to use the registration process. Although the introduction of the 2003 Act, and its Amendment in 2009, has changed the legal position of more than half of the total stateless people in Sri Lanka, the issue has not yet been resolved for many individuals as most of them are not in a position to show their proof of residence.[32] Moreover, discrimination against the plantation Tamils still persists.

Concluding Observations

The discussion in this chapter would make it clear that it is difficult to treat the notion of statelessness as a one-dimensional concept in the context of post-colonial South Asia. A pragmatic approach to statelessness entails rigour in identifying the causes behind statelessness. In fact, it is not advisable to think of stateless persons simply as those who have accidentally been deprived of belonging to a nation-state due to some unavoidable exigency, placing them in some kind of a legal no-man's land. Statelessness is the by-product of the processes of unmaking and remaking of boundaries and borders of nation-states in South Asia. Therefore, some people are stateless in this region on account of certain state policies. These policies and decisions have made some people stateless in one country, while they are unwelcome in another. Perhaps there could not be any better example to prove this point than the case of Indian Tamils of Sri Lanka.

Usually, statelessness emerges as a by-product of succession of states or territorial reorganisation. But it also emerges due to the persecution of minorities and a state's majoritarian bias, which lead the states at times to expel citizens or inhabitants. This condition, reinforced by the protracted refusal of the involved states to take them back creates a situation which, at times, leads to the loss of their nationality and citizenship. The states of South Asia, sometimes referred to as the 'kin states', represent multiple social and ethnic continuities across the borders. As such, one can find cases with overlapping sources of statelessness in contemporary South Asia.

To understand the phenomenon of statelessness, it is also necessary to take a close look at the concept of citizenship. Nationality and citizenship are two words most commonly used to describe the legal bond of membership between an individual and a state. Nationality can only be conferred or confirmed by the states and the states are responsible for protecting the fundamental rights of everybody on their territory, including those of stateless persons. In other words, for all activities relating to statelessness, the states are indispensable actors. Sri Lanka makes an interesting counterpoint to India in this respect. India started out with a relatively inclusive citizenship law and moved towards exclusion, while Sri Lanka started out with an intentionally exclusive law and a deliberately created statelessness problem, and then apparently moved towards inclusiveness in its citizenship law and towards renationalising those stateless persons.

Statelessness most commonly affects refugees. But all refugees are not stateless, and similarly, not all stateless men, women and children may qualify as refugees. Refugee status entails certain extra requirements: a person is a refugee when he/she is outside his/her country of nationality (or country of habitual domicile if stateless), and deserves asylum, based upon a well-founded fear of persecution for categorised reasons that make him or her unwilling or unable to avail of the protection of that country. Some Sri Lankan Tamils living in the camps of Tamil Nadu, who had acquired Sri Lankan citizenship before their flight due to the massacres in the island nation, do not wish to go back to their homeland. Moreover, in some instances, the protracted nature of refugeehood of the Indian Tamils has subdued their identity as a stateless people. They are not willing to go back to Sri Lanka as their legal status has not been clearly confirmed. Due to the fear of persecution they do not want to face once again the fate that they had faced earlier. Under such circumstances, the dividing line between the protracted refugees and the stateless people becomes very thin, and ambiguity prevails.[33]

According to legal experts, the long-staying refugees who acquired Sri Lankan citizenship before they fled and who do not wish to return are not stateless unless they have renounced their Sri Lankan nationality, as there is no safeguard in Sri Lankan nationality law. Those who acquired Indian citizenship before they fled Sri Lanka will not be regarded as stateless if they have been recognised as Indian citizens. There are others, who claim to have acquired Indian citizenship under the pacts but cannot prove this; they could be of undetermined nationality or stateless. In this context, a question arises in relation to those who were entitled to Indian citizenship and repatriation under the pacts, but fled before the repatriation occurred: Are they deemed to have entered as illegal immigrants?

Notes

* This chapter includes content drawn from various Calcutta Research Group publications, which have been used with permission.
The author would like to acknowledge our debt to all our respondents in India and Sri Lanka, who shared their experiences with us. Our researchers arrived at Coonoor on the day when the cyclone 'Thane' hit the region. Due to heavy rain, initially it was not possible for them to walk around the tea estates and talk to the estate workers. We are really grateful to our respondents, who agreed to meet our researchers at the hotel, ignoring that cyclonic weather, to share their experiences of having to resettle themselves in the Nilgiris, an alien place in their 'homeland.' We express our sincere thanks to Rupabardhana of Nuwara Eliya, without whose help as interpreter, it would have not been possible to talk to Tamil estate workers at Hatton. We would also like to thank Dr Nasreen Chowdhory for her suggestions and comments on the draft of this chapter. The author is indebted to Gladston Xavier, Loyola College, Chennai for his insights on the camps in Tamil Nadu.

1. It is to be mentioned in this connection that the Government of India and the state government of Tamil Nadu have not recognised these people as 'stateless.' These people are considered Sri Lankan refugees. Please see LankaNewspapers.com (2007).

2. As of November 2011, the total number of refugees from Sri Lanka staying in 112 camps situated in 26 districts of Tamil Nadu was 68,155. Total number of non-camp refugees is 34,398. Interview with K. Deenabandhu, Commissioner, Commissionerate of Rehabilitation and Welfare of Non-Resident Tamils, Chennai, 2 January 2012.

3. However, legal experts may argue that being a refugee does not preclude one from simultaneously being stateless.

4. It is important to note that there were two amendments and the second one was the Grant of Citizenship to Persons of Indian Origin (Amendment) Act No. 6 of 2009.

5. There are 13 camps altogether in Thiruvannamalai.

6. The Portuguese were the first Europeans to invade the island. But in 1658, the Portuguese lost to the more powerful Dutch. Their rule lasted for 150 years and in 1796, the Dutch surrendered their territories to an expedition sent out by the British. In 1833 different parts of the territory, which functioned independently, were unified by the British for administrative convenience.

7. See note 5, this chapter.

8. It is to be noted that grant of a citizenship certificate was left to the discretion of the minister. This combination of laws effectively discriminated against the up-county Tamils who did not have such long ancestral links in Ceylon. In this context, please see the restrictive conditions for citizenship by registration under Articles 11–14 of Ceylon Citizenship Act 1948. Moreover it is also worth mentioning here that under Section 19 of the 1948 Citizenship Act of Sri Lanka, citizens can renounce their nationality without having acquired a nationality of another State—an act which could render them stateless.

9. Interview with P.P. Devaraj, Chairman, Foundation for Community Transformation, Colombo, and former minister for Hindu religious and cultural affairs (1989–94), Colombo, 2 April 2011.

10. Cited in ibid.

11. As a proof of citizenship a special Indian passport mentioning the Sirimavo–Shastri Pact 1964 on the cover of the passport was issued to the applicant who wanted Indian citizenship. However, in many cases displaced Indian plantation workers who received Indian passports under the Sirimavo–Shastri Pact lost or misplaced their identity proofs in the course of taking refuge. After entering the refugee camps they were not in a position to show their Indian passports to the camp authorities and became refugees in their own homeland.

12. V. Suryanarayan shared these narratives in his interview with the author on 29 September 2011. See also Suryanarayan (2010).

13. It is to be noted in this context that if their children were born in India before 1 July 1987, they would be Indian citizens under the 1955 Indian Citizenship Act, and the children born to one Indian parent would acquire Indian nationality if born between 1 July 1984 and 7 January 2004.

14. Sri Lankan refugees arrived in Tamil Nadu in different phases. The first phase started from 24 July 1983, after Black July, to 29 July 1987. The second phase began with the start of Eelam War II after 25 August 1989, where many Sri Lankan Tamils came to Tamil Nadu. Eelam War III commenced in April 1995, starting the third wave of refugees. The flow of refugees had stopped in 2002 because of the ceasefire agreement.

15. The data are collected from the Commissionerate of Rehabilitation and Welfare of Non-resident Tamils, Chennai.

16. The details of camp experiences discussed in pages 89-91 are attributed to Nasreen Chowdhory entitled 'Belonging in exile and "home": The Politics of Repatriation in South Asia', McGill University, 2007 (dissertation) unless otherwise stated.

17. Data collected from the Commissionerate of Rehabilitation and Welfare of Non-resident Tamils, Chennai.

18. Ibid.

19. Most of the camps in which interviews were conducted had a very good and effective nursery facility. Young mothers were provided with additional nutrition, and infant children were given proper care for seven to eight months after their birth in the camps.

20. Camp officials told the researcher that they regretted the repatriation of refugees because they had lost their jobs after working in the camps for 14 years. However, since 2006, freedom of movement has vastly improved. There are no daily roll calls; in fact, it happens only once a month now. Refugees with permission from authorities are allowed to stay outside the camp for purpose of employment for extended periods.

21. Experts argue that Thomas George has Sri Lankan citizenship, even if it is not effective. However, it should be noted that under Section 19 of the 1948 Citizenship of Sri Lanka, citizens can renounce their nationality without having acquired a nationality of another State—an act that could render them stateless.

22. It was stated in the declaration that: '[t]he agreement reached between the two parties must guarantee the right of all Ceylonese, persons of recent Indian origin domiciled in Ceylon, to enjoy the full panoply of human rights including the right to life, citizenship, property, universal suffrage etc. as well as self-determination as described by the Universal Declaration of Human Rights and upheld in International Law and Practice' (OfERR 2003).

This is important because the Declaration demands the enjoyment of human rights including the right to citizenship (nationality) rather than the term 'citizenship rights' which suggest rights flowing from citizenship.

23. These persons, who were treated as 'stateless' people in Lanka, came to India as refugees prior to 1990 due to the ethnic conflict in the island nation.

24. On 25 May 2007, Ramalingam Chandrasekeran, JVP MP, raised the issue of 28,500 people, who are living in camps in Tamil Nadu and had not received Sri Lankan citizenship although they were entitled to it under the terms of the Sirimavo–Shastri Pact. In Parliament, the motion said that: 'in terms of the 2003 Act, children of people who have lived continuously after October 30, 1964, are entitled to Sri Lankan citizenship. But those who have had to live as refugees in Tamil Nadu owing to the situation in Sri Lanka after 1983 have not been able to meet this requirement. As a result of this, about 28,500 have not received citizenship' (*Asian Tribune* 2007).

Asian Tribune reports that: 'it was realized that 28,500 Ceylon Tamil Refugees in Tamil Nadu would suffer disadvantages unless they were in possession of the Certificate of Citizenship issued under Section 4(2) of the Grant of Citizenship to Persons of Indian Origin Act No. 35 of 2003 confirming their Ceylon Citizenship. Under Sec. 2 of the Act, "Any person of Indian origin, who on the date of coming into operation of this Act, (a) Has been a permanent resident of Sri Lanka since October 30; 1964 or (b) Is a descendent resident in Sri Lanka of a person who has been a permanent resident of Sri Lanka since October 30, 1964, shall be granted the status of citizen of Sri Lanka, with effect from such date and be entitled, in like manner and to the same extent, to all the rights and privileges to which a citizen of Sri Lanka is entitled to, by law". According to Ramalingham Chandrasekeran, most of the Ceylon Tamil Refugees in India fled the island in 1990. Since then, the refugees referred to in the Act as "persons of Indian origin" had been accommodated in the camps run by the Government in Tamil Nadu. While agreeing to consider the JVP's demand to amend the citizenship laws for persons of Indian origin to enable "Ceylon Tamil refugees" now living in Tamil Nadu, the Sri Lankan Government said the subject could be referred to a select committee to rectify loopholes, if any, in the existing Act' (*Asian Tribune* 2007).

25. They were granted Indian citizenship under the Sirimavo–Shastri Pact.

26. Interview with Ramakrishnan, Coonoor, 31 December 2011.

27. The reference is to the special passport that was issued under Sirimavo–Shastri Pact.

28. Interview with Ramakrishnan, Coonoor, 31 December 2011.

29. Interview with Chandramohan, Coonoor, 31 December 2011.

30. Ibid.

31. Interview, Hatton, 12 March 2011.

32. According to Mr Yogarajan—formerly of the Ceylon Workers Congress (CWC) and currently the UNP MP for the Nuwara Eliya district where the maximum number of plantations are to be found—the issue seems to be producing birth documentation that is required in order to obtwwain NICs. Births on the estate are usually registered by the estate management and then notified to the relevant local authorities, but he claims that in many instances these births have not been registered, and therefore it is difficult to obtain the NIC. He also states that the Registrar General's Office is willing to accept other documents that would show residency in order to provide a birth certificate, but individuals need to be assisted with this effort because they do not fully understand the need for these documents. Interview with Yogarajan, Hatton, 6 April 2011.

33. In this context, the UNHCR's view is noteworthy. It says that stateless persons who are refugees should primarily be viewed as refugees as they are guaranteed a higher level of rights (that is, benefit of the principle of non-refoulement). The fact that they are stateless is relevant to assessing the appropriate durable solution.

FOUR

The Chinese of Calcutta

A Case of Statelessness

*SUHIT K. SEN**

The Chinese community has been around in the city of Calcutta (now Kolkata) for well over two centuries. For most of that period, they had been wayfarers—merchants, workers—who would come to the city to work but would not typically settle in the city. It was only around the end of the nineteenth century that a distinct community of Chinese settlers began to take shape around an equally distinct Chinatown in what is now central Calcutta, in an area known as Tiretti Bazaar (Dey 2007: 14–17). When this settlement was destroyed, they moved to Tangra, an area in east Calcutta, and pioneered the tanning and leather-work industry there. A majority of Calcutta's Chinese residents still live in the area, from where most of the tanneries have now been relocated. It is now the centre of a thriving business in Chinese cuisine.

What we are concerned with here is the fate of the Chinese people in Calcutta after India became independent in 1947. In the colonial period, the Chinese people were left very much to themselves, to go about their myriad businesses by the state—there was neither much engagement nor interference. With the advent of Independence, the situation seemed to not have changed significantly, despite the establishment of a nation-state. The Chinese people continued to go about their business quietly. The question of citizenship did not arise. This situation was critically facilitated by the fact that the community was very closely knit, reclusive and disinclined to get involved in matters that were political, or otherwise controversial.

Registration and Statelessness

Things began to change, however, in the late 1950s, when the Union government issued orders concerning the registration of foreigners, consequent to some legislative changes with regard to their status. The Chinese of Calcutta were singled out for special reference. Registration too entailed the need to obtain residential permits for those who had not been in continuous residence for a certain period of time. It was at this point that the ghastly implications of statelessness and alienation came home to the Chinese community, with a number of advisories being issued against Chinese residents in Calcutta and Kalimpong, especially. The change in the situation was caused mainly by border disputes and mutual allegations of cross-border incursions between China and India. Things started coming to a head towards the end of the 1950s and culminated in the 1962 Sino-Indian hostilities, as even a cursory perusal of contemporary newspapers will attest to.

As the governments of West Bengal and India moved against the Chinese in India and Calcutta, a newspaper report said that several thousand Chinese could become stateless in India as a result of the Government of India's decision that Chinese residents in India would have to obtain residence permits in India and passports from the People's Republic of China, after the Chinese Communist Revolution, which most were loath to do. Passports issued by the Kuomintang government in Formosa (Taiwan) would not be recognised.[1]

But, as it happened, this was just the beginning of their travails, which began in right earnest after the 1962 Sino-Indian War broke out. With the outbreak of these hostilities, more restrictions were imposed on the Chinese community, apart from the fact that one group of around 1,500 Chinese people were shipped off to a camp in a place called Deoli in the state of Rajasthan. Others joined them later. In effect, almost all the Chinese residents of India, including the Chinese people in Calcutta, where they were massively concentrated, became undesirable aliens, though most of them had lived most of their lives in India and a substantial number had been born in the country as well. Few had any link with China, especially after the 1949 Communist Revolution.

Among the new disabilities that the newly undesirable aliens encountered were restrictions on employment leading to the loss of jobs, and restrictions on travel imposed by the necessity to obtain travel permits that were granted only in exceptional circumstances. This in itself disrupted the possibility of engaging in normal activities, like being employed or getting an education. But, perhaps, even this was not what brought home to the Chinese the full force of their statelessness and alienation in the land of their birth or long-term, permanent residence. What did was the xenophobic hostility this largely unexceptionably self-engaged community faced from 'Indians'—or should we say other Indians—abuse was quotidian, and attacks on lives and property not entirely uncommon.

There was a paradoxical element that needs to be pointed out here. While the Government of India, on the one hand, insisted that the Chinese residents of India, regardless of their provenance, acquire passports from mainland China—the People's Republic, in other words—it also frequently harassed those who had Beijing passports on the ground that they were *agents provocateurs*. Let us take a few examples. From 1959 onwards, reports originating with the governments of India and West Bengal spoke of propaganda and espionage being carried out by Chinese residents. On 20 November 1959 there was a report about propaganda.[2] A few days later, it was reported that there were 185 Chinese residents in Kalimpong who had infiltrated into India during the Kuomintang rule in China. It was not known, the report said, how many had registered under the Foreigners Registration Act 1946.[3] A few days later, there was again a report that Chinese spies had infiltrated into Kalimpong.[4] Soon after, the chief minister of West Bengal, Dr B.C. Roy, informed the assembly that a close watch was being kept on anti-Indian, pro-Chinese propaganda in Darjeeling district.[5] Many of the Chinese residents there had gone to the hills from Calcutta (see, for instance, Hsieh 2011). A census specifically of the Chinese residents in West Bengal was mooted, listing numbers, distribution, origin and place of birth.[6] A flurry of reports followed. One said that the Ministry of External Affairs had denied in the Rajya Sabha a contention that news had been leaked through the All India Radio to the Chinese Embassy.[7] Within a couple of days, it was reported that the government had issued an order that all foreigners—including the Chinese—should acquire residence permits by 5 January 1960.[8]

There were reports about a sense of uncertainty within the Chinese community. Newspaper reports said that the Chinese Embassy had complained to the Union government in New Delhi that the police had resorted to measures in the guise of vigilance that were hampering trading facilities for Chinese residents, especially in Kalimpong. The Union government subsequently asked the West Bengal government for details. Meanwhile, many Chinese residents in Calcutta who did not have Chinese passports issued by Beijing, and were not Indian citizens, had approached New Delhi for Indian citizenship, given that they had been living in Calcutta—or elsewhere in India—for a long time, in some cases, generations. The prospect of statelessness had created uncertainty among the Chinese, who, by and large, favoured the Kuomintang government in Formosa (Taiwan). Formosan passports were not, however, favoured in India. Many holding Formosan passports had been deported.[9]

Quit Orders and Deportation

'Quit India' notices also became the order of the day in the early 1960s, leading up to the 1962 Sino-Indian aggression in Ladakh and the North-Eastern Frontier Agency (now Arunachal Pradesh).

On 25 January 1961, it was reported that a Chinese couple, for instance, were served these notices. Mr T.I. Ping and Mrs Ping had registered as foreigners in 1957 and were later arrested in Darjeeling and served the notices under the Foreigners Act.[10] A similar fate befell Chang Ju, a school teacher, and He Shing-tu, editor of the *China Review*. They had to leave Calcutta under quit orders, for prejudicial activities. They were escorted to the Tibetan border via Sikkim. The Union government denied that it had been persecuting Chinese residents. As a sort of gesture, it withdrew a case against Chang Wen-keel, manager of the Bank of China, who had agreed to leave India.[11]

The spate of deportation orders continued. In March, the parliamentary secretary to the minister for external affairs, Sadath Ali Khan, told the Lok Sabha that the Government of India had replied to a 'Note' from China on the deportation of Chinese nationals in India. He also informed the House that 70 quit India notices had been issued to Chinese residents—of which 10 had been complied with.[12] In April, four foreigners suspected to be Chinese were held in Naihati, 38 kilometres north of Calcutta, without passports or other papers.[13] Two Chinese residents were deported from Calcutta. They were taken to the Nathu La Pass and sent on from there. The same report that gives this information also mentions that quit orders were served to 50 Chinese residents. Most of them had left India in response, but some had gone to court against the issuance of these notices.[14] A week later, it was reported that a Chinese resident, L.C. Kang, was sentenced for failing to comply with a quit order notice, while another was produced in court in Darjeeling. He had earlier been a resident of Kalimpong.[15] Not long after, a Chinese woman, L.N. Lan, the editor of the *China Review*, was jailed for violating a quit order.[16] In the very next month, a Chinese woman, Ching Mei-fung, and her children had to leave Calcutta under police escort. They had earlier been issued quit orders.[17] A couple of days later, three more Chinese residents had been served quit orders. The article reporting this also said that till May 1961, 50 Chinese residents had been escorted out of India.[18]

A week later, it was reported that Kalimpong was likely to be declared a notified area, to make it easier for the government to protect the security of the state.[19] This was consequent to a series of reports that the hill station had become a hotbed of anti-Indian propaganda and activities. A month and a half later, it was reported that besides expelling Chinese residents suspected to be involved in anti-Indian activities, the Government of India was contemplating fresh steps to ensure that Chinese residents could not carry out such activities. Among these steps, it was contemplated that Chinese residents would not be allowed to buy property or enlarge their business concerns. The report said that the government believed that the number of business enterprises owned by Chinese residents had grown and that these could be used for subversive purposes. Besides, it was reported that a census of Chinese enterprises had been conducted and a comprehensive screening of these enterprises carried out. It did not, however, mention what results had been obtained from these programmes.[20] Replying to a question in the Lok Sabha, a report said that then Union Home Minister Lal Bahadur Shastri replied that small Chinese establishments—especially laundries and shoe shops, two areas of business the Chinese had a large presence in—had been screened on receipt of reports that they were being used as centres of espionage.[21] A press release a couple of months later said that a census of Chinese residents in West Bengal had found that as of 31 December 1960, the number of Chinese residents in the state had been pegged at 11,307.[22] We shall return to the question of the size of the Chinese population in the course of this chapter.

Quit India notices and reports of deportations continued alongside special census operations and measures to contain the activities and mobility of the Chinese residents. In November, it was reported that a Chinese businessman from Darjeeling, Liang Ti-chi, had been told to leave India. It was reported that at that point, 28 Chinese residents from the district had been asked to leave the country.[23] Soon after, four Chinese residents from West Bengal were deported. One was a tailor from Kalimpong, another a shoemaker from Darjeeling, and two more—of unspecified professions—from Calcutta.[24] In 1962, these actions against Chinese residents in India continued. It was reported in April that Liang Pei-chiang, proprietor of a saloon and a resident of Delhi, had been asked to leave India.[25] Clearly, Calcutta, or West Bengal, was not the only arena of the crackdown on Chinese residents. I shall have occasion in the course of this chapter to return to this and some other reports referred to here.

In early August in 1962, two more Chinese residents were expelled. A report said that the total number of those expelled had numbered 30.[26] Later that month, it was reported that 56 Chinese residents had been told to leave between January and June. It also said that as of 1 January 1962, there were 10,867 Chinese people in India.[27] In the run-up to the Sino-Indian conflict that year, actions against Chinese residents became more frenetic. In September, two Chinese were served quit notices.[28] Later that month, it was reported that 184 Chinese residents had been expelled from India till the month of August.[29]

The next month seemed to have registered an escalation in, if not exactly the peaking of, panic among the reportedly 15,000-strong Chinese community of Calcutta. A report said that 4,000 Chinese persons had applied for passports from the Communist China regime; 400 had adopted Indian citizenship; and the rest were recorded as stateless, whose status had been or would have to be regularised with temporary residence permits. Panic had been triggered, the report said, on two counts. First, it was feared that subsequent to the outbreak of hostilities, the public might get enraged; and, second, the government might ask them to obtain valid travel documents or leave the country. Those with documents from mainland China feared deportation, though many did not wish to leave India. The report suggested that many of those who had obtained passports from the Communist regime had done so under coercion by a small section of residents who were vocal votaries of the Peking regime. Many among this latter section, the report went on to say, had been expelled. The panic was compounded by a run on laundries owned by Chinese entrepreneurs, though restaurants continued to be popular. In this situation, the West Bengal government had warned the general populace against any disorder and had assured the stateless that no action would be taken against them. It also said that the panic had reached a pitch that would provoke an exodus, adding that no such thing had actually happened. At the same time it said that it was worried about the activities of 20-odd hardcore Communists. Even before the incursions in the North-East Frontier Agency, the government added, the *China Review* had been publishing adverse editorial content about India.[30]

Despite statements that mixed reassurance and a hard line, Chinese residents continued to be picked up, served quit notices or deported. At the fag-end of October, five Chinese residents were held in Darjeeling for subversive activities.[31] Early next month, a Chinese woman was jailed pending deportation.[32] In Calcutta, following the arrest of one Lee Chin Tha, three associates—named C.P. Hua, P.S. Lin and W.S. Chin—were also arrested and remanded in custody.[33] Earlier, Chinese residents arrested in Calcutta were taken to the camp set up in Deoli, Rajasthan, while one person of Chinese origin was served a quit order.[34] Next month, 18 Chinese residents were taken into custody, prior to being sent to the camp in Deoli.[35]

Some time earlier, the tenor of the government's reaction to the presence of Chinese people on Indian territory became clear in some answers made in the Lok Sabha by then Union Home Minister Lal Bahadur Shastri and his deputy. They said in response to questions that the government planned to take strict action against Chinese people in India who were considered 'security risks.' Shastri also said that curbs and restrictions had been imposed. The minister of state iterated that a watch was being maintained on those Chinese residents whose activities were likely to be anti-national or anti-social. He also said that 24 Chinese residents had been asked to leave India since 30 June 1962, of whom five had left; special steps would have to be taken against the remaining 19. Significantly, in response to another question, the minister could not provide a break-up of these figures into Chinese nationals, Indian citizens and stateless people.[36]

Loyalty and Panic

Equally significantly, the high pitch of the government's attitude to the Chinese people in India came despite public protests by leaders of prominent Chinese residents that their loyalty lay entirely with India, where most of them had been born. For instance, it was reported on 12 January 1960 that Y.K. Cheung, president of the Overseas Chinese Association of India, addressed a meeting and iterated that the Chinese community stood fully behind the Indian people and the Government of India; 85 per cent of the people who attended were in tune with him. This was in the context of a border dispute and Chinese incursions into India. Cheung also said that the Chinese community treated India as its homeland and that the Chinese regarded themselves as citizens of India. He said that of the 15,000 Chinese in India, 12,000 lived in Calcutta and many had applied for citizenship.[37] In October 1962, over 1,000 Chinese residents of Calcutta met under the auspices of the Overseas Chinese Association and resolved to join hands with Indians to fight China. With one K.C. Yap presiding, they said India was their homeland and expressed deep sympathy with the Indian people. Yap said of the 15,000 Chinese people, 12,000 were stateless, 400 were Indian citizens and 300 more had applied for citizenship. Two representatives of the Pradesh Congress Committee attended the meeting.[38]

We have earlier referred to the panic that in this context had gripped the Chinese in Calcutta. This panic was exacerbated in December 1962 with reports that the Chinese consulate in the city would close down. They besieged the consulate to get special visas for the mainland. It was reported that in three days, 250 people had been given visas, with several hundred more waiting for them. Those with Peking visas were finding it impossible to live in Calcutta, though they had been in the city for generations, were unconcerned with politics and considered Calcutta their hometown. Things, the report said, had started changing with the opening of the consulate in 1950 and persistent pressure on Chinese residents to acquire Peking passports.[39] The consulate did, in fact, close shop in 1963.[40] This unsettled state of affairs was exacerbated by a statement from Peking that it would send ships to repatriate Chinese residents in India who were being victimised.[41] The Ministry of External Affairs described Peking's charge that Chinese residents were being ill-treated as 'fake and mischievous', and rejected the charge that they had been interned with 'ulterior motives'. It also said that the 2,000 Chinese people who had been rounded up from Assam and the aforementioned border districts in West Bengal and sent to Deoli would be screened, and those who were not considered risks would be released.[42]

In connection with the panic among Chinese residents, we have earlier mentioned the apprehension of public anger. In fact, with first, the intensification of border skirmishes, and then with the outbreak of hostilities, there was a rash of demonstrations against China. While these may not have been specifically aimed at the Chinese residents of the city, they would have done little to assuage their apprehensions. It was reported that meetings, rallies and other kinds of demonstrations were constantly being held all over the city in connection with Sino-Indian border disputes. Mass demonstrations were also common. Clashes between rival groups were disrupting city life.[43] After the hostilities began in 1962, a mass rally was held against Chinese aggression.[44]

It is important to note one feature that emerges from some of the reports narrated here. Though, unfortunately, most of the reports do not make any mention of who exactly the Chinese residents against whom action was taken were, what their provenance or profession was and how long they had been in India, some of the reports do suggest that a number of people who were being hounded were professionals or small business people—an editor here, a banker there, a laundry-owner, a shoeshop-owner or a tailor. If we combine with these scattered references what we know of Chinese migration patterns as mentioned at the beginning of the chapter, it becomes clear that a large number of ordinary Chinese people who had either lived in India for decades or, indeed, been born in the country, became victims of the government's attentions. This point was, in fact, made by an MP in Parliament when he asked the then Union Home Minister Govind Ballabh Pant whether many Chinese residents living in Calcutta for generations would be registered as Chinese nationals just because of their origin. Pant's cryptic reply was that some had got citizenship.[45] Clearly, the stateless status the Chinese people in Calcutta and India as a whole had to suffer was not the result of a naturally anomalous position, but a result of the Indian government's considered policy of not granting them citizenship and forcing them to register as citizens of Communist China.

Number Games

Let us focus now on the question of numbers. According to some leaders of what we may call Chinese society, there was a massive diminution in the size of the Chinese community in Calcutta. Estimates of the size of the community vary, but community leaders claim that in 1962 there were at least 30,000 Chinese in Calcutta—the actual size could well have been double that number (see, for instance, Hsieh 2011: 199). Now the community is about 5,000-strong. Apart from those who were sent back to China, and many incredibly were, others left Calcutta either for other parts of India or, more usually, for other countries altogether.

Census figures present a different picture, though. According to the decennial censuses conducted in India, in 1951, the Chinese community in Calcutta was 9,215-strong; this grew to 14,607 in 1961. In 1971, despite the Sino-Indian conflict, the number of Chinese in Calcutta did not fall appreciably—it was pegged at 14,000, a fall of less than 5 per cent. By 1981, it had fallen to 12,500, many presumably dispersing to other parts of the country and some going abroad.

The Government of India did a special census of Chinese residents in India just before the Chinese incursion into India. Announcing the results of this special census, Jawaharlal Nehru informed the Parliament that there were 17,373 Chinese living in India, of whom 8,336 lived in West Bengal, mostly in Calcutta, but some in the hill station of Kalimpong as well. As will be clear from the reports cited previously, there were other estimates as well, some from the special censuses and some from Chinese residents. It is not clear why the community's estimate varies so widely from the census figures, or for that matter why the decennial census figures diverge from that of the special census. But it does appear that there was no major exodus of the Chinese in the wake of the war.

Reasons of State

Let us return to the late 1950s, when the government started seriously going about the business of getting the Chinese to register as foreigners under the Foreigners Registration Act. The year 1959 seemed to have been critical for a number of reasons, principal among which was the flight of the Dalai Lama and large numbers of refugees from Tibet to India. To this was added a long-running war of words between the two countries mostly about disputed border positions. There were some border incursions as well, reported in the Indian press as having occurred from the Chinese side. The security of Ladakh, which it was thought the Chinese might try to occupy, was also an important irritant.

In the wake of these diplomatic incidents and unsettled relations, the Indian government claimed that there were a large number of Chinese people who were engaged in espionage both in Calcutta and in Kalimpong, as we have seen. Some of the people were served orders to leave India from 1959, through to the Sino-Indian conflict. As mentioned earlier, a large number of Chinese people were bundled off to a camp in Rajasthan after the outbreak of hostilities and restrictions on movement imposed. The manner in which people were picked up and bundled off to the Deoli camp was traumatic, as has been recorded by one Chinese resident, whose grandfather had come to Calcutta and whose father had lived in India, mostly in Calcutta (Hsieh 2011: 121–37). When they were picked up in Kalimpong, where they had moved, the author's father was working in the shoe trade and he himself was a student preparing for his school-leaving examinations. Their long residence in India and legitimate occupations did not prevent a midnight knock on the door and ultimate transportation to Deoli (ibid.: 173–81).

But even before that, when the drive to register the Chinese in India, including Calcutta, began, they were told that they would have to acquire passports of the People's Republic of China, and that Formosan—Taiwanese—passports would not be recognised. Most Chinese in India, who had come long before the Chinese Revolution, did not want to get these passports, or acquire citizenship of Communist China. The Indian government did grant some passports to those who had been in India for a long time. In the proceedings in Parliament already alluded to, for instance, it was mentioned that 3,601 Chinese in India had Formosan passports and in effect were stateless, while 66 had applied for Indian citizenship. The then Union Home Minister, in response to a question, claimed that some long-standing Chinese residents had obtained citizenship. But clearly, throughout this period, the overwhelming majority of Chinese people in India were either formally or in effect, stateless.

Paul Chung, a leader of the Chinese in Calcutta, said that trying to obtain an Indian passport remained extremely difficult even about a quarter of a century after the Chinese hostilities. He obtained his after applying thrice. The situation has changed now. Apart from a few hundreds who have obtained Chinese passports, the rest of the people are now recognised as bona fide citizens of India, but only after lengthy litigation. But some ambiguity probably still surrounds the Chinese people in Calcutta.

Legal Quagmires

Chung's difficulties stemmed entirely from a legal framework that provided only the most conditional of rights to people who did not qualify for citizenship, either by dint of descent or geography. The Citizenship Act of 1955 specified that eligibility for citizenship would devolve only to those born in India on or after 26 January 1950 (the day the Indian Constitution was promulgated) but before 1 July 1987; or those born in India after 1 July 1987 and before the commencement of the Citizenship (Amendment) Act 2003, with either parent being an Indian citizen; or, finally, anyone born on or after the commencement of the Citizenship (Amendment) Act 2003, both of whose parents were Indian citizens, or one an Indian citizen and the other not an illegal alien (Ministry of Home Affairs 1955, see Annexure 13).

The act then goes on to specify the conditions under which someone is eligible for Indian citizenship by descent rather than by the fact of being born in India. The details of those provisions need not detain us here. But the plot thickens when we come to the provisions of the Act that provide for citizenship by registration. We shall not go into the provisions governing this, but will note that Explanation 2 under Section 5(g) of the Act specifies that a person shall be deemed to be of Indian origin if he/she, or either of his/her parents, was born in undivided India, or any territory that became part of India after 15 August 1947 (ibid.). This, as far as many Chinese residents in India, like Chung, for instance, are concerned, is the crux of the matter. Though neither the Census of India nor the various special enumerations of the Chinese residents in India recorded their length of stay in India or where they were born, it can safely be assumed in the light of the history of Chinese migration to India and some collateral material already cited that a large number of Chinese residents were either born in India or had parents who had been born here.

Let us go back to the first part of the Citizenship Act referred to in this chapter. Clearly, this piece of legislation could not have meant that only those born in India under the specified conditions would be eligible for Indian citizenship. What follows is that there is an unspoken—or unwritten—assumption informing these provisions that one class of people was naturally Indian citizens and that this class of people consisted of those who were naturally Indians. A clue to this problem may be found in a historical enquiry. Paula Banerjee, for instance, points, in a historical vein, to the ambiguities surrounding the notion of 'Indianness' in relation to the Parsis in the colonial period. Though the Parsis had migrated to India as early as the fourteenth century, 500-odd years later, a vigorous debate had been sparked off over whether the Parsis were indeed Indian (Banerjee 2003: 73–77).

Banerjee further argues, in the context of the first Foreigners Act—passed in 1864—that in the second half of the nineteenth century, the colonial state was legislatively devolving upon itself the power to make a distinction between subjects and foreigners/aliens. Nevertheless, she cites an observation that before the First World War, there was no tangible distinction between subjects and foreigners/aliens in the British Empire. Wartime legislation, however, strove to define more clearly the category of the alien and solidify differences between aliens/foreigners and subjects, a project that continued in the immediate aftermath of the cessation of war (ibid.: 84–88). Another round of legislation was triggered by the Second World War to consolidate the project of making the distinction as well as instituting a regime of surveillance (ibid.: 90–93).

Banerjee (ibid.: 94–97) also shows that after the war the interim government comprising Indians, in the run-up to Independence, continued to pursue the colonial projects of emphasising distinction and imposing surveillance and control, but in a more rigorous fashion by passing a new Foreigners Act in 1946.

There are a couple of points to be made in relation to this narrative. The first is that despite the rhetoric surrounding British subjecthood (later Indian citizenship, as we have observed) and alienness or foreign status, nowhere in legislation, colonial or post-Independence, was there any clear definition of what constituted that Indianness on which all these legislative manoeuvres were predicated. Banerjee makes this point in connection with the spate of the First World War and post-First World War legislation. 'However they were yet to define who an Indian was apart from the criteria [sic] of birth. Did that mean that all those who were not born in India were foreigners?' she writes (ibid.: 89). She also notes that there was no real definition of citizenship, other than that which followed from the definition of subjecthood as defined by the Nationality and Status of Aliens Act of 1914 (Banerjee 2003: 95).

Banerjee (ibid.: 98) makes another interesting point: that after independence, the Foreigners Act preceded the Citizenship Act by almost a decade. Was this an accident? We can posit that following the colonial lead, the new constitutional regime that was coming into and then came into being from 1946 onwards was at first more concerned with fixing the boundaries that would define who did not belong, because there was an intuitive understanding of who were 'naturally' Indians and, therefore, would belong, and, therefore, qualify for Indian citizenship. The Chinese obviously fell through the citizenship net, however long they may have lived in India, and, from the late 1950s, came to be subjected to the indignities of the Foreigners Act.

This law, enacted as we have seen in 1946, prescribed fairly stringent measures that state and central governments could use against those designated 'foreigners,' as we have seen in the case of the Chinese in Bengal, especially Calcutta. These included powers of surveillance, curtailment of mobility, documentation and, in extreme cases, deportment. But, as our story shows, and as Banerjee's account historically contextualises, the whole matter remained cloaked in ambiguity. Thus, for instance, many who were served quit notices could and did appeal to Indian courts. Apart from this, some Chinese residents in Calcutta (and elsewhere) in India managed to get citizenship status before 1962 and even in the late 1950s and early 1960s, when relations between the Delhi and Peking were scraping the bottom of the barrel.

It may also be reiterated that even a quarter of a century after the hostilities of 1962, those Chinese residents who weathered the harshest rigours of the late 1950s and 1960s found it difficult to obtain citizenship. As we have seen, under the operation of the Citizenship Act (as variously amended), most Chinese people in Calcutta would be legally entitled to citizenship. But it is far from clear how far legal provisions smoothen the way to actually obtaining passports or other valid documents—in other words, citizenship. It is also far from apparent whether Chinese residents queue up in droves to obtain these documents. Given the reclusive nature of the Chinese networks, it is entirely possible that, as for centuries, the Chinese prefer to go about their business without nitpicking about legal status, until some urgent circumstance necessitates it.

Notes

* This chapter includes content drawn from various Calcutta Research Group publications, which have been used with permission.

1. *Statesman*, 21 February 1960.
2. *Statesman*, 20 November 1959.
3. *Statesman*, 24 November 1959.
4. *Statesman*, 26 November 1959.
5. *Statesman*, 1 December 1959.
6. *Statesman*, 3 December 1959.
7. *Statesman*, 15 December 1959.
8. *Statesman*, 17 December 1959.
9. *Statesman*, 30 December 1959.
10. *Statesman*, 25 January 1961.
11. *Statesman*, 25 February 1961.
12. *Statesman*, 30 March 1961.
13. *Statesman*, 25 April 1961.
14. *Statesman*, 24 May 1961.
15. *Statesman*, 31 May 1961.
16. *Statesman*, 23 June 1961.
17. *Statesman*, 14 July 1961.
18. *Statesman*, 16 July 1961.
19. *Statesman*, 21 July 1961.
20. *Statesman*, 2 September 1961.
21. *Statesman*, 22 August 1962.
22. *Statesman*, 29 October 1961.
23. *Statesman*, 14 November 1961.
24. *Statesman*, 23 November 1961.
25. *Statesman*, 23 April 1962.
26. *Statesman*, 10 August 1962.
27. *Statesman*, 22 August 1962.
28. *Statesman*, 17 September 1962.
29. *Statesman*, 26 September 1962.
30. *Statesman*, 24 October 1962.
31. *Statesman*, 31 October 1962.
32. *Statesman*, 4 November 1962. As mentioned earlier, this crackdown was countrywide. The Government of India, for instance, ordered the

internment of people of Chinese origin in Assam and the five border districts of West Bengal—Cooch Behar, Darjeeling, Jalpaiguri, Dinajpur and Maldah—including those who had been served quit order notices but had not complied. Almost the entire Chinese-origin population of the Bengal districts—313 people—was arrested. *Statesman*, 21 November 1962. In New Delhi, a young Chinese man was arrested for having links with the Chinese embassy and undesirable elements. *Statesman*, 25 November 1962. Another Chinese resident was held in New Delhi the next month. *Statesman*, 12 December 1962.

33. *Statesman*, 1 December 1962.
34. *Statesman*, 25 November 1962.
35. *Statesman*, 16 December 1962.
36. *Statesman*, 15 November 1962.
37. *Statesman*, 12 January 1960.
38. *Statesman*, 29 October 1962. See also *Calcutta Municipal Gazette*, volume 73 (3), pp. 40–51.
39. *Statesman*, 9 December 1962.
40. *Statesman*, 1 January 1963.
41. *Statesman*, 19 December 1962.
42. *Statesman*, 20 December 1962.
43. *Calcutta Municipal Gazette*, volume 71 (1), 26 December 1959, p. 219.
44. *Calcutta Municipal Gazette*, volume 73 (2), 27 October 1962, pp. 25–26.
45. *Statesman*, 18 August 1960.

FIVE

The Stateless Chakmas in Arunachal Pradesh

SAMIR KUMAR DAS and
*ANASUA BASU RAY CHAUDHURY**

Article 1 of the 1954 Convention relating to the Status of Stateless Persons defines that a 'stateless person' is someone who is not recognised as a national by any state under the operation of its law. They therefore have no nationality or citizenship and are unprotected by national legislation and left in the arc of vulnerability. Whether or not a person is stateless can be determined on the basis of an assessment of relevant nationality laws and how these laws are implemented by the state. Since nationality is generally acquired on the basis of an existing, factual link between the individual and the State—some kind of connection either with the territory (place of birth or residence) or with a national (descent, adoption or marriage)—it is important to look at the nationality legislation and applicable practice of states with which an individual enjoys a relevant link, to see if nationality is indeed attributed to the individual under any state's law. If not, then he/she is stateless.

According to the UNHCR current estimates, the number of stateless persons worldwide might be at least 10 million, and it is a phenomenon that can be traced on every continent. As Carol Batchelor states:

> Statelessness is not merely a legal problem; it is a human problem. Failure to acquire status under the law can have a negative impact

> on many important elements of life, including the right to vote, to own property, to have health care, to send one's children to school, to work, and to travel to and from one's country of residence. Many complications arise for those who have no nationality including [for some asylum seekers] indefinite detention in a foreign State when that State cannot determine the individual's citizenship. (Batchelor 1998: 159)

In this regard, it is pertinent to analyse not only the problems related to the legal aspects, rules and developments, but also the human issues and realities they are intended to address.

Brief History

Against this backdrop, this chapter attempts to highlight the distress of the Chakmas in Arunachal Pradesh, who were encouraged by the Government of India to take shelter in the desolate land of the North East Frontier Agency (NEFA) (now Arunachal Pradesh), India, once they were uprooted from the Chittagong Hill Tracts (CHT), Bangladesh (erstwhile East Pakistan) in 1964 (Government of Arunachal Pradesh 1996). This displacement of the Chakmas was caused primarily due to the construction of the Kaptai Dam in connection with a hydroelectric project over the River Karnaphuli with the funding from the United States Agency for International Development (USAID). About 40 per cent of the best agricultural land of CHT was submerged due to the commissioning of this dam. The project displaced more than 100,000 indigenous people, who were forced to evacuate the designated area. According to the Government of East Pakistan:

> According to the survey undertaken by the Rehabilitation Officer, about 10,000 ploughing families having land in the reservoir bed and 8000 landless *jumia* (the tribal people whose means of livelihood is Jumming or slash-and-burn cultivation) families comprising one lakh people (1 lakh = 100,000) were displaced. The reservoir submerged a vast area comprising 125 mouzas. The inundation threw over 54000 acres of plough land out of cultivation. This area

> constitutes 40 percent of the total settled cultivable land of the district viz. Karnaphuli, Chengi, Kasasalong, and Malni have been inundated. (Ishaq 1971: 42)

According to Government of India estimates, by the middle of 1964, at least 140,000 persons—including Chakmas and Hajongs consisting of 2,902 families—had migrated to Assam. The then Government of Assam expressed its inability to settle such a large number of migrants in the state and consequently requested for their shifting to some other place. A suggestion was also made that a substantial number of families could be accommodated in the NEFA as 'some surplus land was available there' and 'NEFA agreed to accommodate some new migrants including the Chakmas and Hajongs under the already approved scheme' (CCRCAP 1995: 2). During 1964–68, 2,902 Chakma/Hajong families were settled in the NEFA in three districts of Lohit, Tirap and Subansiri. The plots of land varying from 5 to 10 acres per family (including 3 to 5 acres of cultivable land), depending upon the size of the family, was allotted to them under a centrally-sponsored rehabilitation scheme of India. A cash grant for each family was also sanctioned by the ministry of rehabilitation.

It is clear that, Arunachal Pradesh was (and still is) a sparsely populated state with the lowest population density (about 13 per square kilometre, according to the 2001 Census) amongst all the states in India. At that time, the NEFA was administrated by the ministry of external affairs of the Government of India with the Governor of Assam acting as an agent to the President of India. Vishnu Sahay, the then Governor of Assam, in his letter no. GA-71/64, dated 10 April 1964, addressed to the then Chief Minister of Assam, Bimala Prasad Chaliha, pointed out that:

> It occurred to me that we may get trouble between the Mizos and Chakmas in the Mizo district. These Chakmas would be quite suitable people to go into the Tirap division of NEFA where there is easily found vacant land in the area about which you and I have often spoken. (Government of Arunachal Pradesh 1996: 9)

The government records of Arunachal Pradesh indicate that between 1964 and 1969, a total of 2,748 families of Chakmas and Hajongs comprising some 14,888 persons were sent to the NEFA. Initially these migrants were settled in 10,799 acres of land in the three districts, namely Lohit (214 families settled: 1,192 persons in total), Subansiri (now in Papumpare: 238 families and 1,133 persons altogether) and Tirap (now in Changlang: 2,146 Chakma families with 11,813 persons in total and 150 Hajong families with 750 persons altogether) (see Basu Ray Chaudhury and Biswas 1997; Government of Arunachal Pradesh 1996: 9). By 1979, these figures increased up to 3,919 families consisting of 21,494 persons. According to the 1991 Census, the total number of the evacuees in Arunachal Pradesh from the CHT increased further to around 65,000, whereas the total population of the state was 858,392. Due to the absence of a census survey since then, the aforesaid figure is quoted in all accounts of the issue.[1]

Early in 1964, a wave of the Chakma Buddhists from the then East Pakistan migrated to Mizoram and Tripura. In the first half of May 1964, 490 Chakma refugees travelled on their own from Tripura to Margherita (Assam) and knocked at the door of the NEFA—where outsiders under all normal conditions were not entitled to visit.

Reflecting on the government's response to the Chakmas, Gautam Chakma observes:

> Within 48 hours the gate unlocked, the next day they were somewhere in Namphai and Mr. Mahavir Tyagi, Rehabilitation Minister, immediately flew to Shillong—then the capital of undivided Assam, directed special trainloads of Chakma refugees coming through Aizawl to Lido. Within 6 months, towards the end of the year 1964, the Lido camp vacated (sic) in favour of NEFA. In 1966, those who had been taken to Bihar, were redirected here. The same year, the Manchera Transit camp cleared (sic) for NEFA. (2005: 89)

The refugees were initially provided shelter in the government camps of Assam. 'They came in a hopeless and pathetic condition, just with the clothes that they wore' (Basu Ray Chaudhury 2003: 258), recalls one senior Mizoram official who was part of the Government of Assam team that received the incoming hill people in the state. Since a large number of refugees had taken shelter in Assam, the state government had expressed its inability to rehabilitate all of them and requested assistance in this regard from certain other states. The Government of Tripura also did not encourage these displaced persons to settle there despite requests from Chakma leaders. At one point, the Chakma leaders toyed with the idea of moving these hill people to the Andaman and Nicobar Islands. However, later they devised a scheme to accommodate these refugees in the desolate land of the NEFA.

P.N. Luthra, the then Adviser to the Governor of Assam, in his letter no. RR17/64 dated 21 April 1965, addressed to all political officers and additional political officers, NEFA, wrote:

> The settlement of people in NEFA will also help in developing pockets that are lying unused and unoccupied by the local population. Besides, the presence of stretches of vacant land along the border is strategically not desirable and the last emergency had highlighted the problem. Resettlement of people in the vacant border areas will help to strengthen our frontiers and their defence. (quoted in Talukdar 2008b)

The decision of settling them in the then NEFA, according to Dutta, was 'unilateral by nature' and 'the indigenous people were neither consulted nor taken into confidence' (2002: 208). The White Paper prepared by the Government of Arunachal Pradesh (1996: ii), for example, accuses that: 'Chakma and Hajong refugees were settled in Arunachal Pradesh in total disregard of the rights, privileges and ethnic values of people of Arunachal Pradesh.' Incidentally, since its NEFA days, even in the pre-Independence era, the state has enjoyed a 'Special Protected Area' status under the provisions of the Bengal Eastern Frontier Regulation of 1873. The state government cites a series of legislative measures taken by the central government to uphold the essentially tribal character as well as the rights of the indigenous people in Arunachal Pradesh—some of these being the Bengal Eastern Frontier Regulation of 1873, the Assam Frontier Tract Regulation of 1880, the Assam Forest Regulation of 1891 and the Chin Hills Regulation of 1876. These regulations, say government sources, prohibit non-locals and non-residents from acquiring interest in land or in land produce, prohibit 'outsiders' from acquiring forest land and empower the state government to extern any person if his/her presence is considered to be harmful to local interest. Arunachal Pradesh became a full-fledged Indian state under the State of Arunachal Pradesh Act 1986. The Inner Line Permit (ILP) system was introduced to ensure that the entry of 'outsiders' into the union was restricted.

The NEFA was directly administered by the Union government and did not have any representative institution till 1969 and a popularly elected government till 1975. Besides, the 'idea of temporary settlement of the refugees in this region was basically a result of an understanding in 1964 between the then Governor of Assam Vishnu Sahay and the then Chief Minister of Assam B. P. Chaliha' (Basu Ray Chaudhury 2003: 256). Sahay felt that the continuing presence of the Chakmas in the Mizo Hills might lead to Mizo–Chakma conflicts, so he suggested to Chaliha that the refugees be settled temporarily in the Tirap division of NEFA which was thinly populated at that time, and, as the Governor maintained, 'where there is easily found vacant land' (Government of Arunachal Pradesh 1996).

There was also an external factor that was by no means unimportant. As Sabyasachi Basu Ray Chaudhury observed:

> Perhaps the policy of settling the Chakmas in the NEFA originated in the idea of erecting a human wall in view of the potential Chinese threat following the Sino-Indian war of 1962, because those seeking support from the Indian State could be expected to provide security in the scantily populated NEFA region. If necessary, a section of these people could also be utilized by the Indian Army and other intelligence agencies for controlling insurgency in the area. (2003: 257)

Thus, 20,000 Chakmas in Arunachal Pradesh reported to the Census of 1971—the first census held in Arunachal Pradesh since the influx of the Chakmas. In simple terms, they were rehabilitated by the Government of India in the then NEFA—now Arunachal Pradesh. A study, for instance, shows the district-wise distribution of the Chakma migrants in 1969 (see Table 5.1).

Table 5.1: District-Wise Distribution of the Chakmas in Arunachal Pradesh

District	Number of Families	Number of Persons
1. Lohit	214	1,192
2. Subansiri	238	1,133
3. Tirap (Changlang)	2,146	11,813

Source: Government of Arunachal Pradesh (1996: 9).

In October 1979, a census was carried out by the government exclusively for Chakma and Hajong refugees. The demographic profile that has emerged after this census is detailed in Table 5.2.

Table 5.2: Demographic Profile

District	Number of Families	Number of Persons
1. Lohit	319	1,900
2. Subansiri	290	1,600
3. Tirap		
(a) Diyun Circle	1,480	8,474
(b) Bordumsa Circle	412	2,248
(c) Miao Circle	1,160	6,131

Source: Government of Arunachal Pradesh (1996: 9).

Since then, the Chakmas and the Hajongs have been living in the designated areas of Diyun and Bordumsa in Changlang district, Chowkham in Lohit district and Kokila in Papumpare district. In his appeal to the MPs made on 8 August 1995, the President of the Committee for Citizenship Rights of the Chakmas of Arunachal Pradesh (CCRCAP) estimated the Chakma population to be 66,000. The Miao subdivision has the largest concentration of the Chakmas in Arunachal Pradesh. In 1981, the tribals constituted a majority in all the districts of Arunachal Pradesh except Lohit and Dibang valley and the number of refugees of all varieties stood at 81,000, although according to the All-Arunachal Pradesh Students' Union (AAPSU)—that was agitating for the repatriation of the refugees to Bangladesh—their number stands at 100,000. By 1991, the tribals lost their majority status in Changlang—formerly known as Tirap—as well, where their fall has been rather sharp and spectacular (from 62.15 per cent in 1981 to 34.83 per cent in 1991). There has been a slight but steady decline of tribal population in all the districts. According to Abu Naser Saied Ahmed, 'today there are 64,000 people of Chakma origin painfully fighting against the fury of the local people of Arunachal Pradesh' (2003: 243). The growth is phenomenal compared to the total population that stood at 858,392 according to the 1991 Census. It is also interesting to note that a small population has registered a phenomenal growth of over 400 per cent in three decades.

The White Paper by the Government of Arunachal Pradesh observes:

> Obviously, it also does not rule out the influx of non-settler Chakmas and Hajongs added during the course of these years under the cover of 'refugees'. The demographic trend has posed a serious threat to the distinctive identity of the indigenous tribal people. (1996: 9)

However, it is important to note that, initially, these people entered India with the intention to settle in Tripura, where other people of Jumia (the name used by the hill people of the CHT deriving from jhum [slash and burn] cultivation, and to claim all the indigenous communities including Chakma, Marma, Tripura and others as one 'nation') origin have already been residing for a long period of time. History reveals that once upon a time a part of the CHT was under the control of the royal family of Tripura. However, in 1964, the Government of Tripura did not show interest towards the resettlement of the Chakmas in that state, despite such requests from the local Chakma leaders. At that juncture, the Government of India pondered over a scheme to accommodate those displaced Chakmas in the sparsely populated land of NEFA considering the fact that by providing them shelter a section of these Chakmas could be utilised in the future by the Indian army and intelligence agencies to monitor and contain, if not control, insurgency in the area (Basu Ray Chaudhury and Biswas 1997: 141; Bhaumik 1997: 131). In addition, the Sino-Indian border conflict of 1962 had also made a fresh scar on psyche of the Indian diplomats.

Such a position of the Government of India could be explained by tracing their origin in the past of the CHT and adjoining areas.

Decolonisation and Statelessness

The memorandum submitted to the United Nations Organization (UNO) by Kamini Mohan Dewan and Sneha Kumar Chakma, President and General Secretary of the Chittagong Hill Tracts People's Association on 15 February 1947 laid down the reasons why the CHT should have been included in India and not in Pakistan. Referring to the religion-wise breakup of the population of CHT, the memorandum concluded that the 'district is a purely non-Muslim and tribal area in Bengal and as the only non-Muslim area with a predominance of tribal population this district presents a very delicate position in Eastern Bengal where there is an overwhelming Muslim majority' (Chakma 1948: 1). It argued that insofar as the area was one with an 'absolute non-Muslim population', it should not go to Pakistan and that since India was the birthplace of Buddha it was in the fitness of things that the area went to India rather than Pakistan.

The Memorandum lay down the reasons in greater detail. That it is not contiguous with West Bengal was not to be entertained as an argument for its inclusion in India:

> Chittagong Hill Tracts though detached from West Bengal was in continuation to the Tripura State in the North, Assam in the East and Burma in the South and the East. It is not that Bengal was being divided but it was that East Bengal was being detached from India to make a Pakistan. So absence of contiguity with West Bengal is not a ground to compel the Buddhistic territory into Pakistan. In fact Darjeeling and Jalpaigury districts also are not contiguous to West Bengal. (Chakma 1948: 2)

Again, that the CHT was more communicable from the other side than from the Indian side, could not be taken as a viable argument. As the Memorandum argued:

> Lines of communication towards the North East and South are no worse than those towards the West. And means of transport are made more by men than by God. It is a matter of few days or months to make highways, Railways or even tunnelways if necessary. (ibid.)

It was also argued that, since there was not a single member in the Indian National Congress from the CHT, the party did not have any 'right to affect Chittagong Hill Tracts by entering into any agreement with the Muslim League regarding Boundary Commission's awards' (ibid.). Sneha Kumar Chakma, as late as in November 1949, continued to urge Jawaharlal Nehru to raise the issue in inter-dominion conferences as he himself expressed dissatisfaction with the award of the Boundary Commission particularly Khulna and CHT to Pakistan.[2]

Against this background, it may be argued that the Chakma issue seems to have evolved through three albeit interrelated stages: first, although the issue has its origins in the decolonisation process in South Asia, it was born with the commissioning of the Kaptai hydroelectric project in the then East Pakistan and the consequent displacement of the Chakmas and other indigenous communities in the Chittagong Hill Tracts in 1964. The Chakmas were settled in some districts of the then NEFA without much of a problem with the indigenous tribes till Arunachal Pradesh became a separate state in 1986. The period between 1986 and 1996 may be regarded as one of contention. It ended in a court battle that in its landmark judgment in 1996 gave the verdict in favour of the right to life and protection of the Chakma refugees. Notwithstanding the landmark verdict, the Chakmas continue to face discrimination since then. We designate the period between 1996 and 2010 as one of despair.

The Birth of the 'Chakma Problem'

In 1994, the AAPSU estimated that there were at least 200,000 'foreigners' in the state. This figure is said to be 'highly exaggerated' (Choudhury 1994: 8). In any case, the Chakma population was put at more than 100,000. It is believed that, initially, the Government of Arunachal Pradesh had a hand in inflating the figure. After all, it was in September 1994 that Gegong Apang, the chief minister, pointed out that the official figure of the Chakma population was around 35,000. This more or less tallied with the state government's projection of the Chakma and Hajong population in 1992 as 30,000. The Refugee Deportation Council (RDC), however, challenged these official estimates. S. Singpho, then a prominent leader of the RDC, said that the government figures relate to the refugee population officially registered in the settlement area. He also claimed that the Chakma influx was a 'continuous process', and that 'they were now scattered in many areas, outside the state the zone originally earmarked for their settlement' (ibid.).

In the years 1966–68, 'the then Government drew up the Chakma Resettlement Schemes. Altogether five schemes were sanctioned for the resettlement of 3100 families'.[3]

Therefore, there is hardly any accurate estimate available for the Chakma population in Arunachal Pradesh. One possible reason could be that census figures carefully avoided any break-up of the total population in ethnic and community terms. It is not clear whether the Chakmas are included in the total population figures of the census. The nearest approximation could be the population figures by religion assuming that most of the settlers including the Chakmas are Buddhists and that there would not be Buddhists amongst the indigenous tribal population. Both these assumptions are too extravagant to be true, for, there are—albeit a minority of—Chakmas, who do not return Buddhism as their religion, as much as there are tribals amongst the indigenes (like the Singphos) who happen to be Buddhists. In the total population of 1,097,969 according to the 2001 census, Buddhists constitute 143,028 (Directorate of Economics and Statistics 2009: 16).

As to the number of Chakma/Hajong refugees in Arunachal Pradesh, according to a report by the Government of Arunachal Pradesh dated February 1995, the Chakma refugee population was 34,493. One later estimate, however, indicated that their number could be larger and in the range of 46,000 to 50,000. In a memorandum submitted by People's Referendum Rally for removal of the Chakma/Hajong refugees in September 1995, it was indicated that the number had swelled to over 60,000. The 1981 Census figures for the Chakma and Hajong resettlement in Arunachal Pradesh indicated that there were 24,083 Chakmas and 1,433 Hajongs in Arunachal Pradesh and in the 1991 Census, 30,062 Chakmas and 2,134 Hajongs were recorded. The decadal growth rate of the Chakmas, according to census figures, has been 25 per cent, compared to the state average of 36.83 per cent. It may be recalled in this context that the experts working on Chakmas in Arunachal Pradesh have cited the number to around 60,000 (Table 5.3).

Table 5.3: District-Wise Distribution of Chakma Population in Arunachal Pradesh (in Approximate Terms), 2005

District	Number
1. Changlang	40,000
2. Lohit	10,000
3. Papumpare	10,000
Total	60,000

Source: From Gautam Chakma in Monirul Hussain M. (ed.), *Coming out of Violence: Essays on Ethnicity, Conflict Resolution and Peace Process in North-East India*. New Delhi: Astral International (P) Ltd., 2005, p. 90. Reproduced with permission from Astral International (P) Ltd.

The Chakma refugee crisis in Arunachal Pradesh allegedly points to the double standard and breach of commitment on the part of the Government of India. Subir Bhaumik et al. (1997: 130) describes it as 'part of Delhi's dual policy on refugees'. As the Indo-Pak War came to an end, Indira Gandhi and Sheikh Mujibur Rahman—the Prime Ministers of India and newly independent Bangladesh—met in New Delhi and issued a joint declaration, which formed the nucleus of the subsequent Pact of Friendship, Cooperation and Peace in March 1972. The refugee question lay at the centre of the aforementioned pact. It was agreed that Bangladesh would receive the refugees migrating to India after 25 March 1971 while all those settled primarily in India during the time of East Pakistan would remain settled in India with the implicit understanding that they would gradually be regularised as Indian citizens. In fact, the Assam Accord that marked the end of the six-year long anti-foreigners agitation targeted predominantly, though not exclusively, against the Bangladeshis provides for the gradual regularisation of these foreigners migrating between 1966 and 1971 into citizens. In September 1992, the then Union Minister of State for Home in a letter to a local MP replied that the refugees who had come to India between 1964 and 1971 were eligible for the grant of citizenship and ruled out any deportation of the foreigners.[4]

East Pakistan/Bangladesh's unwillingness to accept the Chakma returnees from Arunachal Pradesh as its citizens is understandable. Writing in 1997, Bhaumik noted:

> In their homeland, the Chittagong Hill Tracts, the tribespeople's (sic) predicament is no less precarious. Pakistan equated their early pro-Indian assertions as disloyalty. Bangladesh saw in their (sic) less than firm commitment to its liberation struggle as something close to blasphemy. (Bhaumik et al. 1997: iii)

The contribution of the Chakmas to the state's economy, particularly to its agriculture, can hardly be exaggerated. *The Telescope*—then published from Arunachal Pradesh (now discontinued)—dated 18 June 1975, for example, pointed out:

> The Chakmas . . . risked their hard labour, and sold rice at 25 paise per kg in 1965-66 in Arunachal Pradesh where, a decade ago, the only food production, during nine full months of the year, has been air-dropping. By now they have made mustard seeds, a fat business here, and this year they have proved wheat a fine agriculture here. (quoted in Chakma 2005: 90)

It is, therefore, not very surprising to note why there was no significant resentment against the Chakma settlement during the initial years, that is to say, between 1964 and 1986. First, the NEFA, being one of the least sparsely populated of all the administrative units in India, could provide enough land to the Chakmas, so much so that they could be settled in the areas by and large distant from those of the other local communities. There was very little scope of interaction between the locals and the 'foreigners'. Second, since the NEFA was kept out of the ambit of elections till 1979, the opinion of the indigenous people was never taken into account.

The resentment of the locals against the apparently prosperous migrants was first articulated in the Changlang district by the AAPSU when its Changlang district unit enforced an 'economic blockade' upon the Chakmas in 1995, calling upon the natives to not buy anything from the refugees.

The fear of being deported to Bangladesh against their will has led many Chakmas to escape from their designated settlements and this often lands them in the hands of human traffickers who use them as a source of cheap labour. According to Ahmed, 'although [there is] no authentic account of the trade, the present author found about 50 of them as road construction workers near Dibrugarh University campus in 1995-96, living in extremely wretched condition' (2003: 245). As they escaped from Arunachal Pradesh to upper Assam, particularly after they were driven out in 1995, the Government of Assam issued a shoot-at-sight order in Sadiya where they were reportedly seen in thousands.

In September 1993, the Assam government asked the Tinsukia district administration to issue shoot-at-sight orders in order to 'prevent the Chakma refugees from Arunachal

Pradesh entering Assam'.[5] Hiteswar Saikia, the then chief minister of Assam, pointed out that the government would not allow any foreign national driven from the neighbouring state. As he reportedly observed: 'Assam is not the dumping ground for foreign nationals' (*Assam Tribune* 1994). The government clamped night curfew along the interstate and international borders to check the possible influx of foreign nationals. Leaders of the All-Assam Chakma Organization and other groups said that in the eventuality of any attack by the people of Arunachal Pradesh they would resist it by peaceful means. They also appealed to the Government of Assam to provide 'temporary shelter' to them in case of an attack. The Assam Chief Minister urged his Arunachal counterpart, Gegong Apang, to push back the Chakmas to the international border with Bangladesh instead of sending them into Assam (ACHR 2007; *Telegraph* 1994). The Chief Minister of Assam said on 10 October 1994 that his government would oppose any move by the Centre to settle the Chakmas or any other refugees in the seven northeastern states (*Times of India* 1994).

To sum up, there are primarily three sets of argument in favour of the Chakmas claiming their right to protection, if not citizenship: First, the legal argument that the Chakmas need to be recognised on the grounds that the Government of India is bound by the international treaty that it had signed with Bangladesh in 1972 (Government of Arunachal Pradesh 1996). Second, that they have contributed enormously to the enrichment of the economy of Arunachal Pradesh. Third—a purely humanitarian reason—that while the identity of the indigenous people could be an issue per se it does not in any way deprive the Chakmas of their right to life and liberty.

The Resentment

It is only too widely known that 'everyone needs a nationality because nationality serves a basis for legal recognition and for exercise of other rights' (Batchelor 1998: 1). The demographic decline of the local population on the one hand and land alienation on the other were two most crucial factors that gradually led to the brewing of resentment amongst the locals.

Though the state government had no occasion to go through the Indira–Mujib Agreement, it is certain that the Agreement did not take away the rights of 'the State Government to restrict entry of non-locals through the instrument of ILP (Inner Line Permit) and not to allow permanent settlement of the non-locals in the State' (Government of Arunachal Pradesh 1996: 19).

Although the refugee population was settled in a way that did not displace the local, indigenous population from their ancestral habitats, it created a potentially inflammable situation. The refugees were initially granted 10,799 acres of land. As their population increased, they started encroaching on forest reserves as well as pastoral land of the indigenous communities. As S. Dutta observes: 'so far as the community rights over land is concerned, the indigenous population lost the right due to this settlement' (2002: 209). Since in the eye of law they remain foreigners, they have no right to own land given to them. In the words of Deepak K. Singh:

> Grant of citizenship will, of course, put an end to their statelessness, but it would not usher in their fuller integration into the local indigenous society. Unless they are given land deeds and treated at par with the indigenous peoples, they would continue to feel insecure. (2010: 254)

Further, Sabyasachi Basu Ray Chaudhury writes:

> According to Peoples' Rights Organisation, the Chakmas have been suffering forcible eviction and arson since the early 1970s. Reports of Chakma houses being burnt or demolished at the behest of the state government also appeared in the press and in the reports of the other NGOs. Vijaypur, a refugee village in the district of Changlang, was reportedly reduced to rubble on three occasions—1989, 1994 and 1995. (2003: 256)

The influx of Chakmas, according to the White Paper, poses a threat to the local people:

> There is nothing common between the tribal people of Arunachal Pradesh and the Chakma refugees. The Chakmas worship evil spirits. They also believe in and perform witchcraft. Their language is identical with East Bengal language with little phonetic decay mixed with Burmese and Arakanese variety. The Chakmas though Buddhists (Hinayana Sect) do not have set rules and practices. This may perhaps be the reason for their propensity towards crimes and other anti-social activities which the local people residing in the neighbourhood of these refugees have been suffering since their ill-conceived settlement. (Government of Arunachal Pradesh 1996: 4)

In the perception of the AAPSU, the migrants constituted a sizeable non-local population vis-à-vis the small indigenous population and the AAPSU claimed to represent the concerns of the indigenous tribal society regarding the protection of its rights to land and resources and its natural aversion to share these with the non-locals. Some of the concerns of the AAPSU against the migrants were that they were causing serious law and order problems, and threatening the demographic balance, peaceful coexistence and the very identity of the indigenous people of the state. It was in August 1994 that the situation in Arunachal Pradesh underwent a drastic transformation following the ultimatum issued by AAPSU which aimed at evicting the Chakmas and Hajongs from Arunachal Pradesh. With active support from the state administration, the AAPSU, particularly its Changlang District Committee and the RDC, fixed levies on different commercial establishments and village households in order to raise funds for expelling the foreigners. Arunachal Pradesh, in their words, could not be reduced to a 'dumping ground'. In the People's Referendum Rally held on 20 September 1995 at Naharlagun near Itanagar, the state capital, the AAPSU and the leaders of almost all political parties in the state—including the ruling Congress (I) under Gegong Apang, the chief minister—set 31 December as the deadline for the

Centre to evict the refugees from the state. Again in the same rally, the leaders of all existing political parties present vowed to resign from the primary membership of their respective parties and form a 'Common Organisation of Indigenous People' if their demand was not met by the central government before the expiry of the deadline. The AAPSU stand was subsequently supported by the state assembly which had unanimously passed resolutions at least twice to this effect. It may be relevant to note at this point that when the elected government took over in 1979, the resentment of the indigenous people against the settlement of these refugees was voiced through the resolutions passed in the state legislative assembly and zilla parishads (district councils).

In 1980, the state government banned the employment of Chakmas and Hajongs. It stopped issuing trade licenses for members of either community. Furthermore, all trade licenses issued to them were seized in 1994. AAPSU organised an economic blockade of the Chakma and Hajong refugee camps. The state government started dismantling the basic social and economic infrastructure in the Chakma and Hajong settlements. In October 1991, the state government discontinued issuance of ration cards to the Chakmas and Hajongs, most of whom lived in extreme poverty. In September 1994, the state government began closing and burning down schools in these areas, effectively denying them their right to education. Schools built by the Chakmas using local community resources were shut down or destroyed. Health facilities in the Chakma and Hajong areas were all but non-existent.

As Nandita Sardana reports in 1994:

> At a rally at Naharlagun recently Apang [then the Chief Minister] announced to a rapturous audience that his Government had withdrawn all "facilities given to Chakmas": no jobs, no ration cards, no official assistance. According to a September 24 Government order, employment to Chakmas has been banned. Ration cards issued earlier have been withdrawn. Trade licenses are no longer issued to them while those given prior to 1975 are now being

> cancelled. And in schools, Chakma children can only sit at the back, says a bitter Bimal Bhikku, secretary-general of the World Chakma Congress: "The treatment meted out to us is tantamount to apartheid." Or, as other members of his tribe would say, it is the curse of bitter hatred.

In protest against the Centre's inaction, the student leaders in group returned their University degrees apart from organising the rallies and demonstrations, press conferences and other propaganda measures (Basu Ray Chaudhury 2003: 256).

A report by Ratna Bharali titled 'Human Rights: State of Denial' (Talukdar 2008b) has argued that '[t]he opposition of the State government to accommodate them as "citizens" has allegedly led to the gross denial of basic rights, including health care, education facilities, job opportunities and livelihood support'. The report also identified that Diyun Primary School—the 'only secondary school in the revenue circle meant for these refugees'—did not have a proper infrastructure in place and suffered from overcrowding. The student–teacher ratio was an alarming 1350:18; an example cited by Bharali revealed that 'Class VII accommodates 214 children in a single room' (ibid.). She further observes that the only healthcare facility available to refugees and local residents from the Singpho and the Tongsa Naga tribes is a seven-bed primary health centre (PHC) that is run by one homeopathic doctor assisted by three nurses. Beyond this, the area is also prone to malaria and also has a 'severe livelihood crisis'. The plots of land that had been originally allotted to the refugees have now been distributed between their children. To add to all this, refugees are also 'not eligible to work in any government or reputed private farms without having citizenship rights' (ibid.).

The Asian Centre for Human Rights (ACHR) in its *India Human Rights Report* (2007) observed:

> The basic facilities and amenities such as educational and health care facilities and the right to employment earlier withdrawn by the State government have not been restored. As a result, the

socio-economic conditions of the Chakmas and Hajongs remained highly pathetic. (ACHR 2007)

Moreover, Talukdar (2008b) says, 'the erosion in some pockets caused by the river Noa-Dihing has added to the problem of paucity of land for the increasing refugee population.' She talks about how visitors to Maitripur village, which is situated on the bank of the river, are shocked by 'a huge minar-like structure in the midst of the river, about 150 metres away from the bank', which the villagers call 'Qutub Minar of Maitripur'. The structure which was originally the village community well has now taken the shape of a minar following the gradual erosion of land. Several families have also been forced to encroach on reserved forests due to severe land erosion (ibid.).

In a workshop on 'Indigenous/Tribal Peoples' Right to Self-Determination and Self-Government', organised by the North East Indigenous/Tribal Peoples' Forum (NEITF) under the auspices of AAPSU, the speakers emphasised that a situation had arisen where the ruling elites of the so-called mainstream were treating the homelands of the indigenous people as their internal colony (cited in NEITF 1995). These arguments were reiterated in the Referendum Rally for the Deportation of Chakma and Hajong Refugees from Arunachal Pradesh. The influx of refugees, according to the Rally, had diluted the indigenous character of the natives to the point of extinction. It recommended the deportation of the 'foreigners' as the only solution to this problem.[6]

It is in this context that the rights of self-determination and self-government were emphasised by the participants of the workshop organised by the AAPSU in Itanagar. The participants strongly felt that the right to self-determination does not necessarily mean sovereignty or independence or secession, as argued very often by the ruling elites. The workshop declared that the movements for right to land and forest and movements against 'foreign nationals' can also be described as movements for the right to self-determination (ibid.).

The Legal Battle

The Indian Supreme Court has ruled that the Chakmas are not entitled to citizenship under Section 6-A of Citizenship Act of 1955,[7] which contains specific provisions with regard to persons of Indian origin who came to Assam before 1966. Meanwhile, the agitation to deport Chakmas from the state of Arunachal Pradesh gained momentum leading to tension in the area.

On 9 September 1994, the Peoples' Union for Civil Liberties, Delhi brought this issue to the attention of the National Human Rights Commission (NHRC), which issued letters to the Chief Secretary, Arunachal Pradesh and the Home Secretary, Government of India, making inquiries in this regard. On 30 September 1994, the chief secretary of Arunachal Pradesh faxed a reply stating that the situation was totally under control and adequate police protection had been given to the Chakmas.

On 15 October 1994, the CCRCAP filed a representation with the NHRC complaining of the persecution of the Chakmas. The petition contained a press report carried in *The Telegraph*, dated 26 August 1994, stating that the AAPSU had issued 'quit notices' to all alleged foreigners, including the Chakmas to leave the state by 30 September 1995. The AAPSU had threatened to use force if its demand was not acceded to. The matter was treated as a formal complaint by the NHRC. On 12 October 1995 and again on 28 October 1995, the CCRCAP sent urgent petitions to the NHRC alleging immediate threats to the lives of the Chakmas.

On 22 November 1994, the Ministry of Home Affairs despatched a note to the NHRC reiterating its 'intention of granting citizenship to the Chakmas.' It also pointed out that 'Central Reserve Forces had been deployed in response to the threat of the AAPSU' and the state administration had been instructed to guarantee the protection of the Chakmas. 'The direction was ignored till September 1995 despite the standing reminders.'[8]

A joint statement had been issued by the prime ministers of India and Bangladesh in February 1972, following which the Union government had conveyed its decision to confer citizenship on the Chakmas to all states concerned. It further stated that the 'children of the Chakmas who were born in India prior to the amendment of the Act in 1987 would have legitimate claims to citizenship'.[9]

The state of Arunachal Pradesh contended that the issue of citizenship of the Chakmas had been conclusively determined in *State of Arunachal Pradesh v. Khudiram Chakma* (1994 Supp. [1] SCG 615). The Guwahati High Court in its judgment passed on 30 April 1992 categorically held that in view of the laws applicable providing special protection to Arunachal Pradesh, the Chakma refugees are foreigners, that they have no right and claim to have a permanent residence/abode in the place, that the authority concerned may at any time ask them to move or to vacate the place and that the authorities have the right to ask them to quit the state if they desire. However, the Guwahati High Court, on humanitarian grounds, directed the state government to give adequate compensation in case these Chakmas were evicted from this place. It was therefore contended that since the Chakmas are foreigners, they were not entitled to the protection of fundamental rights except Article 21. This being so, the authorities could, at any time, ask the Chakmas to move. They also had the right to ask the Chakmas to move and quit the state, if they so desired.

The Guwahati High Court maintained:

> We are unable to accept the contention of the first respondent (the State of Arunachal Pradesh), that no threat exists to the life and liberty of the Chakmas guaranteed by Article 21 of the Constitution, and that it has taken adequate steps to ensure the protection of the Chakmas . . . The AAPSU has been giving out threats to forcibly drive them out to the neighbouring State which in turn is unwilling to accept them. The residents of the neighbouring State have also threatened to kill them if they try to enter their State. They are thus sandwiched between two forces, each pushing in opposite direction which can hurt them. Faced with the prospect of annihilation the NHRC was moved which finding it impossible to extend protection to them, moved this Court for certain reliefs. (Ishaq 1971: 42)

On the question of rights, the Court clarified:

> We are a country governed by the Rule of Law. Our Constitution confers certain rights to every human being and certain other rights on citizens. Every person is entitled to equality before the law and equal protection of the laws. So also, no person can be deprived of his life or personal liberty except according to the procedure established by law. Thus the State is bound to protect the life and liberty of every human being, he be a citizen or otherwise, and it cannot permit anybody or group of persons, e.g., the AAPSU, to threaten the Chakmas to leave the State, failing which they would be forced to do so.[10]

On the operational part, the Court ordered that it had to be ensured by the State of Arunachal Pradesh that the 'life and personal liberty of each and every Chakma' residing within the state be protected and 'any attempt to forcibly evict or drive them out' of the state by organised groups such as AAPSU be repelled.[11] The Chakmas could not be evicted from their homes and could not be denied domestic life and comfort therein except in accordance with law. The court also clarified that the application made for registration as citizen of India by the Chakma/s under Section 5 of the Act would be entered in the register maintained for the purpose and the application/s would be forwarded by the collector or the deputy commissioner (DC)—who would receive them under the relevant rule, with or without enquiry, as the case may be—to the central government for its consideration in accordance with law. The returned applications would be recalled or fresh ones would be obtained from the concerned persons and processed and forwarded to the central government for consideration, the court ordered (Chimni 2000: 513–14). It was also stated that while the application of the individual Chakma was pending consideration, the State of Arunachal Pradesh could not 'evict or remove the concerned person from his occupation on the ground that he is not a citizen of India until the 'competent authority' had taken a relevant decision.[12]

The Post-Verdict Scenario

The post-verdict scenario is marked by the abject discrimination against and helplessness of the Chakmas. It seems that there is hardly any light at the end of the road for them.

Against this backdrop, Sabyasachi Basu Ray Chaudhury writes,

> 27 Chakmas submitted citizenship applications on 4 May 1998 to the Deputy Commissioner of Changlang district. He refused to accept them and perforce, the Chakmas and Hajongs had to submit applications directly to the Union Home Ministry once again. More than two years later, the Chakmas and Hajongs were yet to be granted citizenship. (2003: 256)

In 2001, the Union government submitted before the Supreme Court of India that the State of Arunachal Pradesh was not complying with the directions of the Court to accord protection to the Chakma refugees and to repel any attempt by organised local groups to forcibly evict or drive them out of the state. Attorney General Soli Sorabjee made a brief submission before a three-judge bench comprising Chief Justice Madan Mohan Punchhi and Justices K.T. Thomas and D.P. Wadhwa during the hearing of a public interest petition by the Arunachal Pradesh Indigenous Tribal Rights (Protection) Organization (APITRO). The petition had said that the granting of citizenship to the Chakmas in Arunachal Pradesh would open the floodgates for illegal migrants and foreign nationals for Indian citizenship and the central government for political reasons could make the state powerless. The petition claimed that the Union government had negotiated with a neighbouring country in order to buy peace on its border by giving a large group of refugees citizenship, and in the process sacrificed the human and legal rights of the protected indigenous communities of the state. The petition further stated that the judgement violated the powers of the state under the 7th Schedule, List 2 of the Constitution and the Court could not pass orders by way of the writ of mandamus ignoring the executive and legislature of Arunachal Pradesh (Government of Arunachal Pradesh 1996).

On 11 February 1999, the Election Commission of India ordered a special revision of electoral rolls across India including Arunachal Pradesh. When a Chakma delegation met the officials of the Election Commission of India, the officials reportedly claimed that they had received not any specific instruction from the Ministry of Home Affairs to enrol members of these two groups. The officials also said they could not act on the basis of statements made by the Ministry of Home Affairs to the NHRC, in which the ministry had recognised the citizenship of the Chakmas and Hajongs under the Citizenship Act. In May 1999, when the Chakmas and Hajongs approached the Electoral Registration Office in Arunachal Pradesh to submit their claims and objections to their exclusion, the local officials refused to accept their petitions.

In 2004, the Election Commission of India issued a directive to the Government of Arunachal Pradesh that 1,497 Chakmas and Hajongs born in India would be enrolled in the state electoral roll from out of a total of 11,360 applicants. The Commission suspended all electoral activities in four Chakma constituencies of Doimukh, Chowkham, Bordumsa and Diyun for non-inclusion of the refugees in the electoral roll. The AAPSU submitted a memorandum to the Commission demanding revocation of the order. The Commission in its order (No. 23/ARUN/2003) held that the non-inclusion of the 1,497 voters implied a violation of the Constitutional mandate given to it by Article 325. In March 2004, the Chakma-Hajong refugee issue took a new turn as AAPSU decided to ban the upcoming elections on 5 May 2004. The Election Commission further ordered special revision of electoral rolls in the four aforementioned assembly constituencies. Chief Minister Gegong Apang resigned from the chairmanship of the all-party core committee on the Chakma-Hajong refugee issue in protest against the inclusion of these voters in the electoral rolls. The CCRCAP welcomed the resignation from the core committee. It also appealed to the AAPSU to withdraw the call for poll boycott. A new history was scripted as the Chakmas and Hajongs voted for the first time. The estimated turnout was 50 per cent of the newly enlisted voters.

Problems started afresh in Arunachal Pradesh after the government declared the conferment of Permanent Resident Certificates (PRCs) to the Chakma refugees on 7 September 2010. Two days later, the government—under tremendous pressure from AAPSU—withdrew its decision.

Other Experiences

In a similar study on the Chakma refugees, displaced by the violence of the mid-1980s in the CHT and now settled in Tripura, Nasreen Chowdhory points out that though initially hospitable, the Government of Tripura gradually considered about 70,000 of them as 'a burden.' Their presence too sparked off nativist outbursts. As she argues:

> Their continued presence created a demographic problem and environmental concerns. The steady rise in birth rate within these camps in South Tripura underwent deforestation, as the refugees were prone to felling and cutting trees for fuel purposes. The local population also faced an acute shortage of natural resources, viz. firewood, wild vegetables, bamboo shoots, wild potatoes, etc., which constituted a primary source of livelihood for them. Moreover, the Government of India had spent 13.5 million rupees on the refugees, which became a source of discontent among the locals, who felt marginalized and harboured resentment for treating refugees as privileged lot. This generated conflict of interests between the local people and the residents of the refugee camp. (Chowdhory 2004: 196)

The phenomenal growth of the refugee population has its impact on the encroachment on forest land. During 1993–94, about 400 hectares of reserved forest land in Diyun, which had been under the illegal occupation of the Chakmas since

1986, was retrieved. Continued presence of the Chakmas and the Hajongs had 'started threatening the fragile eco-system of the State of Arunachal Pradesh' (Government of Arunachal Pradesh 1996: 13).

Tribal people formed 88.76 per cent of the total population of the state in 1961, which fell down to 63.66 per cent in 1991. The rise of non-tribal population in Arunachal Pradesh over the decennial censuses is remarkable (9 per cent in 1951, 12 per cent in 1961, 40 per cent in 1981 and less than 37 per cent in 1991). The demographic decline alarmed the tribal people of the state. Apart from it being the most sparsely populated state, another reason cited was that they could be accommodated under the rehabilitation scheme meant for the refugees from the then East Pakistan. Besides, there was assumed to be cultural continuity: 'The Chakma refugees are Buddhists and some of the locals are also Buddhists'. Further, it was decided that the Chakmas who came to India before 25 March 1971 would not be sent back to Bangladesh (ibid.).

The following narratives need to be assessed in this overall scenario. In fact, one may notice a generational change in the perceptions of the stateless Chakmas in Arunachal Pradesh through their reminiscences. The perception and perspective of the new generation of Chakmas born here appear to be quite in contrast with those who were displaced and resettled in the NEFA (now Arunachal Pradesh). The narratives that have been used in this study can be broadly divided into two categories: voices of the older generation of Chakmas, who still regard themselves as 'refugees' and 'victims of partition' of 1947; and the voices from the younger generation of this community, who faced the anti-foreigners movement led by the AAPSU left their homes and went to metropolitan cities like New Delhi, Kolkata, Mumbai and Chennai, and who are more conscious about their rights, about the legal concept of citizenship, and also about the consequences of being stateless.[13] Without assessing this complexity of the generational response, it is perhaps difficult to understand the state of stateless Chakmas in Arunachal Pradesh.

Unheard Voices from Chowkham

> Yes, we are refugees, refugees from CHT. We are from Sajiacholi village, which is under the jurisdiction of Longodoo police station, district CHT. When the riot broke out in our village we decided to leave our place. Mians were responsible for that. We were altogether eight in our family when we left our village. Like us there were many from other villages, who left their home. We were in a big group. We crossed over to this side in the year 1964. After walking for several days in the group with my ailing parents, wife, our one-year old son, my uncle, aunt and their children carrying whatever belongings that a refugee family could gather before an uncertain journey, we reached Demagri transit camp, set up by the Government of India in the Mizo district [now Mizoram] of Assam. The place is adjacent to our CHT. The moment we registered our names in the refugee list of the camp, we got a new identity—'Chakma refugees'.[14]

Seventy-five-year-old Sashibhusan Chakma (name changed), a resident of Chakma *basti* (village) 1, Chowkham, paused while recalling the experiences of his journey to escape violence from CHT in East Pakistan to India way back in 1964. When we first met Sashibhusan he was relaxing in the *chana*—the open space in front of a traditional Chakma dwelling on a raised bamboo platform—after evening tea. Sashibhusan wearing a *lungi* and a half shirt was smoking his favourite bamboo *hookah*. It was almost dark outside. As we decided to stay at Sashibhusan's house for the next two days, he requested us to take rest after a very hectic journey from Kolkata. Swapna, Sashibhusan's daughter-in-law (wife of his younger son, Paritosh) lit the *chana* with two lanterns. There was no electricity inside and outside the house.

Chowkham, comprising approximately 895 square kilometres of land (District Statistical Office 2009) is one of the eight administrative circles in Lohit district in eastern Arunachal. National Highway 37 connects Dibrugarh with Namsai, the border town of Arunachal via Tinsukia of Assam. From Namsai, a road heads east towards Tezu, the district headquarters of Lohit via Chowkham. The Namsai road divides the whole area of Chowkham into two distinct parts: Chakma *basti*s and Khamti settlements. Apparently these two parts of Chowkham appear identical to the outsider. Lohit is the home of the Adi, Zekhring, Khampti, Deori, Ahom, Singpho, Chakmas and Mishmi tribes. A small group of Tibetan refugees have also settled in Lohit since the 1960s. The Chakma-inhabited area, Chowkham, is surrounded by two rivers, the Kamlang to the north and Barang to the south. As there is no proper bridge on Barang, the Chakmas have to walk on a swinging bridge made of bamboo strips, on which it is very difficult to carry heavy goods. Earlier there was a concrete structure. But the flood of 2004 destroyed the bridge.

In Chowkham, Chakmas are confined within three villages, which they prefer to refer to as *basti* numbers 1, 2 and 3. According to Ramani Mohan Chakma, 58, General Secretary of Chakma Village Council:

> [N]ow we are altogether 5,067 living in these three Chakma *bastis*—2,231 Chakmas in *basti* no. 1, 1,157 in *basti* no. 2 and 1,158 in basti no. 3. There are other 521 Chakmas who are at present landless and they have come from the other parts of eastern Arunachal Pradesh. Out of 5,067 Chakmas only 301 persons (187 male and 114 female) have got the right to cast votes including 13 cases of deletion and 13 cases of additions.[15]

Santosh Chakma, a teacher of Sneha School in Diyun circle, Changlang district, accompanied us all the way from Dibrugarh. Sashibhusan is Santosh's maternal grandfather. Sashibhusan's family has increased in numbers. Now they are 30 altogether. He is staying with his two sons, Mahitosh and Paritosh; two daughters-in-law, Kalpana and Swapna; along with a grandson in the house where we stayed. Later, we came to know that he has other relatives who stay nearby.

Swapna and Paritosh have just come back from Delhi. Paritosh met Swapna in Delhi during his college days. Both completed graduation from Delhi and decided to serve their community in Chowkham. After coming back to their own place Paritosh has started private tuition and established a small private coaching centre within the premises of their designated allotted land.

Swapna teaches Hindi in the government-sponsored primary school situated in Chakma *basti* 1 on a contractual basis. This is the only school for the refugees in Chowkham.

Next morning while he tried to put together fragmented memories of his struggle after crossing the border Paritosh said:

> After staying six–seven days at Demagri we were sent to other transit camps located at Monachera, Hanirpore, Dholar and so on in batches. Each batch had approximately 100–150 refugees with one leader. We walked for the whole day and took rest only in the evening. It continued for four to five days until we reached the next camp. On reaching Monachera, we were put up in camps for 22 days and were given some cash doles and free ration. From there we were taken to Ledo in Badarpur district of Assam where we stayed for nearly eight months in camps. And then, we were finally told that we would be taken to Lohit in NEFA of which we had no idea whatsoever. We came to Chowkham. We were also assured that on reaching NEFA, we would be given land and treated as Indians. We did, however, get land but are yet to be recognised as Indians legally. Each family was given at least 5 acres up to maximum 8 acres of virgin land in Chowkham depending on the size of family. We got 5 acres of land, which took almost five to six years of hard labour to harvest *ahu* paddy. As long as NEFA was under the central government, we were provided with all sorts of facilities, all of which started disappearing once Arunachal Pradesh became a state.[16]

Like Sashibhusan, Nutan Kumar Chakma, the *gaon burrah* (village head) of Chakma *basti* 1; Shanti Kumar Karbari, the *gaon burrah* of Chakma *basti* 2; and several other respondents gathered in that *chana* still believe that they lived peacefully in NEFA under the administration of the central government. They said almost unanimously that when they first came here the local people like the Khamptis, Singphos and even Tangshas were very nice to them. They even had matrimonial relations with them. In schools also, Chakma children were friendly with the children of the locals. The locals were also Buddhists like the Chakmas. But owing to the politicisation of the whole issue of providing citizenships to Chakmas now, such interactions have virtually become impossible. 'The locals have also stopped engaging our people as wage labourers, which was earlier a well-established practice'.[17]

In fact, the areas where the Chakmas are settled were once covered partially by the Public Distribution System (PDS), and ration cards were issued to some of them. But later these were snatched away by the administration in the wake of an anti-foreigners sentiment in 1994. The residents of Chowkham blamed the state government for their destiny. They believe that as they are not regarded as citizens the state is not interested in providing them basic amenities. They don't have any health centres nearby, with the nearest one located in Namsai. In case of an emergency they do not have any other option but to go to Namsai, which is almost a two-hour journey from Chowkham.

These narratives of the respondents in Chowkham over the issue of ethno-religious affinities in Lohit district, a predominantly Buddhist-inhabited area, were overwhelmingly positive. While dwelling upon the common bond between them and the Khamptis and Singphos in terms of religion, almost all our respondents at Chowkham opined that:

> Sharing [a] common religion with the locals helped us to have sympathy, assistance and support at the initial stage from the Khamptis and Singphos. Singphos are few in number as compared to Khamtis in Chowkham. They used to visit our village on several occasions. I can remember the occasion of Buddha Purnima when they actively participated in the festival. We also reciprocated in the same manner. It is true that such commonalties in terms of religion and ethnicity have led to greater understanding and mutual respect for each other in our area. In many cases we used to cultivate their land. However, the situation started changing rapidly since first half of 1990s.[18]

These Chakmas are mostly poor. Due to an increase in the number of members in their families they are facing scarcity of land. They say:

> Five acres of land is not enough for us nowadays. We need land to stay in as well as to harvest. The plot of land originally allotted to us has now been divided among the offspring of the beneficiaries. We are basically cultivators you know. It is true that Khamtis or Singphos are not rich either. However, socially we always face discrimination, be it in the case of admission in the health centre or getting electricity after the major power fault.[19]

It is to be kept in mind that due to the implementation of the Rajiv Gandhi Grameen Vidyutikaran Yojana (RGGVY) since 2005, a process of rural electrification of the non-electrified villages was started by the government in Arunachal Pradesh. During our stay at Chowkham there was a major power cut in that area. Local Chakmas were very agitated as the other side of the road, which was a Khamti-inhabited area, got back their electricity connection while Chakma *basti*s were still in darkness. Although Arunachal Pradesh is considered a potential hub for large-scale electricity generation, the fact remains that a major part of the state is facing irregular electricity supply with low voltage. According to Sashibhusan:

> Sometimes the voltage of the bulbs is so low that it seems there is no electricity in our area. Often we feel that it is even better not to have electricity.[20]

The Chakmas still perceive themselves as victims of Partition of India. They pointed out that they were always pro-Indians. The Mians did not like their pro-Indian stand and that was why the Chakmas faced these consequences. To quote Ramani Mohan of Chowkham:

> We accepted Nehru as our leader. Being Buddhist by religion we always wanted to merge with India during Partition but our homeland CHT was ceded to Pakistan against our will and that was the beginning of our struggle for lives and survival. Our destiny became bleak since the day India was divided. In fact, we can recall the day, when we came to know that our leader Nehru had passed away. It was on our way to Monachera Camp in north Cachar district. It was a great shock

> to us and we suddenly found ourselves in the midst of uncertainty. The man who had allowed us entry into India and had assured us of all possible help was no longer with us. Once we crossed the border and got land from the Indian government we started feeling that we are Indians. In fact, we were issued valid migration certificates by the concerned authorities making our stay legal. In the beginning, the question of conflict never arose as we were settled with the prior consent of the locals. But the politics of citizenship in Arunachal has forced us to regard ourselves as refugees, despite having been staying here for more than 47 years. It was only after Arunachal Pradesh became a full-fledged state of the Indian Union in 1987 that the locals started resenting our presence. Look, we accepted India as our own state but the state did not accept us as its citizens.[21]

Like Sashibhusan, Natun Chakma and Ramani Mohan—the other senior members of the Chakma *basti*s of Chowkham—gathered in Sashibhusan's drawing room that morning also praised the leadership of Nehru for providing them shelter and rations. They expressed their gratitude towards 'their leader' Nehru. While talking to them our eyes were drawn to the photographs kept on the bamboo rack. It was a long and continuous rack running along three sides of Sashibhusan's drawing room, with framed photographs of Nehru, Gandhi and Netaji as well as Gautam Buddha and the Hindu goddess Lakshmi placed together.

Our discussion with these senior members of the Chakma community staying in *Basti*s 1, 2 and 3 made it clear that they still regard themselves legally as the refugees from CHT and Indians in their mind. Their narratives indicated that they have also accepted the fact that it is not possible for them to be a voter of the state in the present political condition. However, they were not in a position to consider themselves as stateless. According to Natun Chakma:

> How can we be stateless? The Indian Government gave us *mati* (land) and if a state denotes a specific land we have that land. Yes, we are refugees and we cannot cast our vote. We are really concerned about our siblings, who were born here after we migrated. What

> will be their future? Without voting rights how will they survive? There is no more land for them to cultivate. Many of our young boys and girls were leaving this place to do something but due to lack of documents they don't get good jobs and we are concerned for that. Our forum for citizenship right is fighting for us.[22]

A Journey from Somewhere to Nowhere

Diyun is one of the 11 revenue circles of the 4,662 square kilometre-large Changlang district of Arunachal Pradesh (Directorate of Economics and Statistics 2009). Changlang is located to the south of Lohit district. It is the eastern-most district of India sharing boundaries with Myanmar. A large portion of the plains of this district is the valley of River Noa-Dihing, a flood-prone area. To reach Diyun from Chowkham (almost 60 kilometres away) it took more than two hours. Santosh wanted to go back to his home at Diyun and we took the opportunity to accompany him. On our way to Diyun, Santosh said:

> The condition of the road is very bad. Many times we will cross the streams, the tributaries of Dihing without any bridge and if you want to go to Miao to visit the Tibetan clustered settlement at Choephelling (30 kilometres away from Diyun) you have to cross Noa-Dihing.[23]

Santosh, 25 years old, was born in Diyun. When his father decided to shift from Diyun to Chowkham, he came along and got admission in Class V in the primary school of Chowkham. However, after six months of his admission the school was closed due to anti-Chakma agitation led by the AAPSU. The agitation gained momentum following the letter written by the Union Minister of State for Home P.M. Sayeed to Nyodak Yonggam, a Rajya Sabha MP from the state—dated 7 July 1994—that indicated that citizenship rights may be granted to Chakmas and Hajongs who settled in Arunachal Pradesh in 1964.[24] This news spread like wildfire and, as a consequence, the AAPSU started strongly opposing the issue of granting citizenship to the Chakmas and Hajongs. The AAPSU leadership took up various programmes to polarise their demand. Santosh said:

> Although the government gave us land, trade licenses, education facilities, ration cards and items of PDS, all our rights were taken away one after another through government notifications since 1980. It was because of the state government's policy of denial and deprivation that we were subjected to scores of human rights abuses such as arbitrary arrests, illegal detention, rape, arson and even genocide.[25]

Santosh's school was closed for three to four years. Like his school, almost all other schools in Arunachal Pradesh were closed for the Chakmas during the period of the anti-foreigners movement. In a bid to oust the Chakmas and Hajongs from Arunachal Pradesh, 49 pre-primary schools (*anganwadi*s) were withdrawn in 1994[26] during the AAPSU agitation to oust the Chakmas and Hajongs from Arunachal Pradesh. The *anganwadi* centres are yet to be restored. It was also true that these had provided employment to 98 women. The withdrawal had resulted in their termination from job without any compensation.[27]

Once the agitation was at its peak, Santosh's brother, Sushanta Chakma, who is one of the founder members of the Shena School in Diyun took him to Delhi. Like many of his schoolmates he also left his place. In Delhi he stayed at Sevadham. After passing his higher secondary examination Santosh went to Tinsukia for his graduation and he came back to Diyun after finishing his studies to help his down-trodden community.

Santosh is not the only one who wanted to come back finishing his course and serve his community. Like Santosh, Bimol, Dilip, Arindam and many other young Chakmas also left their home to escape discrimination and violence that took place in the first half of the 1990s due to the anti-refugee sentiment and, more precisely, due to the 'Quit Arunachal Pradesh' notice circulated by the AAPSU in 1994. Immediately after that notice the Assam government led by Hiteswar Saikia had asked the Tinsukia district administration to issue a 'shoot-at-sight' order to prevent the Chakma refugees from Arunachal Pradesh from entering Assam.[28] More than 16 years after that political unrest, 37-year-old Dilip Kumar Chakma can still easily recall those days of turmoil.

Dilip had been in Class XII at the Diyun Higher Secondary School in those days, and had been a student leader. Under his leadership, a group of Chakma students decided to not leave their place unless Gegong Apang's government issued an order. Meanwhile, the AAPSU declared 31 September 1994 as the deadline to close the entry of Chakma students in all schools. However, Dilip and a few of his friends didn't leave their school. On 28 September 1994, he, along with his friends, was attacked and beaten up mercilessly by the large group of AAPSU supporters within the premises of the school. That day they were narrowly saved as the principal and the vice-principal of the school suddenly appeared on the scene and called the police. However, he was forced to flee from his place when, on 30 December, AAPSU supporters burnt down the boys' hostel of Diyun School. That evening he came to know that the supporters of AAPSU had burnt many houses in Bordumsa and Bijoypur and also got the news that his friend Bhaskar had been killed by them. They also tried to murder him that night. To save his life, Dilip jumped into the River Dihing. He said that he still does not know how he was saved. Nevertheless, he fled to Assam and from Assam to Delhi. He finished his graduation from Dibrugarh and on 23 November 2003 Dilip returned to his own place, Diyun.

According to Arindam Dewan, the Vice Chairman of the Working Council of the CCRCAP (formed in 1991 to demand the citizenship rights of the Chakmas and Hajongs of Arunachal Pradesh), Changlang division:

> In Changlang we are scattered. It is not like Chowkham, where our people are confined within three villages only. Today the Diyun revenue circle has the largest concentration of refugees—around 30,000 people spread over 14 villages. As far as Hajongs

are concerned, they are concentrated in Miao only and there their total number is approximately 3,000. In the Diyun circle, six villages were designated for us at the initial stage. These were: Gautampur, Maitripur, Shantipur, Jyotipur, Avoypur and Dumpani. My own village is Dumpani. My father got land; we got a lease deed for our land too. We paid revenue for the land. But it was only for one time till date. Since then this document is of no use. Even then, I regard myself fortunate in comparison to other members of our community. I have a PAN card, I have a bank account at Namsai. I can cast my vote though I do not have a voter identity card. But just think of others. In Diyun almost 10,000–15,000 Chakmas are now eligible to cast their votes. However, they do not enjoy that right. In more than 40 years of their existence without the protection of any state, the Chakmas clearly see a close link between their statelessness and their increasing vulnerability to human rights abuse.

The state government has deprived us systematically from all sorts of basic amenities. We are just being treated like animals. For example, education . . . we have only one government-sponsored secondary school at Diyun. In the absence of any middle school in the whole Diyun circle, this school has to accommodate all the Chakma and Hajong students passing out every year from more than 10 primary schools operating in our settlement areas. Around 1,350 [students] (probably 18 teachers) are enrolled in this school with virtually no infrastructural facilities. The school building was built by the Chakmas and no grant was given by the state government. No developmental work has been undertaken by the state government. Benches, desks, dusters and other required furniture are self-arranged by the guardians of students. Now in this circle like our Sneha School there are two more secondary schools run privately by NGOs—one is being run by Mahabodhi Society and the other is a Christian school.

Probably you know . . . [Arindam paused, took a deep breath and started again] in 1998 the state government imposed an economic embargo on us. Agricultural products such as ginger, chilli and mustard seeds produced by our people have no market in the local

> areas. They have to be sold in neighbouring Assam. However, to sell these cash crops in Assam permission is required from the state government. But our people are constantly denied that permission or license to sell their products in Assam.[29]

The *Indian Human Rights Report 2006*, published by the ACHR, a New Delhi-based NGO, also points out that the Chakmas and Hajongs irrespective of their legal status face systematic discrimination from the state administration (ACHR 2007). Bharali elaborates that basic facilities and amenities like educational and healthcare facilities and the rights to employment that had been withdrawn by the state government earlier had not been restored. Consequently, 'the socio-economic conditions of the Chakmas and Hajongs remained highly pathetic' (Talukdar 2008b).

Arindam said:

> Acute livelihood risks have made many of our youth go outside in search of work. Without citizenship rights they do not get good jobs anywhere. They mostly work in the informal sector, in textile units, or as security personnel or salespersons. See . . . we have unique weaving skills but most of us don't know how to market the end products. Moreover, restriction on free movement also limits their reach.
>
> In fact, we heard that initially the central government allowed us to settle in this area on the condition that we would be re-settled or go back after the situation improved in East Pakistan. It was not permanent settlement, only transit. But it did not happen. The question of going back to Bangladesh simply does not arise since we never came from there. When we fled our homes in CHT, it was under Pakistan, which is now Bangladesh—an equally oppressive regime.[30]

Arindam's wife Kamini serves her community as a social worker. When we were eager to know about the health status of refugee women in Diyun, she informed us that there are no official records regarding their overall health status. She told us that the only seven-bedded PHC in Diyun caters to the health needs of both refugees and the locals. The health centre lacks an allopathic doctor. It is run by a homoeopathic practitioner and three nurses. While making emergency calls, the team sometimes has to travel to regions over 200 kilometres away. Moreover, this area is very prone to malaria. The local women deliver their babies in unhygienic conditions. Recently, the government announced the Janani Suraksha Yojana Scheme. Under it, pregnant women are entitled to Rs 1,400 for an institutional delivery. However, pregnant women in remote areas simply cannot walk all the way to the PHC and, therefore, end up opting for a local delivery, a report says (Talukdar 2008a). Kamini told us that although she has proper nursing training, she hardly finds the opportunity to implement her expertise. She also said that she helps refugee women to deliver their babies as a *dai*.[31] This situation is almost the same everywhere in Arunachal Pradesh except the towns. Moreover, women in these parts have to walk a long way to collect drinking water during winter when the only sources of water—local streams and the Noa-Dihing river—dry up.

On Citizenship

Arindam further said:

> Despite the clear-cut order of the Supreme Court, the State Government of Arunachal Pradesh has not taken any measure to implement the Court's directions. Rather, it has undertaken various measures to undermine and violate the Supreme Court judgement. As we all know, the subject of citizenship forms part of the Union list as far as the division of power between the Centre and the states is concerned. Therefore, it is the responsibility of the central government to grant citizenship to us. However, it is true that, with the intervention of the Election Commission of India, names of 1,497 Chakma and Hajong youths born in Arunachal Pradesh between 1964 and 1 July 1986, were included in the electoral roll and allowed to exercise their franchise during the 2004 Lok Sabha

polls. The government is yet to take a decision on 4,677 applications for the grant of citizenship, submitted by the Chakma and Hajongs through CCRCAP between 1996 and 2006. In this year 2010, we have got a list from the office of the Election Commission, which shows that the total number of Chakmas and Hajongs enrolled in the list increased further to 1,530 with 105 cases of deletion and only 20 cases of addition.[32]

In this context, it would be pertinent to look back at the Citizenship Act of India 1955, which has been amended twice: first in 1987 and then subsequently in 2003. The Citizenship Act of 1955 is unambiguous on citizenship by birth. Section 3(1) of the Indian Citizenship Act of 1955 states:

Citizenship by birth.-

(1) Except as provided in sub-section (2), every person born in India—

(a) on or after the 26th day of January, 1950, but before the commencement of the Citizenship Amendment Act, 1986;

(b) on or after such commencement and either of whose parents is a citizen of India at the time of his birth, shall be a citizen of India by birth. (Ministry of Home Affairs 1955)

The CCRCAP also reported that the State Election Commission of Arunachal Pradesh had refused to register the eligible voters under Section 3.1 of the 1955 Citizenship Act so far. The CCRCAP requested the NHRC to take into cognisance the difference between (*a*) the Chakmas and Hajongs who migrated from East Pakistan and hence are eligible for citizenship through registration and (*b*) the Chakma and Hajongs who are born between 1964 and 1 July 1986 and are citizens by birth under the Citizenship Act 1955. As mentioned previously, the Citizenship Act of 1955 is absolutely clear that those who are born prior to 1 July 1986 are eligible for citizenship unless '(a) his father possesses such immunity from suits or legal process as is accorded to an envoy of an foreign sovereign power accredited to the President of India and is not a citizen of India; or (b) his father is an enemy alien and the birth occurs in a place then under occupation of the enemy' as provided under Section 3.2 of the Citizenship Act, 1955 (Ministry of Home Affairs 1955). Section 3.2 of the Citizenship Act, 1995 is not applicable in the case of the Chakmas and Hajongs who are born between 1964 and 1 July 1986.[33]

We also visited the house of Purna Kumar Chakma, the *gaon burah* of Jyostnapur village, Diyun circle with Arindam and our conversation about granting citizenship to the Chakmas started again. In our discussion, Purna specified that:

> There are many incidents where Chakma people, though they are eligible to be enlisted as voters, have failed to register their names. You know, we have to apply for registration with duly filled-in form prescribed by the Election Commission. After the submission of the form with valid documents to our village office within a specified date we have to appear for the hearing. It is very interesting to note that in most of the cases our applications have been rejected without showing any valid reason. It has become a continuous process here in Lohit and Changlang. Here DC is refusing to receive or forward our papers to the central level. According to the state government the DC has the power to make initial determinations as to the merits of a citizenship application.[34]

To Arindam, the new amendment to the Citizenship Act of India in 1987 has made the issue more complicated for the Chakmas. He explained it in his own way by saying:

> It has been stated in the new amendment that if either of the parents is Indian then the child will be an Indian citizen. Earlier it was not like that. I was born in 1981 and by birth I have got Indian citizenship. However, I can give you an example of the *gaon burah* of my village Dumpani. He is an old man. After losing his two wives he got married again and had a son with his third wife. He has two more sons from his earlier two wives, who have got Indian citizenship by birth. The *gaon burah* is a Chakma man so is his new

> wife. Now, according to the new amendment, this little child cannot be an Indian citizen as one of his parents is not an Indian citizen. The irony is that in the same family his two elder brothers are Indians by birth and this little boy has become stateless just because one of his parents is not Indian. How can you solve this problem?[35]

While dealing with the issue of citizenship, it is to be kept in mind that a child who lacks a birth certificate or identity document is not automatically stateless. Although it is true that there is a possibility that the children who lack birth registration may be at risk of statelessness if its lack causes them problems in proving their links to a country, not all children without birth registration are at a significant risk. Where a child comes from a dominant ethnic group, it may be undisputed by the authorities that he/she is a citizen regardless of what documentation he/she has. There may, however, be a heightened risk of statelessness, for instance, in cases where an ethnic group migrates across the border.

History shows us that India acceded to two international conventions, which create an obligation to abide by the declaration in this area. While India acceded to the two 1966 International Covenants on Civil and Political Rights, and Economic, Social and Cultural Rights in March 1979, it agreed to the 1989 Convention on the Rights of the Child which deals with refugee children and refugee family reunification in 1992.[36] Since the Covenants have not been enacted into Indian law they do not have the force of law in India and are therefore not enforceable in Indian courts. It is to be noted in this context that courts may take them into account in appropriate cases while interpreting the statute law.

Arindam's anxiety combined with a little bit of anger seemed justified against the backdrop of legal anachronism. Our conversations with Arindam, Dilip, Santosh and with other young Chakmas of Diyun and Chowkham made one thing very clear to us—it is likely that the younger generation of the Chakma community has become more conscious about their rights, about the legal concept of citizenship, and also about the consequences of being stateless. Their education at Delhi,

Kolkata or Chennai away from their home has helped them to have an exposure to the outside world.

Land Question

While discussing the socio-economic condition of the Chakmas in Changlang, Arindam said:

> Changlang is populated by several tribal groups, namely Tutsa, Tangsa, Nocte, Singpho and the Lisu. Initially the Chakmas were allowed to clear limited forest areas for settlement. The areas they cleared were mostly on the plains of the River Dihing. That land was a good place to cultivate. Our people showed the locals how to do wet farming which was not practised before. Only Jhum cultivation was popular there. But, now it has been repeatedly alleged that our people are encroaching on the land of the tribal people. It is true that a major portion of the land that was designated for our settlement initially belonged to rich Singpho community leaders. The Government of India with the consent of these Singphos allotted this land to our fathers and grandfathers. I am not denying the fact that our people are cutting the jungles for *jhum* cultivation. What can be done? They are poor agriculturalists. In this context two points need to be kept in mind: first, they are not efficient enough to do other kinds of jobs, and second, they are not entitled to do other jobs without citizenship. How many local people of Singpho and Khamti work in their agricultural fields? You can count them on your fingers. They all give their agricultural land to the Chakmas for share-cropping. So, before reaching any conclusion it is very important to listen to both sides of the story.[37]

The fact remains that, according to the White Paper on the Chakmas and Hajongs, during 1993–94, about 400 hectares of Diyun Reserved Forest land was retrieved which had been under the illegal occupation of Chakmas since 1986. It also stated that the continued presence of Chakma and Hajong refugees had started threatening the fragile eco-system of the state of Arunachal Pradesh. Even the Namdapha Tiger

Project/National Park area has not been spared. Chakma refugees have been intruding into the Namdapha Tiger Project/ National Park area and were causing destruction to the habitat. Their cattle has also been grazing unauthorised inside the park area and damaging the plantation raised by the government. Apart from this, they have also been indulging in illegal felling of trees. This biotic interference has damaged the flora and fauna of the habitat. The report also says that an area of 24.6 square miles has been adversely affected by the biotic interference by the Chakmas (Government of Arunachal Pradesh 1996: 13).

As per the White Paper, the Chakma and Hajong who had encroached upon 20 hectares of plantation land (1985–86) near Bijoypur under Bordumsa range, were evicted on 31 October 1995. On 18 June 1994, 50 Chakma families were evicted from Manabhum Ridge of the Tengapani Reserved Forest. On 9 August 1994, the Chakma occupants of 20 huts were evicted. On 22 November 1995, notices were issued by the Divisional Forest Officer, Banderdewa, to 20 Chakma refugee settlers to vacate nearly 110 hectares of Drupong Reserved Forest allegedly encroached by them. Between 20 October and 26 October 1995, in all, Chakma encroachers from 46 huts were evicted and an area of 47 hectares of Diyun Reserved Forest retrieved (ibid.).

Bimol, the mathematics teacher of Sneha School, thinks that:

> For the past few months the issue that has been influencing our local politics of Arunachal Pradesh is the land question between the Chakmas and the Singphos residing in and around M-Pen.[38]

According to newspaper reports, a clash occurred on 9 April 2010 between the Singpho community and Chakma refugees after a dispute over land in M-Pen. Following a court order to vacate the area, 60 Chakma families were evicted as some Singphos who had Land Possession Certificates (LPCs) wanted it back. This led to a conflict between these two communities and led to a lot of people getting injured (*Arunachal Times* 2010a). Bimol believes that:

> The problem does not seem to be as big as it has been made. It could be resolved through dialogue involving the concerned parties. The reason for turning it into a big issue is that it involves the Chakma community. We have been reading all the biased reports from some of the Arunachalee dailies. But did they bother to hear the opinion of the Chakmas residing in M-Pen? I will say no, because they are landless and refugees. They took only the opinion of some Singpho leaders and other students' bodies.
>
> I can give you another example, in an Arunachalee daily it has been reported on 11 August 2010 that the Chakma refugees attacked locals returning from a hearing on summary revision of electoral rolls injuring at least 30 on 10 August. No one wants to listen to us. No one really wants to know what has actually happened. How many times does an Arunachalee daily report about the plight of Chakmas, who are leading a miserable life without the facilities of proper education, healthcare, employment, etc.? How many times did they report the atrocities on the Chakmas? Now the Singpho leaders are claiming that they possess the LPC. Where was that LPC two or three years back? Just because they have the political and bureaucratic backing they can get LPC anytime. This is not the case with the Chakmas . . . Previously, in times of our older generation, the situation was not bad, but probably the rise of population among the Chakmas, mainly in the Changlang area is the main cause of change in their behaviour. The younger generation of the Khamtis and Singphos especially is more intolerant . . . government won't listen to any of our problems. Our state government has become a puppet in the hand of AAPSU—six months ago, when some of my friends and I gave documents to open bank accounts, they demand PRC and the Scheduled Tribe status document for this which we lack.[39]

The conversation with Arindam and Bimol discloses more on the dispute regarding issuing of PRC to non-APST (non-Arunachal Pradesh Scheduled Tribes) people—in an office memorandum vide No.POL-193/2004/453 dated 24 June 2010—in Lohit and Changlang districts, which turned the land question into a highly emotive one. The order stated that 'PRC may be issued to non-APST people and their families who have settled down in Lohit and Changlang districts prior to 1968 and in respect of whom proper records are available with the administration' (*Arunachal Times* 2010b). The office memorandum also said that before issuing the PRC, a detailed dossier should be prepared and a proper record of the list of eligible persons maintained. However, the government made it clear that the 'issue of such PRC shall not entitle the non-APST to claim for APST' (ibid.).

The AAPSU gave a 20-day ultimatum to the state government to 'cancel that order, failing which it threatened to launch massive agitation throughout the state' (*Arunachal Times* 2010c). To quote Takam Tatung, the President of AAPSU:

> We had suffered enough due to the refugee problem. Today Chakma has become a majority in many areas of Lohit and Changlang districts. All this happened due to the wrong policy of our central government. This decision of issuing PRC to non-APST people has added to the misery of Lohit and Changlang residents. AAPSU is not against issuing citizenships to Chakmas. We are concerned about the humanitarian aspects. However, if they will be granted citizenship then they have to be deported from Arunachal. There are other places in India where they can be accommodated, and not in Arunachal, as according to the Act of 1873 we enjoy a special status. Every outsider has to collect Inner Line Permit to visit our place even if he/she is an Indian citizen. In fact, the Office of the Deputy Resident Commissioner, Arunachal Pradesh, where one has to apply for the Inner Line Permit to enter into the state, is itself in Guwahati, the capital city of Assam. This office does not entertain any application for ILP for the Changlang and Tirap districts which house the refugee settlements, considering the sensitivity of the issue. The Chakmas have come here as refugees and they cannot reside here permanently as citizens of India.[40]

Newspaper reports reveal that indigenous people of both districts were extremely angry with this decision and felt like they had been betrayed by the state government. The All Mishmi

Students' Union (AMSU) of Lohit and Anjaw districts, the All Tai-Khampti-Singpho Students Union and the All East Siang District Students' Union (AESDU) supported AAPSU on this point. They voiced their protest against the state government's decision strongly. In a memorandum written to State Chief Secretary Tabom Bam, these students' unions stated that this decision of the government was a 'gross violation of rights of the bonafide tribal people of Arunachal Pradesh and . . . against the provision of Bengal Eastern Frontier Regulation Act of 1873'. They also said that the decision had been taken without the consent of the local people of both districts and termed it as 'illegal' and 'against the interest of the local inhabitants of Lohit and Changlang' (*Arunachal Times* 2010d). Further, the Arunachal Citizens' Right (ACR) under the leadership of its chairman, Bamang Tago, proposed a rally in collaboration with AAPSU to protest against the issue of PRC to non-APST. According to Tago:

> The state government is confusing the people of the state. Which order of the Supreme Court was the government referring to? Even if the apex court had passed such an order or directives, it is the prime duty of the state government to file a counter affidavit to protect the interest of its people. The people of Arunachal cannot be 'victims of democracy'. We are sympathetic to the Chakmas but their cause cannot prove bad for the Arunachalees . . . give them citizenship status but they should be properly rehabilitated outside Arunachal Pradesh. The 1873 Regulation proves that we are not open to outsiders. Arunachal Pradesh has a distinct identity and culture which gets hampered for infiltration. So time has come—AAPSU has to sit together with the representatives of state government, central government and also the representatives of CCRCAP and talk for a solution and the Government of India should take the chief part . . . There is a common perception among our indigenous tribes that the Chakmas are criminal in nature; they have killed so many locals. So if they are granted permanent residential certificates, they would dominate the indigenous communities . . . customary laws and traditional rights of indigenous people living in surrounding areas will be violated

> . . . also the encroachment of the forest area is a big issue, we have to see local people's sentiments as well.[41]

Due to mounting pressure from all the students' unions coupled with the resentments from different groups of indigenous people the State Cabinet decided to revoke the order honouring the public resentment on the issue of PRC. The chief minister of the state, Dorjee Khandu, said in a press conference that the decision had been taken on 'humanitarian ground in favour of non-Arunachalees residing in the state with permanent land holdings and was not intended to provide them APST status but it wanted to enable them to get education and job benefits' (*Outlook* 2010; *Arunachal Times* 2010d).

Role of Local Media

The Chakmas in Arunachal Pradesh allege that the media of the state is completely biased towards the local communities or the indigenous tribes of the state. Their claim is that every report in the newspaper is against the Chakmas even if the truth is otherwise. As Arindam states:

> Many people feel Changlang is a disturbed area . . . but this is not entirely true. This should also come up in the media. They always project one side of the story. I feel media should be balanced . . . should bring out balanced news. Even if it is not positive for us the truth must still come out. But the media here is so negative. They portray us as criminal tribes.[42]

Arindam went on to say:

> I can give you numerous instances where the media has acted biased and against us. Like few months back there was this hearing happening on objections to some applicants among the Chakmas regarding gaining the right of citizenship status on 9 June 2010. This is a process whereby persons who have been denied the right to vote are informed about the reasons of some objections. More than

often in the past, officials have not been present in these sessions and as a result we have never come to know what constitutes the basis of addition and deletion of names from the electoral rolls. So on this day, some youths among the Chakmas got a bit carried away and pelted stones towards the vehicles of the officials in charge of the hearing. This was reported with an exaggeration in the media. The whole issue was blown out of proportion and it made big news. The dailies reported that many people have been injured due to the attack by the Chakma youth, which is not true. So the media has a vital role to play but is not doing so.[43]

Dilip Kumar Chakma echoed what Arindam said:

Our people have been agitated because we have been demanding the right to vote and citizenship for long but the authorities constantly deny us. Our children are not being issued birth certificates and hence we are falling short in providing documents to apply for voter's identity cards and so on.[44]

Way Out?

There are at least three major issues that have to be taken into consideration.

First, the federal relations need to re-negotiated. While the central government urges the state government to carry out what it considers as its 'national' responsibility, the state government accuses the Centre of having taken a 'callous and indifferent attitude' towards the 'unanimous demand' of the people of the state (Government of Arunachal Pradesh 1996: 2). The state government, on the other hand, requests the central government 'for removal and dispersal of these refugees by following the due process of law as they were found wanting in "responsible social behaviour" and posed a threat to the very survival of the indigenous tribal people' (ibid.: 23).

The Union and state governments are not on good terms notwithstanding the fact that they are sometimes run by the same political party. It appears that the social dynamics at the local or state level prove to be much more crucial than the federal dynamics and sometimes make the party also ruling at the Centre act against the high command. The crux of the problem, as Sushmita Sengupta (2002: 263) explains, lies in the fact that the rights of the Chakma refugees come into conflict with the rights claims of the indigenous tribes having a 'distinct way of life'. As Rabijit Choudhury (1994: 8) aptly puts it: 'The nationality of the Chakmas may be questioned, but their right to sustain themselves is undisputed. The problem arises when this right is in conflict with the rights of the indigenous tribes who have a distinct way of life'. Deepak Kumar Singh writes: 'both the stateless Chakmas and the indigenous Arunachalis have equally competing claims against the Indian State' (2010: 266).

Moreover, the liberal resolution that contending rights get resolved insofar as 'basic rights' 'trump' other rights does not seem to work. What we see here is that both the communities are involved in a kind of controversy that centres on equally basic rights.

Second, one has to also understand that there is a limit to what the law and law courts can do. The law and law courts do their best but these get stonewalled by the implementing authorities. In a personal interview, Justice Ahmadi (who wrote the landmark judgement in 1996)[45] pointed out the futility of the court verdicts saying that law courts have failed to prove themselves as law enforcing agencies. He expressed his deep sense of dissatisfaction with the way the Court has been overruled by the local administration and his acute sense of 'helplessness' in implementing the verdict.[46] The law cannot initiate any change unless society is ready to accept and implement it. As Sabyasachi Basu Ray Chaudhury comments: 'despite the court judgment, the Chakmas and Hajongs have remained subject to intimidation, harassment, torture and other forms of abuse' (2003: 269).

At the same time one has to understand that the Chakma issue cannot be resolved without addressing the rights claims of the indigenous tribes who feel that recognition of the rights of the Chakmas would result in violation of their own. The options along the legal trajectory seem to have been exhausted. As Singh (2010: 249) argues, 'What accounts for the non-grant of citizenship to the Chakmas is not so much a problem of legal deficiency or lack of constitutional provisions at the domestic level or absence of institutional obligations, as it is a question of political will'. The Government of India's approach to the whole problem is that it should be settled through 'a fair and impartial mechanism' (CCRCAP 1995: 7). But the issue is political—and it should be settled politically (AITPN 1997). The presence of a 'fair and impartial mechanism' per se does not enhance the acceptability of the solution proposed by it.

Third, the civil society inside Arunachal Pradesh is highly fractured—polarised between two centres. Some forces gravitate towards the CCRCAP and some hover around the AAPSU. Singh's argument hardly recognises that 'political will' does not drop from above but is generated from below through a long haul, through a series of almost endless initiatives facilitating dialogues and discussions between these two otherwise contending communities. Endless, because the dialogues cannot afford to fail and have to continue till the issue is resolved. S. Dutta (2002: 211), in fact, pleads for a 'consensual approach' in order to solve this vexed problem. There cannot be any civil society solution. It only reminds us of Carol Batchelor's comment (1998: 159) quoted at the beginning of the chapter: 'Statelessness is not merely a legal problem, it is a human problem'. Bearing this in mind, it is important to examine not only the issues related to legal dimensions and developments, but also the human concerns and realities they are meant to focus on.

How can headway be made in such a situation? One way is to organise a series of sustained dialogues—not necessarily the successful ones. The organisation of dialogue with lower- or medium-level leaders is itself an achievement. It may take place outside Arunachal Pradesh, and must be conducted in a series and in a way that it becomes possible for both the parties to take part in it. Such dialogues should also be multilayered involving different stakeholders in the society and politics of Arunachal Pradesh, i.e., the 'stateless' people in the state, the local communities, Union and state government representatives, civil society organisations, NGOs, media and so on. The CRG is ideally suited to launch the initiative and organise such multilayered dialogues (to begin with) outside Arunachal Pradesh.

Fourth, it is to be seen whether these 'refugees' or 'stateless persons' in Arunachal Pradesh could be treated like the 'mandate refugees' of the UNHCR.[47] In other words, there may be, like in the case of refugees, a mandate category for the UNHCR to protect the stateless persons.

Fifth, the establishment of an Equality Commission as proposed by the CRG in the paper 'An Indian Charter for Minority Rights' (Basu Ray Chaudhury 2009) could ensure a rights-based approach instead of a charity-based one while also considering long-term relief of the Chakmas in Arunachal Pradesh. After all, when other basic rights are more or less secure and protected for the Chakmas, chances of pressing for citizenship rights and exacerbating the conflict may be reduced to an appreciable extent. Conflicts such as these take time to resolve. Therefore, it is important to secure other rights as soon as possible. One can perhaps also draw suitable lessons from the Assam movement in this connection.

Last, but not least, there is also a need for a South Asian Charter for protecting the stateless. After all, these stateless persons are primarily the products of the decolonisation process, the associated boundary-making exercise and the creation of the South Asian state system.

Notes

* This chapter includes content drawn from various Calcutta Research Group publications, which have been used with permission.

1. Interview with D.C., Tezu, 12 September 2010.

2. Letter from Sneha Kumar Chakma, 19 November 1949.

3. *State of Arunachal Pradesh v. Khudiram Charma*, 27 April 1993, 1994 AIR 1461, 1993 SCR (3) 401.

4. On 7 July 1994, Shri P.M. Sayeed, Minister of State for Home Affairs vide his DO (Demy-Official) letter (DO No. 13/12/94.MZ) invited the attention of Shri N. Yonggam, MP, to the debate in the Rajya Sabha on 27 January 1994 raised by him and said that: '[W]e have examined the matter in detail and find that the Chakma-Hajong refugees were settled in Arunachal Pradesh under the Indira-Mujib Agreement of 1972, it was decided that those Chakma Hajong refugees who came to India from erstwhile East Pakistan (now Bangladesh) before 25th March, 1971 will be considered for grant of Indian citizenship' (cited in Government of Arunachal Pradesh 1996: 56).

5. *Assam Tribune*, 13 September 1993.

6. See 'Chakma and Hajong Refugee Problems in Arunachal Pradesh: Why We Demand Deportation?' published by the People's Referendum Rally for Deportation of Chakma and Hajong Refugees from Arunachal Pradesh, September 1995.

7. *State Of Arunachal Pradesh v. Khudiram Chakma on 27 April, 1993*, 1994 AIR 1461, 1993 SCR (3) 401, http://indiankanoon.org/doc/473806/ (accessed on 12 January 2014).

8. *State of Arunachal Pradesh v. Khudiram Charma*, 27 April 1993, 1994 AIR 1461, 1993 SCR (3) 401.

9. Ibid.

10. *National Human Rights Commission v. State of Arunachal Pradesh*, 1996 AIR 1234.

11. *State of Arunachal Pradesh v. Khudiram Charma*, 27 April 1993, 1994 AIR 1461, 1993 SCR (3) 401.

12. Ibid.

13. During the field visit, altogether 20 Chakmas (16 male and four female) from the Lohit and Diyun circles were interviewed.

14. Interview with Sashibhushan Chakma, Chakma *basti*, Chowkham, 23 September 2010.

15. All unaccredited quotes in this chapter are from the authors' fieldwork.

16. Interview with Paritosh, Chowkham, 23 September 2010.

17. Interview with Sashibhushan Chakma, Chakma *basti*, Chowkham, 23 September 2010.

18. From a group discussion arranged in Chowkham, 24 September 2010.

19. Ibid.

20. Interview with Sashibhushan Chakma, Chakma *basti*, Chowkham, 23 September 2010.

21. Interview with Ramani Mohan, Chowkham, 24 September 2010.

22. Interview with Natun Chakma, Chowkham, 24 September 2010.

23. Interview with Santosh, Chowkham, 24 September 2010.

24. *Statesman*, 3 October 1994.

25. Interview with Santosh, Chowkham, 24 September 2010. In this context it is important to note that the state government through its letter no. POL–21/80 dated 29 September 1980 banned public employment for the Chakmas and Hajongs in the state. In 1991, the state government under its order no. FPSO-3/90-91 of 31 October 1991, issued by the circle officer of Diyun, withdrew ration card facilities under the PDS from the Chakmas. In 1994, the state government through its order no. CS/HOME/94 dated 21 November 1994 further directed 'withdrawal of all kinds of facilities from the Chakma Settlement area' (quoted in ACHR 2007). See Prasad (2012).

26. Vide Order no. CS/HOME/94, dated 21 November 1994.

27. http://www.globalpolitician.com/22651-refugees (accessed on 12 January 2012).

28. *Statesman*, 13 September 1994.

29. Interview with Arindam Dewan, Changlang, 25 September 2010.

30. Ibid.

31. Interview with Kamini, Changlang, 26 September 2010.

32. Interview with Arindam Dewan, Changlang, 25 September 2010.

33. Based on a letter from CCRCAP to NHRC on 12 September 1997.

34. Interview with Purna Kumar Chakma, Chowkham, 24 September 2010.

35. Interview with Arindam Dewan, Changlang, 25 September 2010.

36. It is pertinent to mention here that the International Covenant on Civil and Political Rights (ICCPR) declares that 'every child has the right to acquire a nationality' (OHCHR 1966). Further, Article 7(1) of the Convention on the Rights of the Child reads: 'the child shall be registered immediately after birth and shall have the right from birth to a name, the right to acquire a nationality, and as far as possible, the right to know and be cared for by his or her parents' (OHCHR 1989). The Convention was adopted by the UN General Assembly on 20 November 1989.

37. Interview with Arindam Dewan, Changlang, 25 September 2010.

38. Interview with Bimol, 24 September 2010.

39. Ibid.

40. Interview with Takam Tatung, Itanagar, 25 September 2010.

41. Interview with Bamang Tago, 25 September 2010.

42. Interview with Arindam Dewan, Changlang, 25 September 2010.

43. Ibid.

44. Interview with Dilip Kumar Chakma, Changlang, 26 September 2010.

45. On 9 January 1996, the Supreme Court, in its judgement (which was regarded as a landmark one) on a writ petition filed by the NHRC in 1995, instructed the state government of Arunachal Pradesh to ensure protection of the life and personal liberty of every Chakma residing within the state and to enter the facts of the applications made for registration as citizens of India by Chakmas under Section 5 of the Citizenship Act, 1955, in the register maintained for the purpose and forward the application to the central government for consideration.

46. Interview with Justice Ahmadi, New Delhi, 5 May 2001.

47. Those who are recognised as refugees by UNHCR under its statute are termed 'mandate refugees'. Mandate status is especially significant in States that are not parties to the 1951 Convention or its 1967 Protocol (http://www.globaldetentionproject.org/resources/glossary.html [accessed on 28 August 2013]).

SIX

Elusive Home-Thoughts

The Unstable World of the Lhotsampas in South Asia

ATIG GHOSH
*PRAVINA GURUNG**

The post-colonial state-building process in South Asia has been marked by the production of divided communities and mutilated neighbourhoods. The history of these post-partition states of South Asia has been one of consolidating majoritarian elites producing persecuted minorities, of citizenship and the denial of which has led to statelessness, of borders resulting in illegal but not unnatural cross-border movements, and of development policies uprooting millions. This condition, reinforced by the protracted refusal of the involved states to take them back, creates circumstances that may eventually lead to the loss of their nationality. It has made South Asia a region crowded with refugees and the displaced (Bose and Manchanda 1997). The Indian national-territorial space, therefore, is indiscerptible politically and practically from the networks of movement and displacement that span the entire region. If one keeps one's investigative feet firmly planted in the national soil, then what will result is not merely a nationalist myopia, but also serious misrecognition of transnational flows and linkages, processes and provenances. As such, one needs to step out of national(ist) boxes and think in terms of connectivities when dealing with stateless groups. These groups may not be stateless *per se*, but protracted refugeehood can over time push them into situations akin to statelessness. Also, and somewhat alternately, dual deprivation as being simultaneously a refugee and a stateless person may blur the strictures of legal formalism and produce a lived experience that needs to be considered carefully to revaluate, perhaps rethink, our positions vis-à-vis these formal categories. A classic case is provided by the Lhotsampas or ethnic-Nepali Bhutanese refugees in Jhapa, Nepal, who were denied Bhutanese nationality at the same time as they became refugees; that is, they were refugees at the same time as being stateless. We would look into the case in some detail in what follows.

The UNHCR in January 2012 recorded that there are around 800,000 stateless people residing in Nepal, among whom are individuals from Tibet and Bhutan (UNHCR 2012). As has already been indicated, this chapter covers only a section, albeit a very large and significant one, of this group—the Lhotsampas of Bhutan, minority groups of Nepali origin who have been expelled and compelled to lead a life of refugees in Nepal. They were 121,000 refugees living in seven different camps of Nepal in 2012. After 15 rounds of bilateral talks failed between Bhutan and Nepal, they have now been offered the option of third-country resettlement as a durable solution. However, not all the refugees in Nepal have chosen to resettle abroad. The Government of Nepal and development partners who have been closely assisting refugees are still not clear about the status of those staying back in Nepal. There is limited information regarding those who have gone for resettlement in the third countries—about whether it has been a happy choice willingly made or a forced one, leading to the loss of identity.

At a glance, it would become obvious that the Lhotsampas have gone through changing, almost unstably flighty, status reckoning over the years. Here, our endeavour would be to understand and find out about the experience and journey of Lhotsampas from the status of being minority citizens in Bhutan, to refugeehood and eventual statelessness in Nepal, and the new forms of citizenship emerging in the third country of resettlement or even Nepal.

At the outset, it may be useful to frame a set of questions which we may then try to address and answer through the narrative of dislocation and dispossession of the Lhotsampas. These questions may be:

- What were the challenges of living as a minority group in Bhutan?
- How were groups of Nepali-speaking Bhutanese population rendered stateless?
- What were the factors that compelled them to leave their homeland and travel all the way back to Nepal?
- What were the challenges of staying without a nationality in Nepal though they were culturally and religiously similar?
- How do the refugees view the resettlement options: a new identity or a loss of identity?
- How do the refugees staying in Nepal review their situation?
- What will be policy of the host government, Nepal, for the stateless people staying on in Nepal?

The situation is described through the lens of secondary literature; review of books, journals, articles on the internet; and testimonies published on the internet; and also interviews with the Lhotsampas living in camps.

Concepts of Statelessness: A Legal Discursus

Mid-1950s onwards, international bodies were busy forging and implementing laws to deal with the figure of the stateless person. The two milestone international conventions that have attempted to define the status and rights of stateless individuals and groups—sometimes, though not necessarily, in contradistinction to the refugee—in fact, took place in this period: the 1954 Convention relating to the Status of Stateless Persons[1] and the 1961 Convention on the Reduction of Statelessness.[2] As of 20 December 2013, there were 79 state parties to the Convention of 1954[3] and 55 state parties to the 1961 Convention.[4] None of the South Asian countries were party to these conventions. Yet, the conventions, insofar as they provide a working frame for identifying and addressing statelessness, provide an important legal *entrée* into the problem of the Lhotsampas. Further, they help us engage with and interrogate the activism of the South Asian governments, or the lack of it, in comparison to how other states in the world have gone about addressing statelessness.

To begin with, however, one needs to establish if, from the legal point of view, the Lhotsampas qualify as stateless. The International Law Commission observes that the definition of a stateless person contained in Article 1(1) of the 1954 Convention is now an integral part of customary international law. Both the 1954 and 1961 Conventions exclusively deal with the issue of statelessness. Both these legal instruments explain statelessness predominantly in two ways: *de jure* and *de facto*.[5] While defining a stateless person as a person who is not considered a national by any state under the operation of its law, Article 1 of the 1954 Convention generally equates the term with *de jure* statelessness. The issue at stake in Article 1 is not whether the individual has a nationality that is effective or not, but whether the individual has a nationality or not in the first place. Although the line between being recognised by law as a national but not being treated as such on the one hand, and not being recognised as a national at all on the other may be fine, the two problems are nevertheless conceptually distinct: the former is connected to the rights that are attached to nationality, whereas the latter problem is connected to the right to nationality itself.

De facto stateless persons, in contrast, are persons who are outside the country of their nationality and hence are unable—or, for valid reasons, are unwilling—to avail of the protection of that country. Protection in this sense refers to the right to diplomatic protection, exercised by the state of nationality in order to remedy an internationally wrongful act against one of its nationals, as well as diplomatic and consular protection, and assistance generally, including repatriation. This situation may be evidenced in practice by, for instance, the refusal of the country of nationality to allow him or her to return home, even though it still recognises the individual as a national. In such a situation, the person may also fall under the definition of a 'refugee' depending on the circumstances, and refugees are indeed the most numerically important category of *de facto* stateless persons.

As we have seen, the two legal instruments made to address statelessness—the 1954 and 1961 Conventions—have an inherent limitation.[6] In spite of increasing encouragement from the international humanitarian organisations to accede to these conventions, the number of state parties remains low and the South Asian countries are among the non-signatories. Also, one important shortcoming of the 1961 Convention is that it does not prohibit the possibility of revocation of nationality under certain circumstances nor does it address the subject of retroactively granting citizenship to all currently stateless persons; hence, the problem of statelessness has not nearly been resolved. However, these two documents are not the only sources of international norms relating to statelessness. The Hague Convention of 1930, the Universal Declaration of Human Rights of 1948, the Convention on the Elimination of All Forms of Discrimination against Women in 1979, the Convention on the Rights of Child in 1989 and the European Convention on Nationality in 1997 are some of the major attempts at reducing statelessness. Although it may be important to plead for accession to both the instruments of 1954 and 1961, this is not a necessary precondition for action against statelessness, and it is important to develop an understanding of the other legal tools that are available. Such is the case because, conceptually, the idea of the State—and by that logic, 'nationality' and 'citizenship'—cannot be dissociated from the idea of statelessness. 'Nationality' and 'citizenship' are two words most commonly used to describe the same phenomenon: the legal bond of membership between an individual and a State. Nationality can only be conferred or confirmed by states, and States are responsible for protecting the fundamental rights of everybody on their territory, including those of stateless persons. Thus, for all activities relating to statelessness, the states are indispensable actors. If a person is stateless, then by the same token he/she is without nationality and citizenship.[7]

Viewed in the light of this elaboration, the Lhotsampas residing for decades in the Jhapa camps of Nepal are victims of statelessness. Diplomatic *démarches* between Nepal and Bhutan notwithstanding, the latter has refused to readmit the Lhotsampas into its territory. In theory, stateless people enjoy many human rights under international law; however, in practice it has been seen that the non-citizen stateless populations face great difficulty in exercising their rights and therefore suffer a precarious existence (Blitz 2009; also see Blitz and Lynch 2011b). Brad K. Blitz points out that

> under the 1954 Convention, individuals who have not received nationality automatically or through an individual decision under the operation of any state's laws are known as *de jure* stateless persons. There are also countless others who cannot call upon their rights to nationality for their protection and are effectively stateless or *de facto* stateless persons. Often *de facto* stateless people are unable to obtain proof of their national identity, residency or other means of qualifying for citizenship and as a result may be excluded from the formal state. (Blitz 2009: 7; also see Blitz and Lynch 2011b; van Waas 2011)

It is also important to note that 'the existence of stateless populations challenges some of the central tenets of international law and the human rights discourse that have developed over the past sixty years' (Blitz and Lynch 2009: 5). Most significantly, the 'reality of statelessness' is contradictory to the right to nationality that the UDHR guarantees. Blitz and Lynch (ibid.) state that 'Article 15 of the UDHR implicitly acknowledges the principle whereby an individual's nationality is linked to his or her identity, and it states in Clause 2 that "no one shall be arbitrarily deprived of his nationality nor denied the right to change his nationality [Article 15, UN 1948]"' (ibid.).

Normally, statelessness emerges from succession of states or territorial reorganisations. It also emerges from persecution of minorities and a state's majoritarian bias, which lead states at times to expel citizens or inhabitants. This condition, reinforced by the protracted refusal of the involved states to take them back, creates a circumstance which may eventually lead to the loss of their nationality and citizenship. State policies make refugees but, as we have argued, all stateless are not refugees. The basic premise is that states should be held accountable for displacing their citizens. But where displaced people seek refuge across borders, the host state should receive refugees on humanitarian grounds and respect the principle of non-*refoulement*. One of the aspects of statelessness in South Asia is the fact that it is also a product of economic migration between states.

There have been some regional efforts to articulate and implement the notion of state responsibility at the regional level. Regional treaties such as the 1969 American Convention on Human Rights, the 1990 African Charter on the Rights and Welfare of the Child and the 1997 European Convention on Nationality emphasise that '[e]veryone should have a nationality'. These regional instruments also seek to clarify the rights and responsibilities of countries in ensuring these rights in practical terms. The UN General Assembly designated the UNHCR as the national interlocutor in the absence of any other specific organisation dealing with statelessness, both to provide legal assistance to the disenfranchised and to promote the avoidance and elimination of statelessness globally. Recognising the important link between statelessness, security and forced population displacements, the international community has encouraged the UNHCR to adopt a more active role in this area so as to actively promote accession to the 1954 and 1961 Conventions on statelessness as well as to provide relevant technical and advisory services pertaining to the preparation and implementation of nationality legislation.

Statelessness is treated as a politically sensitive issue and often viewed as internal problems of countries. Many countries are unable to ascertain the number of stateless persons on their national territory because states consider this issue politically delicate. Governments do not make accurate counts of these populations. As such, the overall figures are difficult to arrive at. Although statelessness is prohibited under international law, the UNHCR presently estimates that there may be as many of 10 million stateless people in the world. There are an estimated 3.2 million refugees and stateless in South Asia and more than 800,000 stateless persons in Nepal alone.

Migrant History: Nepali Nationals to Bhutan

R. Ramasubramanian (n.d.) remarks: 'Historically, South Asia has witnessed substantial intra-regional movement and dislocation of regional groups fleeing ethnic or religious persecution and political instability'. The 'Nepali-speaking Bhutanese, also called Lhotsampas ("People of the south")', Maya Maxym (2010) explains, 'are Bhutanese citizens of Nepali origin'. Bhutan is a small kingdom surrounded by giant neighbours—China in the north and India to its east, west and south. It is ruled by Ngalongs' Wangchuk Dynasty since 1907. Bhutan is a multi-racial, multi-cultural and religious country and comprises 14 ethnic groups including three major ones: the Ngalongs also called Drukpas, the Sarchops and the ethnic Nepalese or Lhotsampas.

Nepalis had migrated to Bhutan in the nineteenth century. According to lore, it is believed that a Tibetan king had taken some Nepali/Newari families to Tibet to construct monasteries. The same people were believed to have constructed the Kyichu Lhakhang of Paro district in Bhutan and they settled in the fertile villages of western and central Bhutan. Maxym (ibid.) writes:

> The first report of the residence of the Nepalese in Bhutan was around 1620 when Shamdrung Ngawong Namgyal (a Tibetan lama who unified Bhutan) commissioned a few Newar craftsmen from the Kathmandu Valley in Nepal to make a silver Stupa for his father, Tempa Nima. There are no references to any further movement of people from Nepal to Bhutan until the beginning of the nineteenth century.

In the mid-to-late nineteenth and early twentieth centuries, people 'from Nepal were invited to populate the lowlands of southern Bhutan' (ibid.). The Nepali-speaking people were granted full citizenship of the country by the Citizenship Act of 1948 (AHURA Bhutan n.d.). There was limited contact between the Druks (Bhutanese) in the north and the Nepali-speaking Bhutanese (Lhotsampas) in the south. The Lhotsampas retained their 'Nepali language, culture and religion' despite having lived in Bhutan for 'up to five generations' (Maxym 2010). With the initiation of nationwide programmes for development and modernisation in 1961, 'the Lhotsampas, with the development of education, social services and the economy during the 1960s and 70s, rose to occupy influential positions in the bureaucracy' (AHURA Bhutan n.d.). This set off the beginning of their participation in public life as well as in politics to the extent of even reaching important positions of leadership. The Lhotsampas and other ethnic groups in Bhutan coexisted peacefully with other ethnic groups in Bhutan until the mid-1980s, when the king of Bhutan as well as the ruling Druk majority felt threatened by the increasing influence of the Lhotsampa population, believing it to be a danger to their position of majority and to traditional Buddhist culture of the Druk Bhutanese.

'During the 1980s, the Lhotsampas came to be seen as a threat to the political order and the Drukpa culture. The Drukpas of the northwest or the ruling elite began to fear being overshadowed by Lhotsampas of the south' (ibid.). The Drukpas comprised 16 per cent of the total population, the Sarchops 31 per cent, and the rest were the Lhotsampas though the figure, like most demographic statistics in comparable socio-political situations, are somewhat controversial.[8] Then, the Bhutanese government adopted a number of legislative measures and policies to push the southern Bhutanese out of the country. In 1985, a new Citizenship Act was passed by the Government of Bhutan fixing 1958 as the cut-off date for citizenship. Following the introduction of the new Act, a 'census exercise was carried out only in the southern districts of Bhutan in 1988, in which every household of the southern population had to produce documentary evidence of having legal residence, such as land tax receipt of 1958' (AHURA Bhutan n.d.). Failing to produce such documentary evidence led them to be labelled non-nationals. The new act and census policy was aimed towards depriving the southern Bhutanese (ethnic Nepalese) of their citizenship. The Association of Human Rights Activists, Bhutan (AHURA) (ibid.) reports:

> The census team randomly categorised the southern Bhutanese into seven different categories. In many cases, citizenship cards previously issued were confiscated. Many genuine Bhutanese citizens who could not produce a land tax receipt of 1958 were declared non-nationals. Even the village headmen were taken into confidence by dubious means and were not permitted to testify to the credentials of the people of their villages during the census.

An operation, infamously known as the 'One Nation One People' campaign, was initiated by the government to 'strengthen what they perceived as the solidary Bhutanese national identity. The policies imposed the Druk dress code, religious practices and language use on all Bhutanese regardless of prior practices of the Lhotsampa community' (Maxym 2010). These changes affected the Lhotsampa people negatively as they had none of these in common with the northern Bhutanese. 'The use of the Nepali language was prohibited in schools, many Lhotsampa teachers were dismissed, and textbooks were publicly burnt' (ibid.). Driglam Namza—an 'ancient code of social etiquette of the western Bhutanese' that contains instructions on how to eat, sit, talk, dress, bow before authority, and what hair style to adopt—was made obligatory for all the Bhutanese inspite of their cultural diversity (AHURA Bhutan n.d.). A report of AHURA Bhutan poignantly describes:

> In the name of national integration, government's drive for 'One Nation One People' policy made all the southern Bhutanese liable to a fine or imprisonment if they ventured out in anything other than western traditional costume, and Nepali language was removed from the school curriculum. Many southern Bhutanese were fined

> and imprisoned for not complying with this order. The wearing of 'gho' and 'kira', traditional Drukpa male and female garments was unsuited to the heat of southern Bhutan. (ibid.)

The crisis deepened in Bhutan in the 1990s and made the lives of the Lhotsampas extremely difficult. Maxym (2010) elaborates how there were rampant human rights violations, 'including detention, imprisonment without trial and torture'. Further, 'stringent and unrealistic requirements' to prove citizenship were forced upon the Lhotsampa people, most of whom were denied any recognition of their status as citizens 'even when they were able to provide proper documentation' (ibid.). Saurav J. Thapa, contesting the Bhutanese monarchy's attempt to project Bhutan internationally as 'a country of smiling Buddha', writes:

> Little do most outside observers know the dark underbelly of this seemingly innocuous portrayal. It wilfully ignores the history of ethnic cleansing and institutionalized racial intolerance against Lhotsampas inside Bhutan that continue unabated to this day. Between 1987 and 1992, the absolute monarchy and northern Drukpa elite carried out a systematic and sustained campaign of ethnic cleansing against its Lhotsampa minority who live mostly in the south. The Lhotsampas are mostly Hindus of ethnic Nepalese origin whose ancestors migrated to Bhutan two centuries ago during the British Raj. In fact, the Lhotsampas settled in Bhutan even before the current Wangchuk dynasty of Drukpas came to power in 1907. They gradually assimilated into the life of their new homeland and actively contributed to the economic wellbeing of Bhutan. (Thapa 2011)

The stories of fear, dispossession and separation leading to tragedy are legion. The AHURA report recounts the following anecdote:

> Sita Mothe, the wife of Buddhiman Mothe, a Bhutanese citizen of Chirang district committed suicide on fear of being separated from her husband and children when the census team threatened to deport her from the country for being a non-national. Mrs. Mothe

> was an Indian citizen by origin who had married a Bhutanese national. (AHURA Bhutan n.d.)

Clearly, the frenzy to relieve Bhutan of any trace of non-Druk culture was followed through arbitrarily.

As we have discussed, with the introduction of the 'One Nation One People' policy, the Nepali-speaking Lhotsampas were forbidden from wearing their own traditional dress and were forced to speak the Drukpa language only. On 9 April 1988, Tek Nath Rizal—the then Royal Advisory Councillor and people's representative from the south—'petitioned the Bhutanese King seeking a review of the 1985 Citizenship Act and the manner in which the census was carried out'. However, this appeal was treated as an act of treason by the king and Rizal was 'imprisoned and tortured on charges of inciting the southern Bhutanese against the government' (ibid.). Following that incident, Rizal went into exile in Nepal to work for the human rights of the Bhutanese people and under his leadership the 'People's Forum for Human Rights in Bhutan' was formed, which started campaigning against the gross violations of human rights in Bhutan.

On 16 November 1989, Rizal, along with other activists, was abducted from Nepal and imprisoned in Bhutan. There were massive human rights violations in Bhutan. The Bhutan People's Party (BPP) was formed in exile in India in June 1990 with the aim to work for political reforms in Bhutan. At the end of 1990, the BPP organised 'a mass rally throughout southern Bhutan and some parts of eastern Bhutan' (Acharya 2006). Public demonstrations demanding democracy, and human, civil and cultural rights were held across southern Bhutan and hundreds of people took to the streets. The Royal Government labelled such activities 'anti-nationalist' and assigned the responsibilityof crushing the movement to the Royal Bhutan Army (RBA). Ram Lal Acharya (ibid.) writes that 'people participating in the movement were arrested, tortured, raped, harassed, houses were destroyed and their citizenship cards confiscated'.

A resolution was drawn in 1991 in the National Assembly of Bhutan for the eviction of any person who had 'participated in the peaceful demonstrations' or had been 'in any way related to those who had fled from the country' (ibid.). In addition, as mentioned earlier, 'unrealistic requirements' to prove citizenship were enforced on the Lhotsampas, with most being denied citizenship even on providing documentation (Maxym 2010). They were forced to sign the Volunteer Migration Forms at gunpoint and forced to leave their home country without a citizenship and with a lost identity.

Following the discrimination and fear of the security threat, many fled to Nepal passing through India. By the end of 1992, thousands of Lhotsampas landed in the eastern part of Nepal.

Forced Migration to Nepal: Protracted Refugeehood

The life of the Nepali-speaking Lhotsampas did not become easy in Nepal. The arrival of hundreds of thousands of people to Nepal created a humanitarian crisis in the country. At the request of the Nepalese government, the UNHCR established a Bhutanese Refugee Camp in south-east Nepal in 1991.

The Bhutanese nationals, whose forebears had been from Nepal, now ironically became refugees who were at the same time suspended in a stateless void in Nepal. Although they spoke the same language as a native Nepali speaker and had similar cultural ties with Nepal, it was very difficult for the Government of Nepal to absorb all the Lhotsampas as it created a huge pressure on the local community. During a period of 15 years or more, the number of Bhutanese refugees massively increased and reached 107,000. Being a poor country, the Government of Nepal was not able to shoulder the burden of the refugees. They were supported by various humanitarian organisations for food, education and shelter support. While Nepal allowed the Bhutanese refugees to remain on its land, it provided them only some limited rights. Human Rights Watch reports how no provision has been made for 'Bhutanese refugees to acquire Nepalese citizenship' despite the fact that 'many Bhutanese refugees have now resided in Nepal for more than 15 years, and that a significant proportion of the Bhutanese refugee population consists of children who were born in Nepal' (HRW 2007b).

Nationality or citizenship is a legal bond between a state and that country's laws and the individual. As stated by the UNHCR (1997), it:

> entitles the individual to the protection of the state and provides a legal basis for the exercise of many political, social, economic and other rights, as well as the responsibilities of both governments and citizens. In many instances, nationality also enables people to find employment, to make use of public services, to participate in the political process, to have access to judicial system. It is a genuine effective link between the individual and the state for the vast majority of people around the world. The link is easily established and readily acknowledged by the authorities of the states concerned. In situations, where those conditions do not exist, problems of statelessness are likely to emerge.

In the case of Bhutanese refugees in Nepal, they are denied citizenship and do not have the liberty to exercise their fundamental rights.

The Government of Nepal 2005 Survey estimates that over 1 million Nepalese are deprived of citizenship rights, mostly women. Under the Nepali Citizenship Law, the age of eligibility for citizenship is 16, based on descent, subject to endorsement by an immediate male family member. This has been slightly modified in recent years and citizenship is issued in the name of the mother as well, but the number is not very significant. Nepal's citizenship policy is based on descent and *jus sanguine.* However, it might be worthwhile to note that:

> International human rights law is unambiguous about the prohibition of citizenship based on '*jus sanguine*' i.e. based on the nationality of their parents instead of where they are born. The UN Human Rights Committee and UN Committee on the Elimination of Racial Discrimination directed a number of States like Cambodia, Japan and Germany not to practise citizenship based on '*jus sanguine*'. (ACHR 2010)

The issue of citizenship is a politically sensitive one in Nepal and is highly discriminatory based on gender. Statelessness affects men and women in different ways and the situation of women is more complex than that to men. This also applies in the case of a mixed marriage between Nepalese citizens and the Bhutanese refugees. If a Bhutanese refugee male marries a girl holding Nepali citizenship, her husband will not be entitled to a citizenship. However, there are some conditions in which he will be granted citizenship, such as that by naturalisation, which may be achieved though application if the person has resided in Nepal for at least 15 years and also if he is a citizen of a country where there is legal provision or a custom to provide naturalised citizenship to Nepali nationals, among other conditions. However, it is not mandatory and lies at the discretion of the state whether to issue citizenship to that man. The situation is different for men pertaining to the issue of citizenship. For instance, if a Nepali man marries a Bhutanese refugee girl, then she will be eligible to obtain a citizenship. However, the citizenship once issued will not be confiscated even if there is a divorce following a mixed marriage.

Statelessness and the Option of Third-Country Resettlement

In November 1992, Bhutan, Nepal and other relevant actors began negotiations to discuss the return of refugees living in the camps. There were several efforts towards trying to initiate bilateral talks between the Governments of Bhutan and Nepal. Finally, in 2000, under increasing pressure from the international community to find a solution, Bhutan and Nepal agreed to commence a pilot screening of the refugees in one of the camps, to establish their status. In 2001, the 12,173 inhabitants of Khudunabari camp (about one-eighth of the total population in the refugee camps) were screened by the joint Bhutanese-Nepalese verification team. Monitoring by the UNHCR or any independent third party was prohibited. Human

Rights Watch reports, 'The verification exercise was intended to resolve the nationality status of the refugees and open the way for repatriation to Bhutan. The result of the verification process [which was announced in late 2003] was disappointing' as it was limited to only one camp (HRW 2007b). Yet, 75 per cent of those screened were found to be eligible to return to Bhutan. On 22 December, the Bhutanese leader of the verification team reported the conditions of return to the assembled refugees.

- Category 1 (2.5 per cent people) were found to be Bhutanese citizens who had been forcibly expelled. They were allowed to return to Bhutan as citizens, but not to their original houses and lands;
- Category 2 (70.5 per cent) were categorised as 'Bhutanese who voluntarily migrated' which 'supposedly provides for the right to return (though none have yet been allowed back), but without compensation or restoration of lost property' (HRW 2007a). They will have to reapply for citizenship under the challenging terms of the 1985 Citizenship Act after a probationary period of two years spent in a closed camp in Bhutan.
- Category 3 (24.2 per cent) termed as 'non Bhutanese' have their right to appeal the results of the verification unilaterally cancelled. They constitute an 'utterly stateless' people.
- Category 4 (2.8 per cent) includes relatives of those to be charged with criminal acts. '[C]ategorised as "criminals", usually as a result of the nonviolent expression of their political beliefs' (HRW 2007a), these people were to be detained in a designated camp on return—which is effectively a euphemism for arrest. (Photo Voice n.d.)

Human Rights Watch (2007b) further reports,

> Bhutan's attempts to limit the unconditional right of return to people in Category 1 violate its obligations under international law. Regarding the people in Category 2, Bhutan argued that these people had renounced their Bhutanese citizenship voluntarily. However, the circumstances surrounding people's departure from Bhutan in the early 1990s make clear that, far from leaving

voluntarily, Nepali-speakers were either forced to leave, or felt compelled to leave the country to avoid harassment, physical abuse and imprisonment . . .

The verification exercise also brought to the fore questions about the nationality of children. Under the provisions of the 1985 Citizenship Act, only children whose parents are both citizens of Bhutan are citizens by birth. Since only 2.5 per cent of the refugees in one camp have been recognized as citizens, few children will have two Bhutanese citizen parents.

People belonging to Category 2, which is the largest one that would theoretically be allowed to return, would find it nearly impossible to obtain Bhutanese citizenship upon return. They would have to additionally qualify under the 1985 Citizenship Act. Human Rights Watch (ibid.) states, 'Among other strict provisions, the Act requires proficiency in the Dzongkha language, which in almost all cases the children have not heard spoken in their entire lifetime outside primary school language classes in the camps'. The Act additionally requires 20 years of residence in Bhutan (or 15 years for children with one Bhutanese parent)—which no child could fulfil.

After returning, they would have to wait 15–20 years before being able to apply for citizenship. This means that it is likely that most Bhutanese children currently living in the Nepalese refugee camps, if they ever are allowed to repatriate, will most likely remain stateless. As stateless persons, they would face significant restrictions to their basic rights. Under the current Bhutanese ID system, they would not be eligible for higher education or to obtain government jobs, business licenses or for trading without a 'No Objection Certificate'. Such certificates would not be issued to the children of stateless people. They would be reduced to being subsistence farmers, but would not have land and therefore no means to sustain themselves. (ibid.)

Despite being recognised as the best solution, voluntary repatriation 'did not seem to be fruitful and did not materialise for the Bhutanese refugees'. According to Human Rights

Watch, 'Bhutanese Nepali speakers who managed to avoid expulsion and still live in Bhutan shared that they were insecure in their own country. Some were denied citizenship cards following the latest census in 2005 and so they were effectively stateless in their own country' (HRW 2007b). According to a Human Rights Watch submission to the Committee on the Rights of the Child, the situation of ethnic Nepali children in Bhutan is abysmal. It reports:

> Human Rights Watch wishes to bring to the Committee's attention information regarding the following violations of the Convention on the Rights of the Child by the Bhutanese government:
>
> - deprivation of nationality and identity for ethnic Nepali children (arts. 7 and 8);
> - denial of the right to return to one's own country (art. 10);
> - discrimination against ethnic Nepali children in Bhutan (art. 2), including in access to education (art. 28), health care (art. 24), and landownership (arts. 16, 27 [3]);
> - denial of the right of ethnic or linguistic minorities to enjoy their own culture and use their own language (art. 30); and
> - sexual violence and other abuses against girls and women (art. 19). (HRW 2007a)

Even in the face of such hazardous circumstances, and reports of unabated harassment in Bhutan, the dislocated Lhotsampas wish to go back to their home country. They yearn to be back in Bhutan, regardless of the persecution and the antipathy of the Drukpa regime. Many children and young adults who were interviewed consistently reiterated that their 'true desire was to be restored to the status of full citizens with full respect for their political, civil, economic, social, and cultural rights' (HRW 2007b). A young woman in the Goldhap camp in Nepal said:

> We want to go to our country. My motherland where I was born is precious to me. My family feels the same way. I want to go back to a Bhutan that is better than this. Until now, Bhutanese have been

> deprived of their rights. Men and women should be equal and free. If we go back to our motherland, I have the same hope for human rights. (quoted in HRW 2007a)

However, a note of disenchantment has crept in as well in some of the submissions. A refugee student in Kalimpong, for instance, said, 'I feel that even if we go back to Bhutan, since the Bhutanese government is not interested, they will oppress us. Because of that fear, we do not want to go back. We will not be given any citizens' rights in Bhutan' (ibid.). Against the backdrop of such anxiety and the Bhutanese government's consistent efforts to stop the Lhotsampas from returning, the donors who are supporting the Bhutanese refugees have been forced to seek solutions more durable than repatriation. This is not to say that repatriation has lost importance. It still remains the primary desire of the dislocated stateless population. However, other options have had to be thought of, since repatriation has proven extremely difficult.

The most acceptable alternative durable solutions for refugees now are local integration and/or third-country resettlement. The statelessness of some of the refugees—particularly those who were categorised as non-Bhutanese—could be resolved through naturalisation and integration into Nepal. However, the Government of Nepal was not able to shoulder the responsibility due to certain legal and economic conditions. Hence, after 18 rounds of bilateral talks failed between the Government of Bhutan and the Government of Nepal, the US government declared that it would absorb 60,000 refugees in their country. Initially, very few people registered for third-country resettlement. The refugees were divided in their opinion, one group wanting to go for third-country resettlement and the other wanting repatriation to Bhutan with full dignity. Facing a harsh life in the refugee camps, younger individuals are interested in going to a new country. Their choice is shaped by the fear that they might have to live their entire life stranded in the refugee camp. Clearly, the younger generation that has grown up in Nepal and never been to Bhutan does not feel any powerful emotion for its country of origin and is open to the idea of resettlement. However, the older individuals who have fond memories of Bhutan want to go back there. There is also a strong apprehension among them that at their age they might not find it easy to adapt to a new culture and society, far removed from anything they are familiar with. However, often considerations about the future of the children influence the decision of the family as a unit to choose the option of third-country resettlement. If a child or young adult wants to pursue higher education and eventually an independent career, he/she will find it extremely difficult to do so within the boundaries of the crammed existence in camps. Resettlement in another country, however, opens up that window of opportunity for them.

From 2007 onwards, UNHCR and the International Organization for Migration (IOM) started their operation for third-country resettlement. Initially 60,000 Lhotsampas expressed their desire to be resettled. The number, however, gradually increased. By 2010, the 40,000th Bhutanese refugee since the inception of the UNHCR programme departed for resettlement from Nepal (UNHCR 2011: 4). As of August 2012, more than 70,000 refugees have been successfully resettled in various countries such as the United States, the United Kingdom, Canada, New Zealand, Australia, Norway, Denmark and the Netherlands.

In an e-mail interview, one of the resettled Lhotsampas said,

> We are very lucky to build a Bhutanese community in Nebraska. Now we have our own school with over 250 students; every Saturday over 40 adult Bhutanese students come. We teach our culture, tradition, Nepali language and many more. Second, everybody is following their own religion. There are four religious groups, Hindu, Buddhist, Kirat and Christian. Third, Bhutanese have opened a new business store. We call it Druk LCA. Hundreds of Bhutanese Nepalese are shareholders and customers too. We are able to preserve our identity in Nebraska State of America. Most of the states are doing the same. We are very happy to work for our community.[9]

One may express scepticism about such a rosy self-portrayal, for there could indeed be many difficulties in adjustment to a foreign, even alien, setup. However, what is significant in this narrative, and other similar narratives, is the desire to project normalcy and happy fit in the country of resettlement—a desire to move on, so to speak, and not look back. This is particularly clear in the explanation a former resident of Beldangi-II Camp, Damak, Nepal, gives. Abi Siwakoti, now based in Twin Falls, United States, said in a February 2011 interview: 'When you come to America, you are self reliant and you have a better life' (quoted in Davlin 2011b). Another resettled family in Twin Falls has similar emotions to express, reports Melissa Davlin (2011a):

> 'We are very happy', Man Rai declared as his wife Nara Maya Rai served tea in Jerome Title & Escrow coffee mugs. When Nara Maya makes the tea using the electric stovetop, Man said, the house does not fill with smoke—a vast improvement from cooking with wood-fuelled fires in their bamboo hut at Khudunabari refugee camp in Nepal.

Integration of the Refugees Staying Back in Nepal

From Panitanki in India to Kakarbhitta in Nepal is a 10-minute rickshaw ride across the bridge over the Mechi River. From the sweltering heat of the plains, one can descry the distant hills and two patches of human settlement on them. The man ferrying us in the rickshaw identifies them as Mirik and Kurseong and we were already yearning for the cool climes of the hill towns. The dustbowl of Kakarbhitta, however, soon dissolves into miles after miles of sun-bathed fields and sun-dappled wilderness as you take a bus to Damak. One already feels rejuvenated at the prospect of landing up in Damak and then visiting the Bhutanese refugee camps of Beldangi. Reaching Damak, ready help is available from Father Paramasivam Amalraj, Jesuit Refugee Service field director for Nepal. He agrees to take us to a football match at the Beldangi-I camp. Located in the crook of the restless Ratua River's arm and set against the blue hills in the distance, the camp looks peaceful—a nest of tranquillity. With neat, spacious houses tucked away in leafy groves of banana trees, the picturesque setting can indeed camouflage the history of dispossession in Bhutan and of local exclusion in Nepal that the Bhutanese stateless population experiences on a daily basis. Their smiling agreeable faces hide the hard lines of perseverance.

It is unanimously reported that the local community is against assimilation and integration of the Bhutanese population. The local people fear that the refugees, ably educated by the Jesuits, will take away their land and jobs. The fear, it will be noted, is not dissimilar to what the Bhutanese ruling elite felt about these extremely hardworking and talented people.

Nepal is geographically divided into three regions, namely the Himalayas, the Hills and the Terai regions. The people in the Himalayan region are predominantly Sherpas; the people living in the hilly regions are referred to as Pahades; and the people residing in the Terai are referred to as Madhesis. It is in the Jhapa region of the east Nepali Terai, adjoining the foothills of the Himalayas, that the original seven Bhutanese refugee camps were established by the Lutheran World Federation and UNHCR. The refugees were moved from self-settled camps near the town of Maidar to these camps in the Jhapa and Moreng districts in the mid-1990s (Corsellis 2001: 170). Madhesis, who comprise only about 10 per cent of the total population of Nepal (Shrestha 1991), did not take entirely kindly to this influx in their midst, although no overt act of xenophobic violence has taken place. The local Madhesis believe, perhaps not incorrectly, that the Bhutanese refugees are people belonging to the hilly region and if they integrate that will further deteriorate their position and numbers in the Terai.

With the number of refugees expressing their preference for third-country resettlement having swollen to 100,000, it is now estimated that there will be ultimately around 11,000 Bhutanese refugees who will stay back in Nepal. The Government of Nepal does not have a refugee law; however, since Nepal has signed the Universal Declaration on Human Rights, the government will be obliged to take care of the refugees who have opted out of third-country resettlement but, at the same time, cannot be repatriated to Bhutan. So far the Government of Nepal has not made its stand clear on the status of the Bhutanese refugees who would stay on, or on the issue of citizenship. But, the government and UNHCR are working together to develop a programme for those staying back in Nepal. With the agreement of the Government of Nepal to start designing a programme benefiting both host communities and refugees, UNHCR has submitted a revised appeal document of a five-year Community Based Development Programme/Transitional Solutions Initiative (CBDP/TSI) to the government. This offers a 'comprehensive strategy to facilitate the transition from humanitarian assistance to sustainable development in the refugee-hosting and impacted areas, pending voluntary repatriation of the refugees to Bhutan' (UNHCR 2013: 211). The CBDP/TSI focuses on the environment, health, income generation and skill development of both the refugee and the host communities.

It may be said that this is after all a way of integrating ethnic Nepali Bhutanese refugees into Nepalese society. That is, perhaps the UNHCR is expecting that the few who remain in camps would gradually blend into the general population around and the Government of Nepal would not pursue them any further. However, the government has *not* so far promised to provide citizenship to the refugees staying back nor has it openly granted them the status of being refugees. Citizenship, as we have seen, is a very sensitive, even controversial, issue. While Nepal has generously hosted thousands of refugees from Bhutan and other countries for several decades, it is not a signatory to the Refugee Convention of 1951 or its 1967 Protocol. UNHCR continues to advocate for the adoption of a national legal framework to address asylum issues and accession to international refugee and statelessness instruments. Unless such instruments are in place and the government has expressed genuine, unambiguous commitment to succouring and reducing statelessness, the problem of disenfranchisement will linger on. Half-baked and disingenuous 'strategies' like allowing disenfranchised groups to unwittingly blend into the local community cannot wash. A sturdy political will, and a robust legal framework engendered by it, must constitute the basis of combating identitary and locational precariousness.

However, lest we sound uncharitable, it is necessary to end this chapter by timely pointing out that the Government of Nepal has taken a step in the right direction to resolve the embattled issue of establishing and granting citizenship. There were massive changes that followed the 2006 democracy movement, including 'promises of amendments to the citizenship laws' (White 2009: 28).

> Arguably the primary and political objective of the change was to issue citizenship certificates to as many Nepalis as possible in order to facilitate their participation in the Constituent Assembly election. New laws were quickly drafted and adopted, though with limited consultation. They revived the provision for citizenship by birth in Nepal but included a clause making applications for citizenship by birth valid for only two years after the enactment of the Citizenship Act of 2006—until 26 November 2008 (ibid.).

This was followed by a large and 'generally successful' campaign by the government that led to the 'distribution of citizenship certificates to nearly 2.6 million eligible citizens—that is, all Nepali nationals aged 16 and above' (ibid.). The campaign—employing some 4,000 staff—was carried out in all 75 districts of Nepal between January and April 2006. The citizenship certificates were distributed among Nepalis who were not able to acquire citizenship before due to poverty, illiteracy and geographical remoteness. Further, Paul White writes,

> Nepal's citizenship certificate confirms the legal identity of Nepali nationals and proves access (or improved access) to rights, opportunities and services that would not normally be available to non-citizens including: formal sector employment; banking facilities or micro-credit schemes; registration of businesses; civil registration of births, marriages and deaths; registration of property

> transactions; higher education; passports; and government benefits and allowances (for the aged, widowed, disabled, internally displaced and victims of the armed conflict). (ibid.)

While it is true that failure to obtain a citizenship certificate is likely to result in dire consequences that would amount to *de facto* statelessness, it has also to be admitted that the government is playing a proactive role in addressing the issue of citizenship and, by the same token, statelessness. This would certainly have a profound, and possibly positive, impact on the status of the few Lhotsampas who have chosen to stay on in Nepal.

Notes

* This chapter includes content drawn from various Calcutta Research Group publications, which have been used with permission.

1. The Convention was adopted by the United Nations Conference on the Status of Stateless Persons, held at the headquarters of the UN in New York from 13 to 23 September 1954. The Conference was convened pursuant to Resolution 526A (XVII) of 26 April 1954, of the Economic and Social Council of the UN. For the Final Act, recommendation and resolution adopted by the Conference, see UN (1960a: 117).

2. The Convention was adopted and opened for signature by the United Nations Conference on the Elimination or Reduction of Future Statelessness, convened by the Secretary-General of the UN pursuant to the General Assembly Resolution 896 (IX) of 4 December 1954. The Conference met at the European office of the UN at Geneva from 24 March to 18 April 1959, and reconvened at the headquarters of the UN at New York from 15 to 28 August 1961 (see UNHCR 1961).

3. See 'Convention Relating to the Status of Stateless Persons,' Chapter V, 'Refugees and Stateless Persons,' in UN (n.d.).

4. Ibid.

5. It is important to note that *de facto* statelessness is not referred to in the 1961 or 1954 Conventions, but in the Final Act of the 1961 Convention.

6. For a longer critical engagement with the legal definitions, see the introduction to this volume.

7. We are greatly indebted to Samir Kumar Das, Paula Banerjee and Anasua Basu Ray Chaudhury for helping me understand the basic structure of international law on statelessness and its applications.

8. See, for example, the following passage in Piper (1995): '[T]he three main ethnic groups are accepted as together comprising 85–90 per cent of the population, [but] estimates of the percentage of the population represented by each of these groups varies considerably. As an example of the lack of clarity on this issue, Michael Hutt [1994] (who believes it is probable that none of the main ethnic groups is in a majority) points out that estimates of the Ngalong population vary from 10 to 28 per cent, the Sarchops from 30 to 40 per cent and the Nepalis from 25 to 52 per cent' (Piper 1995).

9. E-mail interview, information withheld, August 2012.

SEVEN

Ambiguous Identities

Statelessness of Gorkhas in Northeast India

*ANUP SHEKHAR CHAKRABORTY and SUBHAS RANJAN CHAKRABORTY**

This chapter seeks to look at some current consequences of the treaties signed between the British government and its weak neighbours during the colonial rule in India. The creation of new borders by erecting buffers and barriers failed to prevent cross-migration, especially due to the escalation in the demand of the colonial state for labourers, soldiers, farmers, etc. This produced problems of identity, raised issues of citizenship and created fears of statelessness in the entire northeastern region in post-colonial India. We propose to look at the history of the colonial expansion and the treaties briefly, followed by the processes of migration and evolution of identities and, finally, how these have climaxed over the past four decades in violent movements dealing with the issue of citizenship.

The Historical Context

India was a state and society in transition in the eighteenth century. While the first half of the century witnessed the gradual decline of the Mughal Empire, the second half saw the English

East India Company establish the colonial state by getting the better of the Indian powers who strove to be the inheritors of the Mughal state (Bandyopadhyay 2004: 1–37). It was also the time when changes were taking place in the Himalayan kingdoms with a new process of state formation characterising their development. While Sikkim and Bhutan were old kingdoms, modern Nepal was created by Prithvi Narayan Shah, the ruler of the small kingdom of Gorkha, who conquered the principalities of Kathmandu, Patan and Bhatgaon in 1768 and then proceeded to absorb the small states in both eastern and western Nepal (Pradhan 1991: 89–152). The expansion of Nepal involved the new state in a struggle with the Indian states in the western Himalayas and the Himalayan kingdoms in the east. It was inevitable that the expanding power of the East India Company would come into conflict, resulting in war, with the rising state of Nepal. Nepal invaded Sikkim in 1780 and over the next 30 years they went as far east as the Tista River and annexed the terai (foothills) region. Finally, in 1814–16, Nepal fought a war with the English. Nepal was defeated and made peace by the Treaty of Sugauli in 1815 (O'Malley 1985 [1907]: 19–34).

By the terms of this treaty, Nepal lost territories west of the Kosi River as well as the disputed terai areas in the east. Nepal turned over territories between the Singalila range and Tista River to the Company, which later restored them to Sikkim. The loss of territory and the establishment of a British Residency in Kathmandu were thus accompanied by the drawing of new borders. Nepal lost its common border with the Sikh kingdom of Punjab in the west, and its border to the east, south and west now adjoined territories either under the direct rule of the British or states firmly under their control. Later, as a reward for his help during the siege of Lucknow in 1857, the British restored the lowlands between the rivers Kali and Raptee and the district of Gorakhpur to Nepal (Tyagi 1986: 337).

The British signed the Treaty of Titaliya with the maharaja of Sikkim in 1817 and transferred the hilly country between the rivers Mechhi and Tista, ceded earlier to the company by Nepal in 1815. In 1835 the Raja of Sikkim presented Darjeeling to the East India Company 'out of friendship to the Governor-general'. In 1861 the British government of India signed another treaty, following some raids by Sikkimese subjects and a clash between the British and the Sikkimese, by which Sikkim was virtually reduced to the position of a protectorate. In any case, the triangular contest between Sikkim, Nepal and the East India Company around the early decades of the nineteenth century resulted in the cession of a large chunk of territory to the British. The British set up Darjeeling as a 'hill station' (the curious colonial legacy to India) and sanatorium to begin with (O'Malley 1985 [1907]: 20–23).

The territorial acquisition was rounded off when the British took on Bhutan, the other Himalayan kingdom. The Bhutan War in 1864–65 was followed by the Treaty of Sinchula by which the Government of Bhutan agreed that:

> the whole of the tract known as the eighteen Dooars, bordering on the districts of Rungpoor, Cooch Behar and Assam, together with the Talook of Ambaree-Fallacottah and the Hill territory on the left bank of Tista up to such points as may be laid down by the British Commissioner to be appointed for the purpose is ceded by Bhutan to the British Indian Government forever. (quoted in Samanta 2000: 217–20).

The British government in India later annexed these territories through a Proclamation, and, in return, agreed to make an annual payment of Rs 50,000 to the Government of Bhutan. Afterwards, according to the Treaty of Punakha in 1910, the amount was raised to Rs 100,000, while the Bhutan government allowed the British the right to control their foreign relations. In effect, even Bhutan was reduced to the position of a protectorate (Labh 1986: 388).

Thus, in the course of the nineteenth century, India's frontiers in the eastern and northeastern parts were redrawn and redefined by the colonial state. Of course, the changes were the result of deliberate British policy of establishing hegemony over the entire Himalayan region. The basic motives were both economic and strategic. The Company had been trying to open up China trade since the 1770s with little success. Access to

Tibet was one reason why Sikkim had to be brought under control. Tibet, like Afghanistan in the northwest, was to be involved in Britain's 'Great Game' with Russia.

Gorkha/Nepalis in Darjeeling and the Quest for Identity

The territories ceded by Nepal, Sikkim and Bhutan were clubbed together to constitute the district of Darjeeling in the province of Bengal. While the Company's administration decided to set up a sanatorium in Darjeeling to begin with, they soon came to appreciate the strategic and commercial importance of the area. Darjeeling had the potential to emerge as the 'entrepot of the trans-Himalayan trade, surrounded as it was by Nepal, Sikkim, Bhutan and Tibet' (Chakraborty 2005: 174). The successful introduction of tea plantation was a strong stimulus to growth of the Darjeeling area. In 1872, the number of tea estates was only 74, but by 1901 the number rose to 170 (O'Malley 1985 [1907]: 36). During the Nepal War, the British were greatly impressed by the valour of the Gorkha soldiers. 'The Anglo-Nepal war of 1814–6 is a critical reference point for . . . it was during this war that the British officially "discovered" the Gorkhas' (Caplan 1991: 571–97). So the recruitment of the Gorkhas to the British army acquired priority, especially after the Great Revolt of 1857. Darjeeling, to begin with, was the obvious choice as the centre for recruiting them.

The rapid growth of Darjeeling as a town was understandably accompanied by a flow of immigrants. The beginning of the tea industry created a heavy demand for labour which was met by the immigrant population. Recruitment to the army, the growth of trade and commerce, and sundry employment opportunities 'attracted settlers to Darjeeling, not only from Nepal, but also from the foothills and the plains of Bengal and Bihar. Clearing and reclamation of land for agriculture provided additional scope for employment' (Chakraborty 2005: 175).

Darjeeling in the process became that 'curious' entity which came to be called the 'hill station', other prominent 'hill towns' being Shimla, Mussoorie, Almora or Kodaikanal. Juxtaposed against the white settler society were the original inhabitants—the Lepchas and Bhutias of Sikkim—who lived in inaccessible tracts of forest. Lloyd had called Darjeeling 'the old Gorkha station' and this would indicate the existence of the Nepalis/Gorkhas as well. The British sought to incorporate them within the greater colonial framework and these people found themselves in a new setup merged where migrants poured in from surrounding regions. It was a paradox that the demand for labour acted as a pull factor for the migrants and they found employment as servants, porters, shopkeepers, traders, water carriers, masons, butchers, washer-men, dandy bearers, butlers, ostlers, battiwallas, carpenters, blacksmith, construction workers and labour for the tea gardens. The crowd of native immigrants also included middle- and upper-class Bengalis, the *bhadraloks*.[1]

Like in other parts of the colonial world, the British employed several tactics to attract the gullible Nepalese migrants to occupy largely insecure unmanned frontier spaces of the Raj.[2] The British employed the 'Gallawalahs' to convince the Gorkhas to migrate to the plantation sites in and around the Darjeeling Hills. Prospects of food security, regular wages and incentives attracted greater mobility of people in a highly fluid region where borders and boundaries made little sense. All these can be best summed up by the circulation of proverbs and sayings among the Nepali-speaking population such as *Cha ko bot ma paisa phaleko cha* ('Money blossoms in the tea bush'). Thus 'food security' in the British territory was an important factor that acted as an added attraction for migration (Sinha and Subba 2003: 14–15). Alongside the 'food security' angle was the British construction of the 'myth of the invincible Gorkha warrior': the martial race that encouraged the inflow of the Gorkha (cf. Hutt 1988: 21–32; also cf. Caplan 1995; Forbes 1964; Marks 1971).

Post-independence, Darjeeling was merged with the state of West Bengal, following which a separate district of Darjeeling was established consisting of the hill towns of Darjeeling, Kurseong, Kalimpong and some parts of the Terai region. The region of North Bengal[3] has remained ethnically sensitive with the hill population comprising the ethnic Nepalis who mostly migrated during British times, and the plains occupied by ethnic communities such as Bengali, Santhali, Kamtapuri, etc.[4]

The large-scale immigration into the area, particularly from the eastern part of Nepal, was also the result of political and social evolution of Nepal in the post-unification era. As Kumar Pradhan (1991) has so elegantly described, the political and social consequences of the unification of the kingdom of Nepal may be seen as a push factor. Among these may be mentioned the emergence of a new political elite in Nepal, evolution of new land-tenurial systems in supersession of the old communal land tenures and the plight of the tribal groups, particularly in eastern Nepal. The Lepchas and Bhutias were soon outnumbered by the Nepalese through large-scale immigration from eastern Nepal in particular. Nepalese settlers 'slowly evolved into a community which developed a sense of identity, both unique and separate'. It is interesting to note that there was a 'gradual shedding of tribal identities in favour of an overarching and inclusive Nepali identity'. A major cementing factor which helped the emergence of this identity was the 'Nepali language which increasingly superseded tribal languages/dialects to emerge as the lingua franca for the entire Himalayan region' (Chakraborty 2005: 175).[5]

A significant point to note at this juncture would be the merger of Sikkim, which became the 22nd Indian state, with the Indian Union. This altered the old political geography of the region and was an indirect stimulus to the demand for a separate state in Darjeeling. A new political formation, the Gorkha National Liberation Front (GNLF), now emerged under Subhash Ghishing who spearheaded a violent movement for statehood. The hills of Darjeeling were literally aflame for three years, at the end of which an agreement was signed by the state government, the Government of India and GNLF to create the autonomous Darjeeling Gorkha Hill Council in 1988.

Subhash Ghishing, the leader of the GNLF, raised certain questions regarding citizenship. They referred to the whole of Darjeeling as 'ceded territories' and Kalimpong, Western

Dooars and Assam Dooars as 'leasehold territory' which had not been formally integrated into India. The GNLF President filed a suit in the Supreme Court of India

> seeking appropriate directions to the central government for passing the relevant parliamentary legislation under Article 4 and/or Article 368 of the Indian Constitution for the formal absorption/incorporation of the leasehold territories of Kalimpong, Assam Dooars and Bengal Dooars; as also the ceded territories of Darjeeling, obtained pursuant to the treaties signed between India and Bhutan on the one hand and India and Nepal on the other. As per the treaties which are conditional in nature the govt. of India is paying to the Govt. of Bhutan lease-hold amount/compensation annually of Rs 5 lakhs till this date, a fact that has been accepted and admitted by the Union Home Minister vide his letter dated 11.3.1992. (Pradhan et al. 1996: 7–19)

This was followed in December 1994 by a letter to all the MPs, leaders of political parties and 'leading citizens' exhorting them to raise the issue of non-incorporation of the impugned lands. In May 1995 followed an open letter to the Government of India and the Government of Nepal, urging them to go through the articles of the Indo-Nepal Friendship Treaty of 1950, particularly Article VIII. The Article, it was imputed, cancelled all previous treaties, agreements and engagements entered on behalf of India between the British government and the Government of Nepal. It was contended in the letter that 'neither was the disputed land of Darjeeling included in the British India till the date of 15th August,1947 nor was it formally included in the present independent country of India till date, by the enactment of parliamentary legislation'. In the circumstances, it was further argued, the legal status of these territories in question remains ambiguous and uncertain, leaving the majority of the Gorkhas without a state/citizenship (ibid.: 2). The home minister of the Government of India wrote to assure him that the treaties did not create an anomalous situation. Yet, the issue was a political one, raised by GNLF when it suited them politically.

The constitutional position is not that of an impasse. The problem that the treaties contracted by the colonial state could create for the successor state/s is, however, underscored by the issues raised.

Social History of the Gorkha in Northeast India Over the Years

Locational, Positional and Situational Ambiguities

We may now turn our attention to the northeastern states of India and see how migration across the new frontiers created by the colonial state resulted in demographic changes. The migrant communities much later faced situations that questioned their citizenship. One commentator has called it 'fei-ization of the Nepalis of north-east India' (Nag 2009: 184). This is a term from Confucian China whereby a rebel is declared as *fei* or a non-person. Sajal Nag argues that although the Nepalis are an integral part of the history of the region, they are treated as 'migrants' and not as 'people', thereby denying them any history. He points out that the growing literature on the history and society of the region hardly gives space to these 'migrants'. This historiography also excludes the Bengalis, Marwaris, Sikhs and ex-tea garden workers as they are considered non-indigenous to the northeast (ibid). The Nepali presence in the Northeast has a long history and their role in the development of the region has been crucial.

The politics of Northeast India has been deeply influenced by the influx of people from other regions.[6] Ever since the colonial encounter, there has been a steady flow of the Nepali population into Assam (Devi 2007: 3005–07; Nath 2003). However, it would be misleading to read the presence of Nepalis in Assam and the neighbouring regions as a consequence of immigration alone.[7]

Though the Treaty of Sugauli (1815) is often cited as the watershed year that opened the floodgates of migration from Nepal into the Northeast, it was the Treaty of Yandaboo (Aleaz

2005; Bose 1979: 82–86; Gait 1906) that actually spurred the migration of the Nepalis to Northeast India. The open-door policy of the British in the matter of recruitment of the Gorkha soldiers coupled with the subsequent formal agreement reached with the king of Nepal on the issue ensured the availability of the hardy, good-natured and faithful soldiers whom the British considered somewhat of an asset to contain revolts and extend and preserve their domain in India, particularly in the Northeast. L.W. Shakespear (1977) aptly writes:

> [W]hether it was Sylhet or the Shillong plateau, Naga hills or Lushai hills, Chhitagong Hill tracts or Sadiya frontier tracts, the Bhutan wars or the Manipur rebellion, the *Gorkha*s constituted half the Assam rifles and were always there in operation.

The first direct contact, according to Sinha (2003: 42), between the Nepalis and Assam appears to have occurred in 1817 when the Gorkhas formed part of the Cuttack legion (later known as Assam Light Infantry) which took part in the Sylhet operation. It is recorded that a non-commissioned officer of the Eighth Gorkha Platoon in Sylhet settled down in Shillong as early as 1824. The Gorkhas played an important role as part of the Assam Rifles in the process of British expansion through the Shillong plateau, Naga or Lusai Hills, CHT or Manipur. Their contribution was recognised by the fact that the crossed *khukri* became the emblem of the Assam Rifles. Besides the Assam Rifles, the Gorkha Training Centre and various battalions of the armed forces were stationed in and around the district towns and strategic locations in the hills. The Assam Rifles alone rehabilitated its soldiers in at least 40 sites in Assam, Manipur, Mizoram, Meghalaya and Nagaland. The Nepali ex-soldiers were encouraged to settle down in the foothills, forest fringes and other strategic points on the frontiers. In this way certain compact pockets of Nepali settlement emerged in different states of the region. With hard work they were able to turn their newly acquired settlements into thriving agricultural communities. As far as the plains from the Bengal Dooars to the Barak valley are concerned, in terms of Nepali settlement, a distinct trend may be noted. The less skilful and marginal farmers and pastoralists turned to pastoral grazing on the hilly and forested tracts of the region. The Nepali herdsmen and marginal farmers trickled down to Assam from the first quarter of the twentieth century (Sinha 2003: 45). As early as 1930, the chief secretary of the government of Assam noted that 'the immigration of the Nepalis into Assam may be described as an administrative nuisance rather than a political menace' (ibid.: 46). A policy was initiated soon in Nagaland to remove Nepali settlers on economic and not political grounds. Uncontrolled Nepali immigration was seen as a threat to the economic sustenance of the indigenous population. The intelligence department reported that 'there has been great infiltration of Nepalis eastwards from Nepal'.[8]

D.B. Chhetry states:

> The British adopted a policy of encouraging the settlement of Nepali/Gorkha soldiers particularly in the foothills after their retirement as this served two purposes—one, the ex-soldiers acted as a buffer between the British administration and the restive tribal chiefs and two, families of the ex-army men provided a more dependable source and channel for fresh recruitment. (2009: 353)

Sinha (1982) talks about how almost 3,000 Gorkha ex-soldiers were rehabilitated on at least 40 sites, some of which like Aizawl (Mizoram), Mantripokhari (Manipur), Mokokchung (Nagaland) and Sadiya (Assam) are over a hundred years old. It would not be right to assume, however, that 'the Nepali settlement in Northeast India in general and Assam in particular comprised the ex-soldiers or their families alone' (Chhetry 2009: 353). Encouraged by the soldiers' stories of 'abundant land, dense jungles and hills in the region', more people made their way here 'to try their luck and took to cattle-breeding, dairy farming, sugarcane cultivation'. Many were employed in 'odd jobs in government offices' such as that of '*chowkidar*s, peons, gardeners and the like' (ibid.).

Chhetry further states:

> Amongst this group of migrants, mention must be made of the graziers or the *khutiwalla*s whose presence was substantial in the

> Brahmaputra valley, the districts of Karbi Anglong and North Cachar Hills in Assam as well as in Khasi and Jaintia hills, Garo Hills, Nagaland and Manipur. It is pertinent to note that during 1919-20, of the 1.25 lakh cattle population in the Brahmaputra valley for which grazing tax was realized, the overwhelming bulk belonged to 6319 professional graziers of whom, excepting a few hundred, all were Nepali migrants. (Chhetry 2009: 353–54; cf. Devi 2007)

It was the colonial encounter that proved to be a catalyst for an organised migration from Nepal hills to the Indian frontiers (Sinha and Subba 2003). What is interesting to note is the fact that the very term 'Gorkha' is basically the name of a district in present-day Nepal, and later the term acquired a special meaning in British martial discourses. The term 'Gorkha' became a community appellation and, in the process, transformed its cultural-historical underpinnings into an ethno-political one (cf. Bidhan Golay 2009: 73–94; Pravesh Jung Golay 2009: 49–62). The Gorkhas, eulogised as a 'warrior community', received preferential treatment in terms of recruitment in the Army; and this form of outmigration continued from the colonial through the post-colonial times (English 1983; Muktan 2002; Nath 2003; Palit 1984; Pradhan 1991; Sen 1977; Shakespear 1977; Sinha and Subba 2003; Tyagi 1974).

Another striking point to be noted is that though geo-politically closer to the 'Northeast', the region of north Bengal which serves as the gateway to it through the 'Siliguri-Coochbehar corridor'[9] has not been clubbed into the Northeast, but the desire to be included within the region remains strong among some people (Chetri and Sundas 2009: 14–15). For instance, in 2007, when the West Delhi Police published a book titled 'Security Tips for Northeast Students/Visitors in Delhi' (Dholabhai 2007; *Times of India* 2007) which claimed 'to help the people from the region to overcome the handicap of their "foreign" features', it generated much anger among the students and the people of Darjeeling. It is in the light of this observation that including Darjeeling within the framework of the 'Northeast' for an analysis of the statelessness of the Nepali-speaking population in Northeast India becomes urgent and convenient.[10]

'The history of the permanent settlement of the Gorkhas in Mizoram began in the year 1891 though they had been active in the region throughout the initial encounters between the British and the "Kuki-Chin-Lushai tribes"' (Chakraborty 2008; also see Sinha and Subba 2003). The expansion of territories by the Kuki, Chin-Lushais towards south and southwest from Hakka and towards eastern Mizoram from the Tiddim Falam region of Burma (Myanmar) in the beginning of the nineteenth century and the gradual extension of the British frontiers towards the Northeast led to the confrontation between the 'wild tribes' and the 'Colonial world'. The British developed the ingenious method of protecting the frontier by establishing 'fortified posts[11] in the hills'. Such a move would call for import of manpower, and the experience in Darjeeling and elsewhere made the Gorkhas the chosen workforce. T.H. Lewin summed up the reasons for the migrations of the Gorkhas into the Zo Hills as follows:

> I had formed a high opinion of the little Ghurkhas who, under Colonel Macpherson, had done the fighting of the expedition, and I obtained permission to send to Nepal and get immigrants from there to colonize my frontier wastes . . . The country where these villages were located had previously been uninhabited, through fear of marauding Lushais, and my idea had been to establish there good stockaded villages of courageous, stiff-necked people like the Ghurkhas, who should serve as the buffer between the Mong Raja's territory and the independent Lushais to the east. (1912: 445)

The British employed similar tactics even in the Zo Hills. Thus Gallawalahs were employed to convince and assure the Gorkha of 'security and prosperity'. The Zo Hills were projected as a land of ample opportunities and attractive incentives where the Gorkha would get the best. Such projections were further solidified by sayings such as *Doodh le mooh dhunu* ('mouthwash with milk'), *Patha ko sikar, rah pakwah* ('lots of mutton, and gizzards') and ample opportunity for *Ladai khelnu* ('to play battle, for in the Gorkha tradition a battle is to be played not fought'), etc.

After the construction of stockades at Lunglei and Aizawl, peace was restored in most parts of the hills especially near and around the stockades by the spring of 1891. The expansion work at Aizawl and Lunglei as well as the setting up of an administrative machinery required the increase in the inflow of immigrants, that is, 'the trusted Gorkhas' as mentioned by O.A. Chambers in his *Hand Book of the Lushai Country* (2005 [1899]). The colonial system of administration required manpower as *dak*-runners, *chowkidar*s, peons, cart-drivers, traders, masons, etc. and such work being unknown to the local people, it was felt advisable to introduce migrant labour. The migrant Gorkhas resembled the natives to an extent and the factor of external beauty/attractive physical features and fair skin made them more acceptable to the 'native wild tribes' or *garkhola*s ('arse flaunters') as the Gorkhas called them. Though the Gorkhas were not allowed to settle outside the allotted areas, many Lushai chiefs were eager to have them in their villages.[12] They even entreated the Superintendent of Lushai Hills to permit the Gorkhas to reside in their villages. Accordingly, a few Gorkhas were given permission to settle in some of the Lushai villages.[13] The settlement of the Gorkhas and the *Santhal*s (*Midum* [Blacks]) led to the beginning of wet rice cultivation in the plains of Champhai.

The terms of the Chin Hills Regulations[14] and the Inner Line Permit (ILP) (Bose 1979; also cf. Acharyya 1984; Sangkima 1995, 2004) were twisted and flouted as reflected in the rapid increase in the flow of outsiders in and around Aizawl during the early part of the twentieth century. A large number of these outsiders were the descendants of the discharged military policemen and colonial staff. As had happened with the indentured labour of the sugar plantations in the Caribbean islands, many ex-servicemen were lured by the colonial administration to remain in Mizoram and were allotted plots and privileges at par with the Lushai Chiefs with hereditary right of succession (McCall 1980 [1939]). For instance, Dhojbir Rai was awarded the whole area of Survey Tillah (now Dinthar-II); Sriman Rai, the whole area of Sriman Tillah (now Zotlang); Singbir Rai with holdings in Chawnchhim (Champhai); Lalsing Lama was made the chief of Hrangmual (area around present-day Synod Book Room, Aizawl) and Joy Bahadur given the Tuisenhnar Leilet (paddy field) settlement (Chawngbuanga 1990, cited in Sinha and Subba 2003: 298). The Gorkhas were in the majority in Aizawl town during the colonial days and naturally the names of places were in Nepali/Gorkhali. It was only later in the course of the evolution of identity consciousness among the Zo/Mizo tribes that these names were changed in keeping with Zo/Mizo nomenclature (Singh et al. 1995: 54).

The institution of *Gorkha Maujadar* was introduced in course of time to exercise some administrative coordination over the Gorkha population with the aim of easy collection of foreigner's tax; and later abolished in 1953 with the end of Chieftainship. The initiation of village council politics was followed by the emergence of Gorkha Panchayat, with an autonomous sphere of action and minimal interference of the magistrate of the district (McCall 1980 [1939]). When the village council was introduced, the Gorkhas were represented fairly through election or nomination and some influential Gorkhas even managed to hold the posts of the president of the village council. For instance, Bir Bahadur Limbu of Sriman Tillah (Aizawl) was the first Gorkha Village Council president in 1958. The Gorkhas were able to get a political platform alongside the Zo/Mizo during the initial phases when the Zo/Mizo did not realise the potential threat of the migrant population. With the gradual advancement in the political education of the natives, the true nature of a contested terrain encapsulating every aspect of life began to unfold and the Gorkhas gradually began to be trimmed to size in the political arena.

Culturally, the Gorkhas have, to an extent, successfully assimilated the local customs and practices (Singh et al. 1995; Bareh 2001) while retaining their distinct cultural identity.[15] The Gorkhas in Mizoram have succeeded at crossing the threshold of the stigmas of the boundaries faced by the 'Vai' (Bengali Muslim community) or the 'Burma mi' ('Poi', Burmese) community.[16] The recognition of the Gorkha as 'Denizens' in Mizoram is clearly reflected in the common conversational phrases used for denoting their historicity, *Sap hun lai* ('from the colonial times'), and their assimilation into the Zo/Mizo world, *Mizo ang chiah* ('just like the Mizo'), *Zo rilru an pu* ('they think and feel like the Mizo'), etc.

The settler communities began to be perceived as a threat by the host societies from the 1970s in particular. The status of the Nepalis in the region was questioned. Were they Indian nationals or foreigners residing in India? The 1950 Treaty did not help because it allowed immigration into India as well as emigration to Nepal. As the Nepalis migrated and settled mainly in the hilly areas in the northeast, labourers, farmers and petty traders from the plains of the Indian states of Uttar Pradesh and Bihar cleared the terai of Nepal and turned the region into an economically viable one. These people (Madhesis or plainsmen, as they are called) face identical problems in Nepal. Are they to be considered Nepalis or Indians residing in Nepal? It has become a political issue and these people have now formed their own political party, the Sadbhavna Party. The 1950 Treaty has been seen by many in Nepal as an unequal treaty, a successor virtually to the earlier treaties imposed by the colonial power. The problem faced by the Nepalis has also been faced by many Bengalis, particularly Bengali Muslims, especially after the creation of Bangladesh. Such people are called illegal immigrants, but to draw a line between legal citizens and illegal migrants is often impossible. The real situation, as T.B. Subba puts it, is that there are many 'Nepalese'—in the sense of being of and from Nepal—who must be differentiated from the Indian Nepalis, born in India and probably living here for a few generations. The 1950 Treaty allows the former to come, live and work in India, but this jeopardises the position of the Indian Nepalis. To obviate this difficulty R.K. Sharma had suggested that the Indian Nepalis may be called the Gorkhas, while Subba has coined the term 'Nepamul' to connote such people (Subba 2003: 62).

The whole problem snowballed two decades after the transfer of power when Nepalis were made targets as illegal immigrants in the northeast. In 1967, 800 Nepalis were driven out of Mizoram and in 1978, 200 houses of Nepalis burnt in Nagaland; about

2,000 Nepalis fled Manipur in 1980; large numbers of Nepalis were deported from Assam in 1979 and from Meghalaya in 1987 (Sinha 1982: 91–92; Subba 1992: 115–16).

'The political aspirations of the Nepalis in northeast India are therefore woven around the struggle for economic and political rights equal to that of other Indian citizens' (Subba 2003: 65). The terms of the 1950 Treaty are categorical, yet ambiguities about the recognition of the Nepalese as citizens persist, transforming it into a political-legal problem. The consequence is making many of these Nepalis, particularly those who had lived in parts of the northeast for generations, stateless.

Bhutan and the Lhotsampas: The New Refugees in India and Nepal

Nestling between Tibet and India, Bhutan—the small Himalayan kingdom—is commonly portrayed as *Shangri-la* or abode of peace. Migration of Nepalis to Bhutan must have been old given the contiguous borders and unstable political situation in the late eighteenth and throughout the nineteenth and twentieth centuries. Nepali sources claim that the Dharmaraja settled some Nepalis in the Dalimkote region of Bhutan in the seventeenth century. However, effective Nepali colonisation started after the Bhutan wars of 1864–65. The *Dzongpas* (district administrators) invited sturdy and industrious Nepalis to clear the difficult terrain. Charles Bell, the settlement officer in Kalimpong, noted that in Siphchu and Sangbe there were 750 and 50 Nepali houses, respectively. The Nepali thikadars—Nandalal Chhettri, Garjaman Gurung and Lalsing Gurung—could have under their command 800, 1,000 and 130 Nepali households, respectively. Bell's estimate is that the Nepali population in Bhutan was about 15,000 in the early twentieth century.[17] Three decades later, Capt. T. Morris estimated the population to be 60,000 or 20 per cent of the total population of Bhutan (Morris 1932, quoted in Sinha 1982: 42).

In the early 1930s, Weir, the political officer in Sikkim wrote to the Government of India that Sikkim and Bhutan had no written nationality laws. In Sikkim, he wrote, immigrants (chiefly from Nepal) had been settled for some generations and comprised three quarters of the population. Domicile appears to have been the only criterion there. In Bhutan, Weir added, settlers (chiefly ethnic Nepalis but possibly born in British India or Sikkim) constituted about one-fifth of the population. There domicile, acquisition of immovable property and payment of state dues were the criteria for being considered a Bhutanese national and a person could have only one nationality under Bhutanese law.

Until 1985, despite the ethnic diversity, there was no record of any animosity in Bhutan, and the country was indeed peaceful. A crisis situation emerged following the passing of a new Citizenship Act, which was discriminatory. The subsequent census (1988) in the southern districts, where most of the Nepalis live, revoked the right to nationality of a large number of people rendering them (known as Lhotsampas) virtually without home and livelihood. The next step was to force the non-Bhutanese to adopt Bhutanese dress and culture to create homogeneity. Even Nepali language was dropped from the school curriculum.

The Lhotsampas petitioned the king through their representative T.N. Rizal to seek review of these policies and the manner in which these had been carried out. But these did not produce the expected response. On the other hand, a number of human rights activists were arrested in 1990 when they organised a peaceful public demonstration. The Lhotsampas also demanded political rights. The consequence was oppression of these people and their forced eviction. As a result more than approximately 100,000 Bhutanese refugees live in India and Nepal. Over 90,000 of these have been living in UNHCR-supervised camps in Jhapa and Morang districts of eastern Nepal since 1991. Another 30,000 live outside camps in India and Nepal (Acharya 2004: 11–17).

The citizenship issue is the key issue. The Bhutanese government does not recognise the Lhotsampas as Bhutanese citizens. These are men of Nepali origin and, in effect, are deprived not only of a state but also of their land as they are basically farmers.

'The closer one comes to the present, the more contentious all history inevitably becomes, and when the recent past is characterized by conflict, its history splinters into contradictory narratives' (Hutt 2003). The policies the Bhutanese government adopted on citizenship, education and culture in response to the perceived threat meant that Bhutan's history and destiny were conflated with those of the dominant element of its population. Other elements were marginalised, subjugated and excluded for what the dominant group considered to be legitimate historical and geographical reasons.

Citizenship and Statelessness of the Gorkhas in Northeast India

Accentuating Degrees and Fault Lines in the Contentious Politics of 'Manufacturing of Spaces'[18]

The notion of citizenship in the 'Northeast' in general is strongly accompanied by the notion of the 'other' vis-à-vis the 'self'[19] that has evolved in the region. This, it bears mention, has changed through time. Politically, 'identities' are the product of how power is organised; and how it defines the parameters of the political community, telling us who is *included* and who is *excluded*; it also differentiates the bounded political community internally. Through this process of identification we exclude the other from our shared space of imagination or existence, thereby, consciously or unconsciously, outlining the politics of *inclusions* and *exclusions*. And this becomes intrinsically interwoven within the sub-text of 'insider-outsider' politics. As a result, the uncertainties surrounding their status as citizens and the general non-acceptance have moulded Gorkha consciousness in northeast India, compelling them to take steps to locate a space where their 'identity, notion, tone and content of citizenship' converge perfectly with a territory.[20] The desire to have a territory or a place named after their people thus remains a highly emotional enterprise.

Following the ethnic clashes between the Nepali/Gorkha and the predominant local populations in the states of Assam and Meghalaya through the mid-1970s, the Nepali/Gorkha suddenly found that they were being labelled as 'foreigners'. Although initially the Assam movement spearheaded by the AASU (All Assam Students' Union) during 1979–85 on the issue of 'foreigners', was directed against the Bangladeshis, eventually the Nepali/Gorkha too could not escape the test of citizenship[21] resulting in their large-scale displacement and experience of statelessness.[22] Consequently, during the intensive revision of electoral rolls prior to the 1985 general elections in Assam, thousands of Nepali names were unceremoniously struck off (Chhetry 2012). All this led to a decline in the 'degree of citizenship' and an increase in the 'degree of statelessness' of the Nepali/Gorkha community in the region.

The harrowing experience of the Nepali/Gorkha in Assam was replicated even in the Bodo agitation. Like the AASU, the All Bodo Students' Union (ABSU), in order to prove the majority of the Bodos, started an ethnic cleansing following which the Nepali/Gorkhas in the interior of the districts of Kokrajhar, Bongaigaon, Nalbari and Darrang were victimised (Chhetry 2012).

It would perhaps not be wrong to say that the Assam movement was the precursor of similar agitations in other states of northeast India in which Nepali/Gorkhas were the principal targets. In 1980, Nepali/Gorkhas, who were accorded domiciled status in as far back as 1947 in Manipur, became targets of attack compelling them to flee for safety. Similarly, during 1987, violence erupted in Meghalaya, and Nepali/Gorkhas living in Shillong, Jowai and other parts of the state became the targets. The Khasi Students' Union (KSU) and the Government of Meghalaya together deported about 7,000–10,000 Nepalis in February–March 1987 (Chhetry 2012). In the 1990s, all Nepali/Gorkha settlers were categorised as 'foreigners' in Meghalaya. Similar moves were systematically directed in Nagaland, Mizoram and elsewhere in the Northeast to brand the entire Nepali-speaking people in the region as foreigners residing there illegally. In Nagaland, for instance, in the 1980s, extortion was used as a means of terrorising the Nepali/Gorkhas who had settled in the state before 1940 and were treated as indigenous non-Naga local residents. Consequently, they were forced to resort to distress sale of their property. In the Merapani region located on the border of Wokha of Nagaland and Sibsagar district of Assam, about 200 Nepalis lost their lives in clashes.

In order to strengthen their claim to citizenship, the Gorkhas participated in the constitutionally recognised as well as the shadow or parallel Mizo National Front (MNF) politics of Mizoram. For instance, in the parallel MNF politics, a large number of Gorkhas from the Assam Rifles and the Assam Regiment posted in Mizoram supported the movement (Verghese and Thanzawna 1997: 54). And in the constitutionally recognised Zo/Mizo politics, the Gorkhas had representation in the village council elections. This trend continued till the ushering in of a higher, more sophisticated politics of the union territory model. The nomination of Kapur Chand Thakuri to the Mizoram Legislative Assembly in 1972 was the last significant entry of the migrant Gorkhas into the revered arena of 'Zo/Mizo politics', which is reserved exclusively for *political insiders*. Thereafter, the Gorkha community took to the politics of appeasements and camouflaging.

During the 1970s and the 1980s, many Gorkhas left Mizoram to re-settle in Dehradun and other hilly areas of Uttar Pradesh as well as Darjeeling. During this period, the Mizoram Gorkha Sangh requested the Mizoram (union territory) government for the first time to recognise the Gorkhas of Mizoram as one of the tribes of Mizoram, but this was not accepted. Later, in the year 1984, a renewed demand for inclusion of the Gorkha community in the Mizoram Official Handbook so as to prove their citizenship in India and residence in Mizoram was made to Lal Thanhawla's Congress government. The Congress leaders showed some muted support for the issues and concerns of the Gorkhas in Mizoram.

With the attainment of statehood and the change in power-positions in the form of the rise of the MNF, the Gorkhas openly declared their total support for the MNF and publicly made statements that criticised the Congress. For instance, a number of Gorkhas working for the Congress switched sides thinking the tide would be in their favour. With the re-entry of the Congress (I) in the second state assembly elections, the Gorkhas realised their political mistake and once more switched sides. This time the Gorkha leaders in the Congress (I), like N.S. Chettri, J.P. Thapa, M.K. Limbu, B.K. Thapa and others, demanded the 'Conferment of Equal Facilities to the Permanent Gorkha Settlers of Mizoram'. The Congress did not want to lose its traditional minority vote-bank at this point and decided to accord certain facilities and decided that there should be a fresh census with the co-operation of the Gorkha community residing in Mizoram as on 26 January 1950 and the direct descendants of those people. The Cabinet meeting of 20 December 1991 resolved to extend certain facilities to the Gorkhas of Mizoram who had been residing in Mizoram prior to 26 January 1950. Lal Thanhawla announced the decision before a large crowd in the Gorkha School premises in Khatla, Aizawl. The facilities extended included granting of post-matric scholarships; extension of facilities in the matters of education; land settlement certificates including transfer of ownership, employment and trade and commerce at par with the Mizos and the issue of Permanent Residential Certificates (cf. Government of Mizoram 1992). The Students' Joint Action Committee vehemently criticised the government and forced it to review its decision to grant facilities to the Gorkhas 'at par' with the Mizos.

The *second tension* between the Vai and the Mizo/Zo in the 1990s did not spare even the Gorkhas. The immunity of the Gorkhas was lost through the action and vocality of the students' union. Several shops and small businesses owned by the Gorkha community were burnt including the shop of Kapur Chand Thakuri, the political face of the Gorkhas in Mizoram. The Mizo Zirlai Pawl (MZP)[23] forced many Gorkhas to roll down shutters and move out of business. To counter the trimming mission of the agencies, the Gorkhas conveyed full support to the actions of the MZP to move out the Vai from Mizoram. The Gorkha youth and students' union came out with pamphlets supporting the cause of the MZP, even though it meant that the

Gorkhas were also affected. They declared all losses were for greater glory of both the communities which have been living in peace since times immemorial. The tensions were followed by the strategy of mass conversions. Many Gorkhas converted as they thought conversion to be an effective mechanism to gain their lost grounds in Mizoram. *Ka piangthar a, Khristiana hi a changkang zok tlat, kan him zok* ('I converted, to be a Christian is more safe and will lead to faster progress and security'), says Sheela Chhetri a widow and a mother of three.[24] *Mizo nupui ka thlang zok, mizoramah awmnan a him zok, hna ka hmu pha anga* ('I prefer a Mizo wife [over a Gorkha] as I have to live in Mizoram, it will fetch me security and a job'), says Zorama (Gorkha name 'Kamal') a third-generation Gorkha resident from Zarkawt (Aizawl).[25] The MNF Party promised the Gorkhas that it would be granted an Other Backward Class (OBC) status under the constitutional provisions of the Mandal Commission Report (Engineer 1991; Maheshwari 1995) if the Gorkhas acted as their vote-bank in the 1998 elections (Zoramthanga 1998). The Government of Mizoram accepted 4,453 as the number of the permanent Gorkha settled in Mizoram prior to 26 January 1950 and approved the issue of Land Settlement Certificates (LSCs)/Passes in respect of land traditionally held by them (Government of Mizoram 2001).[26]

From the 1980s onwards, the Gorkha have faced serious challenges (cf. Pradhan 2009: 225–36) to their existence in Mizoram owing to the unchecked flow of migrants from Nepal. The government, after the Peace Accord, clubbed both the categories as 'foreigners' being unable to distinguish between 'old settlers' and 'new migrants'. Such a move triggered the need to consolidate the permanent Gorkhas and make their positions clear in terms of 'genuine citizenship'[27] traced back to the colonial times. The Mizoram Gorkha Youth Association (MGYA)[28] and other Gorkha organisations have been approaching the different governments from 2002 onwards 'to push forward their demand of being granted and recognized as OBCs in Mizoram' (for details, cf. MGYA 2002, 2004a, 2004b, 2004c, 2005, 2006a, 2006b). To substantiate their arguments for OBC status, they appended documentations from other states and regions where the Gorkha have been recognised as OBCs, such as Meghalaya, Nagaland, Assam, Haryana, Punjab, and the Mandal Commission Report which listed the Gorkhas as one of the Backward Classes in Mizoram.[29] The following news report from 2007 reflects the ongoing tussle between the Zo/Mizo and the Denizens:

> The Gorkhas of Mizoram in 2007 criticized the state government of refusing to recognize the Permanent *Gorkha* residents as an OBC category though the Mandal Commission had identified and recommended them as the OBCs in Mizoram as early as 1992. Despite the repeated pleas of the various *Gorkha* organizations, spearheaded by the Mizoram *Gorkha* Students' Union (MGSU), the state government has failed to do so. 'This came a few days after the Rajya Sabha had been informed that the states of Mizoram, Arunachal Pradesh, Nagaland and Lakshadweep have no OBCs.' Mr. Subba, (MGSU Adviser) added that as far as language, religion, economy, education, politics and social life are concerned, *Gorkha*s in Mizoram are backward classes. He emphasized that provisions of the historic Peace Accord, signed between the Mizo National Front and the Indian Government in 1986, stated that the social and economic advancement of minorities in Mizoram shall be preserved, protected and ensured. Mr. Subba further highlighted that during the period of Mizo district council under the Assam state, the '*Gorkha*s' enjoyed equal rights with their Mizo counterparts without any discrimination. As a result, many *Gorkha*s could contest and indeed got elected in the village council election. The *Gorkha*s came to settle in Mizoram along with the British colonialists in the 1890s, Mr. Subba said and added that, as far as the general people are concerned, the *Gorkha*s were not treated as outsiders. (*WebIndia123* 2007)

OneIndia (2008) reported that the Central Young Mizo Association (CYMA) went up in arms against the Gorkha community being given OBC status in Mizoram. Reacting to Minister H. Vanlalauva's remarks that 'the Mizoram government would do anything to ensure the inclusion of Gorkhas in the OBC category, CYMA leaders met Chief Minister Zoramthanga and strongly opposed any move to include the Gorkhas in the OBC category'. The CYMA leaders felt that it would not be wise to offer 'OBC status to the Gorkhas as it could result in demographic invasion' given the nature of free flow of people between India and Nepal (*OneIndia* 2008). The recognition of the Gorkhas as OBC in a few states has thus created a major positional rift.

The politics of social inclusion and exclusion in the Northeast largely determines the degrees of citizenship and statelessness of the Gorkha population in the region, further substantiating the argument that the migrant experience does not end with the first point of settlement. It is handed down through generations, consciously or unconsciously making its contribution to the ways in which those in the diaspora negotiate their existence in the host societies in which they and their cultures are in minority. Being part of a diaspora means living in a cross-cultural context. Those aware of the complexities of this recognise the need to redefine their identity and the necessity of discovering a medium through which they can articulate their progress. For instance, the Gorkhas in Mizoram use the *politics of camouflaging* which include a wide spectrum of strategies ranging from adopting Zo names, to converting to Christianity, to marrying local tribal women. The strategic deployment of such tactics act as a bargain counter to improve their status in the Zo world.

The politics of camouflaging helps the 'migrant others' to negotiate their existence in the Zo world; at the same time there is a constant attempt at 'back-linking' with the past, the country of origin in terms of rituals, practices and values, relationships and family ties (Thapan 2005: 15). It may or may not solve the complex problem of acceptance in the battle of identities. For instance, migrants employ the tactics of marrying local women. While it has helped the Poi and the Gorkha, it hardly acts as a foolproof strategy for the Vai. The Vai continue to be a 'permanent pariah', fit only to serve the realms of economy. The very nature of the historical linkages and the spectre of the insurgency and counter-insurgency mould and shape the everyday lived-in relationships between the Vai and the Zo/Mizo or the Zo hnahthlak.[30]

Even though historically speaking the Gorkhas are migrants, they have succeeded in camouflaging their identity with that of the majority Zo/Mizo. For instance, the Gorkha organisations in Mizoram like the MGYA, formed in 1976 on the lines of the Young Mizo Association (YMA), aim at cultural assimilation with the majority Zo/Mizo culture while maintaining the distinct Gorkha characteristics, further substantiating the argument that migrations do not imply a complete break from the past; rather the migrant must be understood as inhabiting two worlds simultaneously (Thapan 2005: 15).

Many of the Vai from Cachar and Karimganj who come to Mizoram as menial labour often do not possess legal documents, or their documents have expired making them illegal migrants. The vanguards of the Ideal Zo Christian state target this group of people and exploit them for selfish ends, including physical assaults. Of late, the Vai have been regulating their presence by emulating the twin model of YMA and MGYA to chisel out its space within the ambit of the Ideal Zo Christian state in Mizoram. The predominantly Muslim Vai people have formed the Mizoram Muslim Welfare Society (MMWS)[31] in order to consolidate their voices, and have attempted to work in collaboration with the YMA. However, the YMA continues to set the terms of negotiation during conflicts between the Vai and the Mizo/Zo. For instance, in the case of assaults or manhandling of the Vai by the MZP or YMA or Khristian Thalai Pawl (KTP),[32] the first thing that the victim of mob-rule has to do is 'non-reporting', that is the victim should not report to the police or legal agencies. Instead, the victim should bring the case to the notice of the Central YMA and the Church. Failure to do so makes the case unfit for discussion at the negotiation table and the victim has to face the music.[33]

By marking the Muslims as 'OBC', the Mizo government seemed to have alienated the Gorkha community, which then turned to depending on the 'Tini Mohini factor' (*Lelte Weekly* 2010; *Tawrh Bawm* 2010) thinking that this would enable the Gorkhas to have a better bargaining position and retain their coveted position as Denizens in Mizoram. The Gorkha were confident that Tini Mohini Thapa representing Mizoram in the fifth season of *Indian Idol* would enable them to make a mark for their community just as the 'Prashant Tamang factor' during the third season of *Indian Idol* had reinforced the Gorkha sentiment in Darjeeling.

The case of the third season of *Indian Idol* can be of interest in our discussion of the 'contentious and fluid nature of culture, identity and politics' where Prashant Tamang from Darjeeling (West Bengal) was pitted against Amit Paul from Meghalaya. Interestingly, in this particular case, Meghalaya was represented at a cultural level even in the most limited sense (that is on television) by a *dhakar*, that is, a non-local, an 'outsider'. And the sentiments in West Bengal also echoed similar feelings of a 'Gorkha' (that is, Prashant Tamang) representing the 'Bengali' when it came to pitting one state against the other. The internal dynamics within West Bengal, however, strongly voiced the wedge between the 'Gorkha' and the 'Bengali' during the 'final three' when West Bengal was represented by two contestants namely Prashant Tamang from 'North Bengal' and Emon Chatterjee from 'South Bengal'. Here it is important to strongly focus on the geographies of identity and *geographies of anger* (Appadurai 2006) and ethnic consciousness which is rooted in the sense of *relative deprivation* (Gurr 1970; Rapley 2004: 1–16; Runciman 1966), internal colonisation and protests (Gamson 1995; Johnston and Klandermans 1995b; Swindler 1995) and anti-outsider psychology (Weiner 1978). Drawing parallels, we find that the pulse of the Zo/Mizo people soared high when the 'Zo/Mizo-Gorkha' singing sensation Tini Mohini Thapa made it to the 'theatre rounds in Mumbai' in the fifth season of *Indian Idol*. Strangely enough, the Zo cultural nationalists did not feel the pinch of being represented at a larger level by the 'Gorkha' community and instead jubilantly campaigned for Tini Mohini Thapa calling her a worthy 'Zo/Mizo-Gorkha'.[34]

These coping mechanisms[35] are in fact geared towards attaining degrees of citizenship so as to overcome the degrees of statelessness[36] by the Vai, the Poi and the Gorkha in present-day Mizoram. An important area of concern in contemporary readings of identity discourse has been the study of food, the culinary tastes, consumption patterns, and food as linked to a culture and identity. 'Food and cuisine' have not been considered prominent markers of identity and naturally, unlike the prominent markers of identity like clothing and festivals, they have not been at the centre of debates on identity markers till recent times. However, of late, food is increasingly being recognised as playing an important role in demarcating a distinct cultural identity, especially in the context of diaspora citizens.[37]

The Vai, unlike the Gorkha, has largely been unable to cross the threshold of gastronomical divide even though the Zo/Mizo has been by and large able to by incorporating Indian spices, etc. into their food. The pungent smell of fermented delicacies and the local food continue to be repulsive to the Vai (a large majority of whom are Bengalis). Gastronomically adjusting to local situations remains an uphill task for the Bengali for whom 'Bengali food' (*Bangali ranna*) is the ultimate culinary destination. The Vai is yet to overcome the subtle divide and chisel out their space in the Zo world and cross the threshold of the permanent pariah. The Gorkhas have over time incorporated Zo/Mizo food into their diet and this culinary proximity has to a large extent blurred the gastronomical divide. The Gorkhas in Mizoram have to an extent assimilated themselves to the local customs, practices and food habits, thereby making them acceptable as 'Denizens' in a citizenship regime that demands closer assimilation in terms of identity.[38] Naturally they have succeeded in crossing boundaries faced which the Vai or the Poi failed to cross. The everyday use of language by the Zo to refer to the Gorkha such as *Mizo ang chiah* ('just like the Mizos') speaks volumes about their place in the hierarchical ordering of citizenship as full, partial (Denizens), or non-citizens in the Zo/Mizo society.[39]

The Gorkhaland movement which has been relentlessly trying to bring all the diaspora Nepali/Gorkha communities (Bhattarai 2009; Chhetri 2011; Khati 1994; Lama 1996; Rawat 1996) under a common platform thus has become an attractive option for the Nepali-speaking community in the Northeast in general. No doubt the Gorkhas in Mizoram have continually supported the idea of the creation of Gorkhaland in and around Darjeeling,[40] be it under Subhash Ghishing in the 1980s[41] or under the aegis of Bimal Gurung post-2007.[42] However, a word of caution that needs to be given a patient hearing is that the creation of a new state named after a particular community in the region around Darjeeling Hills would naturally have a rippling effect on the marginal communities in north Bengal and boost similar contending/contesting demands.[43]

Some Closing Observations and Recommendations

The expansion of the British colonial state in India in the eastern Himalayan region produced a new political geography and created new boundaries by appropriating land which belonged to Nepal or Bhutan. These boundaries were legitimised—as wars of expansion always are—by treaties that were plainly unequal. These kingdoms being virtually subordinate to the British Indian government, frictions were kept to the minimum by the power of the British, while free movements of population followed a natural pattern. This also changed the demographic profile of the region as Nepalis (from Nepal) as well as people from Bengal, Bihar and even north India migrated in search of work and living. The majority, however, were the Nepalese, settled in British India, Sikkim and Bhutan.

The old treaties were redrawn as 'friendship treaties' with Bhutan (1949) and Nepal (1950) by the post-colonial Indian government. Sikkim became a part of India in 1975. It was from the 1970s that the citizenship of these settler communities, particularly the Nepalis, was questioned in the northeastern states and then in Bhutan. This resulted in conflict and forced migration of these ethno-linguistic groups from these states/kingdoms. The exodus from Bhutan has produced a fairly large number of refugees living mostly in Nepal in camps, but also in India clandestinely. On the other side of the border, the issue of the fairly substantial *madhesi* population in the southern districts of Nepal threaten to snowball into a major problem.

The contemporary critical-theoretical debate surrounding identity and culture politics (Barker 2000, 2002; Grossberg et al. 1992b; Hall 1992; Lane and Ersson 2005) has to be kept in mind and used as a tool to unravel the braided relationship between citizenship, identity, community recognition, etc. All these different claims are directed towards consolidating the community's bargaining power in the contest over citizenship and the benefits bestowed by the state (Greenblatt 1995).

Further, the discussion accentuates the potent role played by media in a globalised scenario in thawing the relations and attitudes among cultures and between people. Media in its myriad format provides the necessary connectedness as well as disconnectedness for maintaining as well as retaining the spatiality of cultures and identities in the form of reawakening or reigniting primordial consciousness which till then may have been largely dormant. In other words, it acts as the potent social force or the catalyst for levelling as well as accentuating identity consciousness among contending communities in a culturally embattled terrain (Curran and Gurevitch 1991; Goodwin and Whannel 1992; Holt and Perren 2009; Keane 1991; Shrum 1994: 50–73; Fairclough 1995; Folkerts and Lacy 2004; Rose 2007; Wilson 1982).

Coming to the issue of the insider–outsider debate vis-à-vis migration, one has to note that the hallmark of migration is its ambiguity. Even as migrants struggle to transform themselves and their families, they are torn between competing ideals: to separate their families and gain access to the power and resources of new places or to remain together, to retain links with their villages; in other words, to return or to stay. Migration always involves relations of power, whether these are between states, cities and rural areas, or regions; between migrants and non-migrants or would-be-migrants; or between individuals within a migrant's household or family (Gardner and Osella 2004).

Some changes at the policy level can help reduce the trauma of statelessness and non-belonging. For instance, the terms and conditions of the Indo-Nepal Treaty of Peace and Friendship of 1950,[44] the 'Plantations Labour Act (1951), etc., may be reconsidered so that the domicile Nepali-speaking population in India could be armed with valid documents.[45] The changes in the terms and conditions, which are by and large hangovers of colonial policies, will enable the community to overcome the disadvantaged position in the experience of citizenship and enjoy the benefits of full citizenship. Being clubbed into the OBC group would also enable them to pursue higher education to have an edge in the competitive job market, something like the experience of the Meena community in western India which has the distinction of being predominantly a bureaucratic community. Likewise, the government should act strongly and check the tendency to retain the *nagrikta patra* (citizen card) of Nepal[46] while simultaneously holding Indian documents like passport, ration card, voter's card, etc. unless it is clearly recognised that these people are permitted to have dual citizenship.[47] The government and the community itself should discourage the common practice of 'earn in India, invest in Nepal' among the Nepali/Gorkha population in the region. Rather, they should pay tax in the country in which they are earning.[48] A distinction has to be made in the experiences in Darjeeling where an institutional structure (the Gorkhaland Territorial Administration [GTA]) ensures the recognition of identity, and those in the northeast, where such recognition, and consequent perception of security, is not automatic.

The case of the Gorkha in the Northeast supports the understanding that citizenship, identity and community recognition is affected by conversion, migration, modernisation, westernisation, partition and the politics of the dominant group. The positional and situational complexities faced by the Nepalis in the absence of a holistic treatment as understood from the aforementioned discussions can be best described as 'Here, There, Everywhere Yet Nowhere' in a citizenship regime that demands the peopling of territories following the Westphalian blueprint.

Notes

* This chapter includes content drawn from various Calcutta Research Group publications, which have been used with permission. All unaccredited quotes in this chapter are from the authors' fieldwork.

1. The English society was represented by different classes of people. At the apex were the members of the Indian Civil Service; below them were those in the top-ranking military posts like the colonel or brigadier; and the rest consisted of uncovenanted officers, businessmen, missionaries, railway engineers, police superintendents, planters of tea, clerks, shopkeepers and doctors. A number of Eurasians or Anglo-Indians were also part of the White society. The different classes of British women who had settled in Darjeeling hills were those with official connections; female missionaries; widows; unmarried women employed as teachers, nurses, governesses at boarding houses, hotels; and grass widows whose husbands remained at their post in the plains. I acknowledge Dr Devika Roy Lama, Associate Professor, Department of History, St Joseph's College, Darjeeling, for this insight.
2. It is to be noted that colonial documents may occasionally prevent correct understanding precisely because of regional variations in documentation style. However, when styled as 'Gurkhas', one can say with conviction that they are from the Kingdom of Nepal. Discrepancies arise when colonial documents style the entry on caste lines, where the nationality of the individual becomes concealed.
3. North Bengal consists of six districts: Malda, Uttar (north) Dinajpur, Dakshin (south) Dinajpur, Darjeeling, Jalpaiguri and Cooch Behar. As per the 2001 Census, the total population of the districts was 14.72 million, which was 18.35 per cent of the state. The decennial growth rate of population is higher than the state average and this is partly due to the influx of immigrants from bordering Bangladesh and Nepal into the districts. There is a high percentage of population comprising Scheduled Castes (SCs) and Scheduled Tribes (STs). The percentage of SC population is 29 per cent as per the 1991 Census, which is 5 per cent higher than that of the state average. The SC population is mainly concentrated in the districts of Cooch Behar, Jalpaiguri and West Dinajpur. The proportion of tribal population in the North Bengal districts is also higher than the state average of 5.6 per cent (Planning Commission 2002). Jalpaiguri and Darjeeling districts account for a high percentage of tribal population—21 per cent and 13.8 per cent, respectively.
4. A strong sense of discontent has emerged among the prominent ethnic communities in North Bengal reverberating itself in the form of demands for smaller states, certain other concessions from the Union and the state governments, etc. The rationale put forward is that the formation of separate states would protect linguistic and cultural identities and also facilitate rapid development. The Nepalis in the hills of Darjeeling have been demanding a separate state of Gorkhaland, while in the plains there is the demand for the state of Kamatapur and Greater Cooch Behar. Darjeeling Hills, for instance, has invited much attention both at home and abroad not just for the natural beauty and tea but also because of

the protracted 'sometimes dormant, sometimes active' Gorkhaland movement.

5. Census reports would indicate that in 1901 there were only 45,000 *khas-kura* or Nepali-speaking people, while thrice the number spoke other languages/dialects. In 1961, the number was 352,000 out of a total population of 404,000 in the hill areas of Darjeeling.

6. The most striking development has been in Tripura. Over the years, owing to the migration of the Bengali Hindu population from East Bengal the tribal autochthones were outnumbered. The tribal population dropped from 64 per cent in 1874 to 29 per cent in 1971. The Bengali population became 68 per cent of the total population in 1971. From all available accounts, the Bengali percentage is now 70. The result has been that political and administrative power passed from the hands of indigenous tribals to immigrant Bengalis. The transfer of land from the tribal population to the Bengali migrants proved to be the most critical factor in deteriorating social relations and a flashpoint was reached in June 1980 at Mandia leading to a carnage, initiated by the tribals, with Bengalis taking retaliatory measures, in which several hundreds lost their lives and 300,000 were rendered homeless. There is widespread apprehension in the minds of the Assamese caste-Hindus that in the near future they will lose political power in favour of numerous migrants. The other states of the region also share the Assamese fears. In a democratic framework of one-person-one-vote, the role played by demographic factor remains crucial in bringing about spectacular changes in power politics (Singh 1987: 257–82). The fear of Tripurisation continues to haunt every state in the Northeast. As echoed by North East Students' Organization, 'the entire region has been smothered by aliens migrating from other parts of India . . . the native population is on the verge of being smothered' (also cf. *Statesman* 1997; Hazarika 1992).

7. The ties between ancient Assam and Nepal have been mentioned in several ancient texts as well. Such texts reaffirm matrimonial ties between their ruling families. There is no doubt that the British facilitated the systematic inflow of people of Nepalese origin into the region. The colonial rulers as an integral part of the policies of expansion encouraged the Nepalese to occupy the buffer zones and provide some sort of security to the British as they could not fully trust and rely on the local tribal population for providing such security. Another view cites the aspect of Nepalese immigrants contributing to the government exchequer. There are numerous strands explaining the reasons for the ready immigration by the Nepalese into the region. One, for instance, is the military-economic explanation. Nepal being an economically backward country the poor Nepalese from the mountainous regions have been migrating to India in general and Assam in particular seeking means of livelihood. Many of these Nepalese in the course of time settled permanently in the forest lands as graziers and cultivators. Similarly, the British too facilitated the process of Nepali migration as they needed soldiers for their army and labour for the plantations and other enterprises. As such, the 'martial' tribes of Nepal were recruited in the military force and many of them, after retirement settled in different parts of the country, including Assam'. For details, cf. Sinha and Subba (2003).

8. Report No. 61/24, April 1946 of the Central Intelligence Office, Government of Assam; quoted in Sinha and Subba (2003: 46).

9. Often referred to as the 'chicken-neck', the 'Siliguri–Coochbehar corridor' symbolises the nebulous zone of 'the beginning' as well as 'the end' of the territorial demarcation between the 'Northeast' and 'Mainland India'.

10. The logic of geopolitics fails to address the mental mapping of ethnic consciousness in north Bengal. There is an invariable inclination to cling to the post-colonial construct of the 'Northeast'; that is, there is a strong tendency to locate oneself within the Northeast rather than the 'mainland' especially when Sikkim has been conveniently placed under it as the younger brother of the seven sisters. When Sikkim can be clubbed into the 'Northeast' why can north Bengal not be included as well is the question that looms large.

Many would undoubtedly question the wisdom of engaging in a debate over citizenship and related statelessness of the Nepali-speaking population in the region. It is true that such engagements divert contending arguments into polar directions; however, it is also true that the experiential facts of the said community cannot be brushed aside or wished away for the simple fact that they fail the tests of the conceptual moorings of legality. Historically, tensions emanating from such debates and associated disaffection can be traced to the times of Damber Singh Gurung's 'Assam Chalo' slogan of 1943.

In this context the extracts from Dozey's account are worth citing: 'In order to discourage emigration the Nepalese Durbar has placed a ban on women leaving the country on any pretext whatever'. This shows the status of the people and the attitude of Nepalese authorities towards the people in the study. For details, see Dozey (1917: 47).

11. Col. Skinner selected Aizawl for the construction of a permanent post in the North Lushai Hills. Once the construction of the post was completed, the column retreated to Silchar leaving behind a garrison of 200 riflemen, mostly Gorkhas of the Surma Valley Military Police Battalion. This garrison was later renamed the First Assam Rifles and set its base in the North Lushai Hills. Likewise in the South Lushai Hills, the 400 Gorkha soldiers of the 2/2 G.R attached to the 9th Bengal Infantry led by Brig. F.V.G. Treagears set their base in Lungleh via Demagiri (Tlabung). With these expeditions began the official migration of the Gorkhas into the Zo Hills.

12. Through my interviews, I was able to get the answer to the question why the local chiefs wanted the Gorkhas within their villages. Most evidently this was because most of the Gorkhas working with the British armed forces (and later the Indian armed forces) even after retirement could be utilised for obtaining cheaper goods, food, clothing and foreign liquor easily from the Army canteens. The local chiefs could buy these goods through the Gorkhas, and keeping in view the difficult terrain and the lack of ready available goods (during that time), this made the option of having a permanent source of procurement in the form of the Gorkha a blessing.

13. The Superintendent of Lushai Hills, Order No. 31 of 1922, in *Mizo leh Vai Chanchinbu*, 1923, p. 33.

14. The Chin Hills Regulations was passed on 13 August 1896. It authorised the superintendent or the deputy commissioner to order any undesirable outsider to leave the area and tax the residents, permanent or temporary; houses; clans and villages.

15. Many of the Nepali-speaking people who reside in the northeast of the Indian subcontinent come originally from a variety of castes and ethno-linguistic groups that have traditionally inhabited the eastern hills of Nepal. But post-migration, generations have attained a high degree of cultural uniformity and are unified by their use of the Nepali language as a common tongue (English 1983; Hutt 1997: 101–44).

16. However, this does not mean that the Gorkha has been accepted unconditionally. The diaspora Mizo/Zo or the Zo hnahthlak from Tripura, Manipur and elsewhere have been voicing their concerns over the issue of accepting the Gorkha as Denizens, while they in spite of being Zo hnahthlak remain at the threshold of carving a niche for themselves within the larger ambit of Zomi identity. For similar arguments, cf. Pudaite (2006: 8–9).

17. C.A. Bell, 'Report on Special Duty in Connection with Bhutan,' 21 July,,India Office Library and Records (IOR), Mss//EUR/F80/5C,1904. Cited in Sinha (2003: 41).

18. Cf. Chakraborty (2008).

19. Interestingly, the usage of the term 'self' in a tribal context is itself debatable. Here the individual gains his identity through the collective and historical identity of the tribe which has been preserved and transferred through generations. Hence, the notion of 'self' transcends to that of collective good and rights rather than individual rights.

20. 'Notion, tone and content of citizenship' all taken together refer to the right to citizenship/nationality and also the associated rights that flow from such privileged status. For further details, please see Chhetri (1986); Nepal (1998).

21. 'Test of citizenship' refers to the everyday challenge that the Nepali-speaking community has to ritually undergo in terms of clarifying their alleged nationalism in the region. Instances are replete where even prominent members of the community have shared their experiences of having been asked to show 'Passports,' legal documents, etc. to prove their nationality. Failure to show such proof results in failing the test of citizenship and therefore, being classed as 'illegal'. For instance, see Ganguly (1986), in Lama (1996: 38–39).

22. Legal experts may soundly argue that the parameters of legality do not consider this 'experience of statelessness' weighty enough to drive in the arguments in favour of statelessness of the said community. However, it is the demand of the times and contemporary legal debates should venture out of the confines of the texts or 'the books' and move ahead and enter into the mode of activism in legality, and fasten the mode and tone of judicial proceedings related to persons experiencing statelessness. Statelessness is a 'lived experience' and experiences 'weigh more than a ton of theory'.

23. The MZP is the largest students' representative in Mizoram and also the most active agency of the nexus of patriarchy in the state. It acts as a mechanism of systemic control through which the politics of 'exclusions' and 'inclusions' is put to function. The MZP was originally formed on the lines of the Assam Students' Union back in 1942 as the Lushai Students' Union in Shillong. It shifted its base to Aizawl in 1970. The MZP came to public prominence from its earlier role of a partner in collection of donations for the MNF movement in the 1980s.

24. Informal discussion with Sheela Chhetri, Dinthar Veng, Zarkawt, Aizawl, 10 February 2008.

25. Interview with Zorama (Kamal Chettri), Babutlang, Zarkawt, Aizawl, 9 February 2008; 12 March 2010.

26. However, most of my elderly respondents during my field visit narrated personal experiences of difficulties that they faced in order to prove their citizenship in Mizoram. For instance, they had to painstakingly produce and preserve the 'Domicile Certificate' given to their great-grandparents by the British to prove their historical roots in Mizoram. Failure to produce such documents led to difficulties to claim their authentic citizenship in Mizoram as well as in India.

27. 'Genuine citizenship' refers to those with proper documents. In the case of Mizoram, this includes any colonial document mentioning the names of the individuals' forefathers. The early Gorkha settlers in the state of Mizoram tended to style themselves as 'genuine citizens' as a class apart from the later entrants from Nepal and elsewhere who came to Mizoram taking the benefits of the 1950 provision between the two countries. The 'genuine citizens' are the first movers in terms of historical timeframe among the migrant Nepali-speaking population in Mizoram.

28. The aims and objectives of the MGYA mentioned in its Constitution openly declare the total submission of the community to the larger Mizo community and the subservient position within Mizoram.

29. Based on a series of telephonic interviews with Shiva Kumar Thapa—a prominent leader of the MGYA and an activist for recognition of the Gorkhas as OBCs in Mizoram—in 2007, and also informal discussions on 27 January 2008 at his residence.

30. A popular statement discouraging marriages with the Vai says *Ali a fapa chu Ali a ni* ('the son of Ali is Ali' meaning that the child born out of inter-community marriages will have his father's name and be of mixed blood, and therefore an 'outsider'). The mother being a local does little to help the children born out of such marriages. But as is the spirit of the Zo/Mizo society, every problem has a solution or 'compensation'. The most easy solution is to make the children adopt a series of strategies to overcome their 'otherness', including using a name echoing their Zo linkages. For instance, most children born in such marriages are christened with names beginning with a prefix 'Zo', changing the father's name or adopting the maternal grandfather's name as the biological father in school and other certificates (so as not to hamper the possibilities of the child to enjoy the benefits of reservation in future). Adopting the religion of the mother is the most ready and obvious solution. All these strategies are geared to make the children enjoy the benefits of the state in terms of affirmative action, scholarships, quotas for higher education, etc., *to make life secure.*

31. The Muslim Welfare Society was established in 2001 at the Bara Bazar Mosque Complex, Aizawl. It was registered as a society on 13 October 2004. What comes as a surprise is that this nascent organisation has managed to secure the status of OBC to the Muslim minority in Mizoram. The activities of the Muslim Welfare Society can well be summed up by glancing at the letters and correspondences made by the body over the years. See Muslim Welfare Society (2001, 2006, 2007); Muslim Welfare Society and Aizawl Mosque Committee (2005) (see Appendix VI of Muslim Welfare Society [2006] for an example of the content of the request letter).

32. The KTP is a religious wing for the youth organised under the Presbyterian Church, much like Thalai Khristian Pawl (TKP) among the Baptists in Mizoram. This organisation works to instil Christian ethics among the youth.

33. Interview with Mammon Mazumdar, General Secretary, Mizoram Muslim Welfare Society, 17 February 2008; 20–21 March 2010.

34. An interesting point to be noted is that most Gorkha in Mizoram identify or define themselves as Zo/Mizo-Gorkha rather than as just a Gorkha. The definition as a Zo/Mizo-Gorkha has enabled the Gorkha to cross the threshold of the exclusion-inclusion divide and attain the position of Denizens in Mizo/Zo society, further substantiating the argument that the issue of 'self-definition' and the recognition of that 'self-definition' by 'others' help to authenticate that group identity.

35. The acculturation strategies employed by 'diaspora citizens' in Mizoram revolves around the nostalgia of imagined communities, 'mental spaces', return to 'home' (*desh*; *pi pu ram*), culinary tactics, etc. all geared to counter the hegemonic politics. The immigrants through these strategies continuously dabble with a more or less dual cultural background walk/live through the trapeze of the 'two worlds'. It becomes essential to explore aspects of the ways in which everyday life becomes invested with meanings as they play out in the social, political and economic relationships and symbolic transactions between the peripheral cultures and the dominant cultures. Further confirming the argument that in identity politics, the migrants ('others') and their ways of life are not simply a passive symbol but something imbued with a distinctive potency in the trajectory of imagining communities.

36. This theoretical/legal incoherence rightly addresses what the writer attempts to point out, that is, the difference between theory and its actual application.

37. Aihwa Ong (2003) argues that it is essential to distinguish between the conceptual meaning and political implications of the term 'diasopra'. Diasporic communites implies a homogenous group with similar 'imaginaries'. Diaspora today refers to a 'wide range of fluid spatial, cultural and political locations' of people or communities. For details, see Walsh (2003: 11).

38. This gastronomical perspective enables us to explore the minute yet often overlooked, mundane, taken-for-granted issues in everyday life that do contribute to the complex, layered web of identity politics. For instance, through these gastronomical changes we can see that there is a gradual, often slow acceptance of the Vai and Indian identity from the side of the micro level, that is, from a small, elite section from within the community. At the same time there is a very miniscule change in the acceptance of the 'Zo/Mizo' by the larger community that is the Indian. The Zo/Mizo through the Peace Accord has been able to except the Indianness and add it as a prefix or suffix to its *generic* or *phonetic* identity ('Indian-Mizo' or 'Zo/Mizo-Indian'); but the Indian has not been able to accept the appendages to the identity of the said group. 'Zo/Mizo of a certain age group are gradually crossing the gastronomical divide and gradually accepting Vai culture via globalization via the West and not directly through Delhi. As the West is openly accepting India and its cultures, so Zo/Mizo are also following the trend', says Vanramchhuangi. The Zo/Mizo have been able to identify with India over the past 10 years, but Indians are yet to identify themselves with this part of India. These instances provide an insight into acculturation processes of the migrants and the 'natives' by taking the 'gastronomical highway' or examination of the culinary behaviour. Information in this note is based on informal discussions with officers from mainland India who had a chance to serve the people of Mizoram and also their children, most of whom were born in Mizoram and spent a substantial part of their lives there.

39. Again, this theoretical/legal incoherence addresses what the writer attempts to point out, that is, the difference between theory and its application in ground zero.

40. The project of chiselling a separate state of Gorkhaland enters into the narratives of the nationalist discourse of the Gorkhas and is also interpreted as the triumph of Gorkha nationalism over the 'other', namely the Bengali and the state of West Bengal. The whole project is also interpreted as a public effort to cut the 'other' down to size. The territorial space is selected as the final battleground where the Gorkha and the 'other' will contest their spatial domain. The map of Gorkhaland is thus held to be endowed with the capacity to exhilarate and express symbols and cultural icons of the Gorkha.

41. The first phase (1980s onwards) of the Gorkhaland movement under Subhash Ghishing ended only after an agreement between the governments (West Bengal and the Centre) and the GNLF, resulting in the establishment of an elected body in 1988 called the Darjeeling Gorkha Hill Council (DGHC), which received autonomy to govern the district. Though Darjeeling became peaceful, the issue of a separate state lingered, fuelled in part by the lack of comprehensive economic development in the region even after the formation of the DGHC.

42. The second phase (post-2007, under Bimal Gurung) of the Gorkhaland movement in Darjeeling Hills has entered the negotiation tables in changed times after the exit of the Left-Front government in West Bengal; a pact was signed leading to the formation of the Gorkhaland Territorial Administration (GTA), a hill council armed with more powers than its predecessor DGHC. Interestingly, even the GTA has evoked strong contestations among contending communities in north Bengal. Gurung and the Gorkha Janmukti Morcha (GJMM) are also unhappy about the power sharing of the GTA with the state government. There is still a lot of uneasiness in the relationship and the demand for a separate state is periodically reiterated.

43. People in the hills of Darjeeling have been demanding a separate state of Gorkhaland, while in the plains there is the demand for the state of Kamatapur and Greater Cooch Behar. Darjeeling Hills, for instance, has invited much attention both at home and abroad not just for the natural beauty and tea but also because of the protracted 'sometimes dormant, sometimes active' Gorkhaland movement. The Gorkha, the Kamtapuri and the Koch have been rallying their identity against their perceived notions of 'backwardness' and non-representation and perplexed notions of self-defined identity.

44. The treaty allows for the free movement of people and goods between the two nations and a close relationship and collaboration on matters of defence and foreign affairs. While India values the treaty as deflecting the influence of its regional competitor, the People's Republic of China, the treaty has been unpopular in many segments of Nepal, which often regards it as a breach of its sovereignty.

45. Valid documents to show their status as either citizens or migrants and confer to them associated privileges. These are suggestions.

46. Such cards are acquired by paying money to the middlemen and bribes to officials in Nepal. Even the Nepali-speaking community from India has acquired these cards and makes use of the privileges such as easy access to jobs abroad and in the British Army, buying property in Nepal, etc.

47. Again, the paradoxes in theory and practice prevail.

48. This is the crux of the debate on the status of the people in study. A major accusation is that the said group of people earn in India and send remittances back to Nepal and invest there instead of in India. This trend evokes strong feelings of ill-will towards them and generates the politics of otherisation. This feeds into the general suspicion of the said group as 'foreigners', leeching the economy of India, etc.

Bibliography

Primary Sources

Court Disputes and Judgements

Bachan Lal Kalgotra v. The State of Jammu & Kashmir and Ors, AIR 1987 SC 1169.

Chairman, Railway Board & Ors v. Chandrima Das & Ors, 2000 AIR 988.

Committee for Citizenship Rights of the Chakmas of Arunachal Pradesh (CCRCAP) (1995) *Counter Affidavit of Union of India on the Chakmas and Hajongs of Arunachal Pradesh in the Supreme Court of India (Civil Jurisdiction) Writ Petition Civil No. 720 of 1995,* New Delhi.

Karnataka High Court Judgment in *Tenzin L. C. Rinpoche v. Union of India & Anr.,* WP No. 15437/2013 (GM-PASS) and Delhi High Court Judgement *Namgyal Dolkar v. Govt. of India,* WP (C) 12179/2009.

Izhar Ahmad Khan v. Union of India, 1962 AIR 1052.

National Human Rights Commission v. State of Arunachal Pradesh, 1996 AIR 1234.

State Of Arunachal Pradesh v. Khudiram Chakma on 27 April, 1993, 1994 AIR 1461, 1993 SCR (3) 401, http://indiankanoon.org/doc/473806/ (accessed on 12 January 2014).

Parliamentary Proceedings and Conference Papers

Calcutta Municipal Gazette, volume 71, no. 1, 26 December 1959.

Calcutta Municipal Gazette, volume 73, no. 2, 27 October 1962.

CR 1B2-3/53 (2057-84, January 1955), Government of India, New Delhi, 1992.

Decisions taken at the 17th Chief Secretaries' Conference held at Dacca on the 29 and 30 August, 1950, CR 3C2-5/50 (2237-55, March 1953).

Decisions taken at the Chief Secretaries' Conference held at Calcutta on the 7-9 April, 1949, Sixth Conference, CR 3C1-4/50 (September 1961).

Decisions taken at the Chief Secretaries' Conference held at Calcutta on the 21 and 22 April 1950, Fourteenth Conference, CR 26A-1/50 (1050-69, December 1952).

Memorandum to the United Nations Organization, The Chittagong Hill Tracts People's Association, 1948.

Question no. 169, Proceeding 2821, Rajya Sabha, Government of India, 22 December 1993.

Question no. 197, Proceeding 2127, Rajya Sabha, Government of India, 1 December 2002.

Question no. 198, Proceeding 617, Rajya Sabha, Government of India, 26 February 2003.

Question no. 204, Proceeding 3634, Rajya Sabha, Government of India, 27 April 2005.

Question no. 207, Proceeding 1699, Rajya Sabha, Government of India, 8 March 2006.

Question no. 211, Proceeding 2369, Rajya Sabha, Government of India, 5 September 2007.

Question No. 194, Proceeding 1714, Rajya Sabha, Government of India, 5 December 2001.

The Superintendent of Lushai Hills Order no. 31 of 1922 in *Mizo leh Vai Chanchinbu*, 1923.

Tin-Bigha Lease Terms Agreement, 7 October 1982.

Reports and Documents

Asian Centre for Human Rights (ACHR) (2007) *India Human Rights Report: 2006*, New Delhi: Asian Centre for Human Rights.

Biswas, Sailendra, Birendramohan Dasgupta and S.C. Sen Gupta (1988) *Samsad Bengali-English Dictionary*, Calcutta: Sahitya Samsad.

Central Intelligence Office (1946) *Report No. 61/24 April*, Government of Assam.

Chakma, Sneha Kumar (1948) Memorandum to the United Nations Organization, Chittagong Hill Tracts People's Association.

Chittagong Hill Tracts (1947) *A Memorandum Indicating the Political Demands of the People of Chittagong Hill Tracts (Excluded Area) Bengal*, Rangamati: Chittagong Hill Tracts.

Department Of Rehabilitation (n.d.) *Information Handbook Under Right To Information Act 2005*, Chennai: Department Of Rehabilitation, Government of Tamil Nadu.

Department of Census and Statistics (2009) *Statistical Abstract 2009*, Colombo: Ministry of Finance and Planning, Treasury of Sri Lanka.

Directorate of Economics and Statistics (2009) *Statistical Abstract*, Itanagar: Government of Arunachal Pradesh.

District Statistical Office (2009) *Lohit District at a Glance*, Itanagar: Government of Arunachal Pradesh.

Government of Arunachal Pradesh (1996) 'White Paper on Chakma and Hajong Refugee Issue', 12 March, Itanagar.

——— (2009) *Statistical Abstract of Arunachal Pradesh*, Itanagar: Directorate of Economics and Statistics, Government of Arunachal Pradesh.

Government of India (1991) 'Census Report', New Delhi.

——— (2001) 'Census Report', New Delhi.

Government of Mizoram (1992) *The Mizoram Gazette*, Extra-Ordinary, 3 February vide Regd. No. NE907, volume 21, Friday, 20 February, Phalguna 9, S.E. 1913, issue no. 24, Aizawl.

——— (2001) *The Mizoram Gazette*, Extra-Ordinary Notification, 17 May vide Regd. No. F20215/85/94-HM-Vol-II, volume 30, Friday, 18 May, Vaisakha 28, S.E. 1923, issue no. 19, Aizawl.

Government of Pakistan (1951) 'The Pakistan Citizenship Act, 1951', http://www.refworld.org/pdfid/3ae6b4ffa.pdf (accessed on 25 March 2015).

High Commission of India (1992) 'Tin Bigha — A Proper Perspective', Intelligence Report, CR 1B2-28/52 (85-89, July 1955), Dhaka.

Intergovernmental Panel on Climate Change (IPCC) (2008) *Climate Change 2007: Impacts, Adaptation and Vulnerability*, Geneva: Intergovernmental Panel on Climate Change.

Ishaq, Muhammad (1971) *Bangladesh District Gazetteers: Chittagong Hill Tracts*, Ministry of Cabinet Affairs, Establishment Division, Government of Bangladesh.

Majumdar, Durgadas (1977) *West Bengal District Gazetteer: Cooch-Behar*, Calcutta: West Bengal Government Press.

Ministry of External Affairs (1958a) 'Instrument Signed by the Governments of India and Ceylon regarding Proposals for Immigration into Ceylon and Citizenship Rights of Persons of Indian Origin', 18 January, Government of India, http://mea.gov.in/bilateral-documents.htm?dtl/7812/Instrument+Regarding+Immigration+and+citizenship (accessed on 26 March 2015).

——— (1958b) 'Agreement Relating to Border Disputes (East Pakistan)', 10 September, Government of India, http://www.mea.gov.in/mystart.php?id=53051914&pid=&flg=1&sz=b (accessed on 29 February 2012).

——— (1964) 'Agreement on Persons of Indian Origin in Ceylon', 30 October, Government of India, http://mea.gov.in/bilateral-documents.htm?dtl/6426/Agreement+on+Persons+of+Indian+Origin+in+Ceylon (accessed on 26 March 2015).

——— (2011) 'Protocol to the Agreement between India and Bangladesh Concerning the Demarcation of the Land Boundary between India and Bangladesh and Related Matters', 6 September, Government of India, http://www.mea.gov.in/bilateral-documents.

htm?dtl/5256/Protocol+to+the+Agreement+between+India+and+Bangladesh+concerning+the+demarcation+of+the+land+boundary+between+India+and+Bangladesh+and+related+matters (accessed on 29 February 2012).

Ministry of Foreign Affairs and Commonwealth Relations (1952) *Pakistan o Bharater Maddhye Jatayater Janye Passport o Visa Niyamabali* [Rules for the Issuance of Passport and Visa for Travelling between Pakistan and India], Dacca: Government of Pakistan.

Ministry of Home Affairs (1955) 'The Citizenship Act of India 1955', 30 December, Government of India, http://mha.nic.in/pdfs/ic_act55.pdf (accessed on 23 February 2012).

—— (1956) 'The Citizenship Rules, 1956', Government of India, http://admis.hp.nic.in/himpol/Citizen/LawLib/Amendments/citizen_ship_rules/MAIN.htm (accessed on 25 March 2015).

Mizoram Gorkha Youth Association (MGYA) (2002) 'To the Honourable Home Minister, Government of Mizoram', Letter No. MGYA(C)/OBC/2002-03/02, 28 November, Aizawl.

—— (2004a) 'To the Honourable Home Minister, Government of Mizoram', Letter No. MGYA(C)/OBC/2003-04/1, 15 February, Aizawl.

—— (2004b) 'To the Secretary, Home Department, Government of Mizoram', Letter No. MGYA(C)/OBC/2003-04/3, Mizoram Gorkha Youth Association, 30 April, Aizawl.

—— (2004c) 'To the Honourable Home Minister, Government of Mizoram', Letter No. MGYA(C)/OBC/2004-2005, 10 December, Aizawl.

—— (2005) 'To the Honourable Home Minister, Government of Mizoram', Letter No. MGYA(C) 1/ 2005/A/1, 11 January, Aizawl.

—— (2006a) 'To The Honourable Home Minister, Government of Mizoram', Letter No. MGYA(C)/OBC/2004-2005, 11 January, Aizawl.

—— (2006b) 'To The Honourable Chief Minister, Government of Mizoram', Letter No. MGYA(C)/OBC/2004-2005, 16 January, Aizawl.

Morris, C.J. (1932) *Report on Immigration of Gorkhas into Bhutan*, Gangtok: Office of the Political Officer.

Muslim Welfare Society (2001) *The Constitution of the Muslim Welfare Society Mizoram*, Aizawl.

—— (2006) 'To The Director, Barak Valley Cement Ltd. Badarpur, Assam', Letter No. /Ref No: MWS/06-07/07, 17 March, Aizawl.

—— (2007) Memorandum for Opening of All India Pre-Medical Entrance Test Centre at Aizawl and Allotment of Seat in the Aligarh Medical College for the Minority Community Living in Mizoram, 2 November, Aizawl.

Muslim Welfare Society and Aizawl Mosque Committee (2005) Memorandum to the President of India (Dr A.P.J. Abdul Kalam during his Maiden Visit to Mizoram), Aizawl, 24 September.

North East Indigenous/Tribal Peoples' Forum (NEITF) (1995) 'Summary of Workshop on Indigenous/Tribal People's Right to Self-Determination and Self-Government', organised by North East Indigenous/Tribal Peoples' Forum and All-Arunachal Pradesh Students' Union , 1–2 April.

O'Malley, L.S.S. (1985 [1907]) *Bengal District Gazetteers, Darjeeling*, New Delhi: Logos Press.

Office of the High Commissioner for Human Rights (OHCHR) (1966) 'International Covenant on Economic, Social and Cultural Rights', 16 December, United Nations.

——— (1976) 'International Covenant on Civil and Political Rights', 16 December, United Nations.

———(1979) 'Convention on the Elimination of All Forms of Discrimination against Women, 1979', 18 December, United Nations.

——— (1989) 'Convention on the Rights of the Child, 1989', 20 November, United Nations.

——— (2005) 'Human Rights and Arbitrary Deprivation of Nationality', Human Rights Resolution 2005/45, UN Commission on Human Rights, 57th Meeting, 19 April, E/CN.4/RES/2005/45.

Organisation for Eelam Refugees Rehabilitation (OfERR) (2003) 'Nallayan Declaration: The Return of Ceylon Tamil Refugees in South India and the Current Peace Process in Ceylon (Sri Lanka)', 26 February, http://www.oferr.org/content.php?id=189 (accessed on 20 June 2015).

Planning Commission (2002) *Annual Report 2001–02*, New Delhi: Government of India.

Pradhan, Rukesh Mani, Darjeeling Gorkha Hill Council (DGHC) and Department of Information and Cultural Affairs (1996) *Continuous Political Struggle for a Separate Constitutional Status of Ceded Land of Darjeeling*, Darjeeling: Department of Information and Cultural Affairs and Darjeeling Gorkha Hill Council.

Singh, K.S., B.B. Goswami, C. Nunthara, N.N. Sengupta, and Anthropological Survey of India (1995) *People of India: Mizoram*, volume 33, Calcutta: Seagull Books.

United Nations (UN) (1948) 'Universal Declaration of Human Rights', 10 December, http://www.un.org/en/documents/udhr/index.shtml#a15 (accessed on 15 November 2012).

——— (1960a) 'Treaty Series', volume 360.

——— (1960b) 'United Nations Convention on the Status of Stateless Persons 195', G. A. Res. 429 (V), 360 U.N.T.S. 117, United Nations Treaty Collection, http://treaties.un.org/pages/ViewDetails.aspx?src=TREATY&mtdsg_no=V- 4&chapter=5&lang=en (accessed on 12 March 2012).

——— (1966) 'International Covenant on Economic, Social and Cultural Rights, International Covenant on Civil and Political Rights and Optional Protocol to the International Covenant on Civil and Political Rights', United Nations General Assembly Resolution 2200 A (XXI), 16 December, http://www.ohchr.org/Documents/ProfessionalInterest/cescr.pdf (accessed on 17 March 2015).

——— (1975) 'United Nations Convention on the Elimination or Reduction of Future Statelessness 1967', United Nations Treaty Collection, http://treaties.un.org/pages/ViewDetails.aspx?src=TREATY&mtdsg_no=V-4&chapter=5&lang=en (accessed on 12 March 2012).

——— (2004) Report of the UN Committee on the Elimination of Racial Discrimination, *General Recommendation 30: Discrimination against Non-Citizens*, 1 October.

United Nations High Commissioner for Refugees (UNHCR) (1954) 'Convention Relating to the Status of Stateless Persons', http://www.unhcr.org/3bbb25729.pdf (accessed on 12 March 2012).

——— (1961) 'Convention on the Reduction of Statelessness', http://www.unhcr.org/3bbb286d8.pdf (accessed on 12 March 2012).

——— (1995) 'Resolution Adopted by the UN General Assembly [on the Report of the Third Committee (A/50/632)] A/RES/50/152', Office of the United Nations High Commissioner for Refugees, 21 December.

——— (1997) 'Statelessness and Citizenship', in *The State of the World's Refugees: A Humanitarian Agenda*, Oxford: Oxford University Press.

——— (2006) 'Conclusion on Identification, Prevention and Reduction of Statelessness and Protection of Stateless', UNHCR Executive Committee Report, 6 October.

West Pakistan Refugees Action Committee (2012) 'Memorandum, Charter of Demands of West Pakistani Refugees of 1947', 22 July, on file with the author.

Secondary Sources

Books

Acharya, Jagat Mani (2004) *Bhutanese Refugees in Nepal: A Sourcebook*, Kolkata: Calcutta Research Group.

Acharyya, N.N. (1984) 'Modernization of Mizoram', Proceedings of North East India History Association (NEIHA), 5th Session.

Agamben, Giorgio (1993) *The Coming Community*, trans. Michael Hardt, Minneapolis: University of Minnesota Press.

——— (2000) *Means Without End: Notes on Politics*, Theory Out of Bounds, volume 20, trans. Cesare Casarino and Vincenzo Binetti, Minneapolis: University of Minnesota Press.

Ahmed, Imtiaz, Abhijit Dasgupta and Kathinka Sinha-Kerkoff (eds) (2004) *State, Society and Displaced People in South Asia*, Dhaka: University Press Limited.

Aleaz, Bonita (2005) *Emergent Women: Mizo Women's Perspectives*, New Delhi: Mittal Publications.

Anand, A.S. (2011) *The Constitution of Jammu and Kashmir: Its Development and Comments*, Delhi: Universal Law Publishing Co.

Appadorai, A. (1982) *Select Documents on India's Foreign Policy and Relations, 1947–72*, Delhi: Oxford University Press.

Appadurai, Arjun (2006) *Fear of Small Numbers: An Essay on the Geography of Anger*, Durham, NC: Duke University Press.

Arendt, Hannah (1989) *The Human Condition*, Chicago: University of Chicago Press.

Bains, Joginder Singh (1962) *India's International Disputes: A Legal Study*, New York: Asia Publishing House.

Bandyopadhyay, Sekhar (2004) *From Plassey to Partition: A History of Modern India*, New Delhi: Orient Longman.

Barker, C. (2000) *Cultural Studies: Theory and Practice*, London and Thousand Oaks, CA: Sage Publications.

——— (2002) *Making Sense of Cultural Studies: Central Problems and Critical Debates*, London: Sage Publications.

Bauböck, R. (2007) *Migration and Citizenship: Legal Status, Rights and Political Participation*, Amsterdam: Amsterdam University Press.

Bhattarai, Ganga Prasad (2009) *Ragat Le Lekheko Itihaas*, Siliguri: Shivakoti Printing Press.

Bhaumik, Subir, Meghna Guhathakurta and Sabyasachi Basu Ray Chaudhury (eds) (1997) *Living on the Edge: Essays on the Chittagong Hill Tracts*. Kathmandu: South Asia Forum for Human Rights.

Blitz, Brad K. and Maureen Lynch (2009) *Statelessness and the Benefits of Citizenship: A Comparative Study*, Geneva: Oxford Brookes University.

——— (eds) (2011a) *Statelessness and Citizenship: A Comparative Study on the Benefits of Nationality*, Gloucestershire: Edward Elgar.

Bose, M.L. (1979) *Historical and Constitutional Documents of North-East India*, Delhi: Concept.

Bose, P.K. (ed.) (2000) *Refugees in West Bengal: Institutional Practices and Contested Identities*, Calcutta: Calcutta Research Group.

Bose, Tapan K. and Rita Manchanda (eds) (1997) *States, Citizens, and Outsiders: The Uprooted Peoples of South Asia*, Kathmandu: South Asia Forum for Human Rights.

Bryant, Jennings and Mary Beth Oliver (eds) (1994) *Media Effects: Advances in Theory And Research*, New York: Routledge.

Caplan, Lionel (1995) *Warrior Gentleman: 'Gurkhas' in the Western Imagination*, London: Berghahn Books.

Chakrabarty, Saroj (1974) *With Dr B.C. Roy and Other Chief Ministers: A Record up to 1962*, Calcutta: Benson's.

Chambers, O.A. (2005 [1899]) *Hand Book of the Lushai Country*, Kolkata: Firma KLM; Aizawl: Tribal Research Institute.

Chhetri, Hira (2011) *Bharathya Nepali Patra Patrika Ko Shatapdi 1887–1986*, Kalimpong: Impression Printing.

Chhetri, Lil Bahadur (1986) *Brahmaputra Ko Cheu Chaw*, Kathmandu: Sajha Prakashan.

Chimni, B.S. (2000), *International Refugee Law: A Reader*, New Delhi: Sage Publications.

Curran, James and Michael Gurevitch (eds) (1991) *Mass Media and Society*, London: Edward Arnold.

Daniels, Roger (1993) *Prisoners without Trial: Japanese Americans in World War II*, New York: Hill and Wang.

Das Choudhury, R.K. (2007) *Human Capital and Manpower Planning in North East*, Itanagar: Himalayan Publishers.

Dozey, E.C. (1917) *A Concise History of the Darjeeling District Since 1835*, Darjeeling: Gorkha Press.

Engineer, Asghar Ali (1991) *Mandal Commission Controversy*, New Delhi: Ajanta Publications.

English, Richard (1983) *Gorkhali and Kiranti: Political Economy in the Eastern Hills of Nepal*, Ann Arbor: University Microfilms International.

Fairclough, Norman (1995) *Media Discourse*, London: Edward Arnold.

Folkerts, Jean and Stephen Lacy (2004) *The Media in Your Life: An Introduction to Mass Communication*, New Delhi: Pearson Education.

Forbes, D. (1964) *Johnny Gurkhas*, London: Robert Hale.

Gait, E.A. (1906) *A History of Assam*, Calcutta: Thacker, Spink & Co.

Gellner, David N., Joanna Pfaff-Czarnecka and John Whelpton (eds) (1997) *Nationalism and Ethnicity in a Himalayan Kingdom: The Politics of Culture in Contemporary Nepal*, London, Amsterdam: Harwood Academic.

Ghosh, Lipi (ed.) (2009) *Political Governance and Minority Rights: The South and South-East Asian Scenario*, New Delhi: Routledge.

Goodwin, A. and G. Whannel (ed.) (1992) *Understanding Television*, London: Routledge.

Gopalan, T.N. (1995) *Repatriates in Nilgiris: A Saga of Struggle*, Kotagiri: Dalit Action Research and Extension Services Centre (DARES).

Grossberg, Nelson L.C. and P. Treichler (eds) (1992a) *Cultural Studies*, London: Routledge.

Gurr, Ted Robert (1970) *Why Men Rebel?* Princeton, NJ: Published for the Center of International Studies, Princeton University [by] Princeton University Press.

Guterres, António and Louise Arbour (2007) *The Hidden World of the Stateless*, Geneva: United Nations High Commissioner for Refugees.

Hathaway, James (2005) *The Rights of Refugees Under International Law*, Cambridge: Cambridge University Press.

Hazarika, Bolin (ed.) (2003) *Human Rights in India: Socio-Political and Legal Dimensions*. Jorhat: J.B. College Human Rights Study Cell.

Holt, Jennifer and Alisa Perren (eds) (2009) *Media Industries: History, Theory, and Method*, West Sussex: Wiley Blackwell.

Hsieh, Ming-Tung (2011) *A Lost Tribe*, Milton Keynes: Author House.

Hussain, Monirul (ed.) (2005) *Coming out of Violence: Essays on Ethnicity, Conflict Resolution and Peace Process in North-East India*, New Delhi: Regency.

Hutt, Michael (2003) *Unbecoming Citizens: Culture, Nationhood, and the Flight of Refugees from Bhutan*, New Delhi: Oxford University Press.

Jha, Dinesh Chandra (1972) *Indo-Pakistan Relations (1960–65)*, Patna: Bharati Bhawan.

Johnston, Hank and Bert Klandermans (eds) (1995a) *Social Movements and Culture*, Social Movements: Protest, and Contention, volume 4, Minneapolis: University of Minnesota Press.

Keane, J. (1991) *The Media and Democracy*, Cambridge: Polity Press.

Khati, Tika (1994) *Nepali Bhasha Manyata Andolan Ka Pratham Senani: Anand Singh Thapa*, Darjeeling: Darjeeling Printing House.

Kumar, Lalit (1977) *India and Sri Lanka: Sirimavo-Shastri Pact*, New Delhi: Chetana Publications.

Ladduwahetty, Neville (2010) *Sri Lanka's National Question: A Collection of Articles*, Colombo: Vijitha Yapa Publications.

Lama, Mahendra P. (1996) *Gorkhaland Movement: Quest for an Identity*,

New Delhi: Department of Information and Cultural Affairs, Darjeeling Gorkha Hill Council.

Lane, Jan-Erik and Svante Ersson (2005) *Culture and Politics: A Comparative Approach*, Aldershot: Ashgate Publishing Limited.

Lego, N. (2006) *Modern History of Arunachal Pradesh (1825–2006)*, Itanagar: Ponung Lego.

Lestricchia, Frank and Thomas McLaughlin (ed.) (1995) *Critical Terms for Literature Study*, Chicago: University of Chicago.

Lewin, T.H. (1912) *A Fly on the Wheel, or How I Helped to Govern India*, London: Constable & Company Ltd.

Lynch, Maureen (2005) *Lives on Hold: The Human Cost of Statelessness*, Washington: Refugees International.

Maheshwari, S.R. (1995) *Mandal Commission Revisited: Reservation Bureaucracy in India*, New Delhi: Jawahar Publishers & Distributors.

Marks, J. (1971) *Ayo Gurkha*, London: Oxford University Press.

McCall, A.G. (1980 [1939]) *The Lushai Hills: District Cover*, Aizawl: Tribal Research Institute.

McLean, Pascale (2005) *Incomplete Citizenship, Statelessness and Human Trafficking: A Preliminary Analysis of the Current Situation in West Bengal*, Kolkata: Calcutta Research Group.

Muktan, K.K. (2002) *The Legendary Gorkhas*, Guwahati: Spectrum Publications.

Nadesan, S. (1993) *A History of the Up-Country Tamil People in Sri Lanka*, Hatton: Nandalala Publication.

Nath, Lopita (2003) *The Nepalis in Assam: Ethnicity and Cross Border Movements in the North-East*, New Delhi: Minerva Associates Publication.

Nepal, Fanindra (1998) *Nepal: Teesta Dekhi Sutlej Samma*, Naya Baneshwar, Kathmandu: Sankhala Offset Press.

Nepal, Padam and Anup Shekhar Chakraborty (eds) (2012) *Politics of Culture, Identity and Protest in North-East India*, volumes 1 and 2, New Delhi: Authors Press.

Okoth-Obbo, George (ed.) (2007) *Collection of International Instruments and Legal Texts*, volume 1, Geneva: United Nations High Commissioner for Refugees.

Osella, Filippo and Katy Gardner (eds) (2004) *Migration, Modernity and Social Transformation in South Asia*, Contributions to Indian Sociology Occasional Studies, volume 11, New Delhi: Sage Publications.

Palit, D.K. (1984) *Sentinels of the North-East: The Assam Rifles*, New Delhi: Major General D.K. Palit.

Phukon, Girin (ed.) (2002) *Ethnicity and Polity in South Asia*, New Delhi: South Asian Publishers.

Pradhan, Amar Roy (1995) *Rule of Jungle*, Kolkata: Published by Sanchayita Roy Pradhan.

Pradhan, Kumar (1991) *The Gorkha Conquests: The Process and Consequences of the Unification of Nepal, with Particular Reference to Eastern Nepal*, Calcutta, New York: Oxford University Press.

Rapley, John (2004) *Globalization and Inequality: Neoliberalism's Downward Spiral*, Boulder, CO: Lynne Rienner Publishers.

Rawat, Bhagirath (1996) *Baans Salki Rahe Cha*, Darjeeling: Department of Information and Cultural Affairs, Darjeeling Gorkha Hill Council.

Ray, N.R. (ed.) (1986) *Himalayan Frontier in Historical Perspective*, Calcutta: Institute of Historical Studies.

Roohi, Sanam and Ranabir Samaddar (eds) (2009) *Key Texts on Social Justice in India*, New Delhi: Sage Publications.

Rose, Gillian (2007) *Visual Methodologies: An Introduction to the Interpretation of Visual Materials*, Los Angeles: Sage Publications.

Roy, Anupama (2010) *Mapping Citizenship in India*, Oxford: Oxford University Press.

Runciman, W.G. (1966) *Relative Deprivation and Social Justice: A Study of Attitudes to Social Inequality in Twentieth-Century England*, Berkeley: University of California Press.

Samaddar, Ranabir (ed.) (2003) *Refugees and the State: Practices of Asylum and Care in India*, New Delhi: Sage Publications.

Samaddar, Ranabir and Helmut Reifeld (eds) (2001) *Peace as Process: Reconciliation and Conflict Resolution in South Asia*, New Delhi: Manohar.

Samanta, Amiya K. (2000) *Gorkhaland Movement: A Study in Ethnic Separatism*, New Delhi: A.P.H. Publishing.

Sangkima (1995) *Cachar-Mizo Relation (AD 1832–1890)*, Proceedings of North East India History Association (NEIHA), 16th Session, Silchar, Shillong: Modern Offset.

——— (ed.) (2004) *Cross-Border Migration, Mizoram*, New Delhi: Shipra Publications and Maulana Abul Kalam Azad Institute of Asian Studies, Kolkata.

Seagull Arts and Media Resource Centre (2004) *The Line Between: The Experience of Partitions and Borders*, 10 April, Kolkata.

Sen, Jahar (1977) *Indo-Nepal Trade in the Nineteenth Century*, Calcutta: Firma KLM.

Shakespear, L.W. (1977) *History of the Assam Rifles*, Calcutta: Firma KLM.

Singh, Deepak K. (2010) *Stateless in South Asia: The Chakmas between Bangladesh and India*, New Delhi: Sage Publications.

Sinha, Awadhesh Coomar and Tanka Bahadur Subba (eds) (2003) *The Nepalis in Northeast India: A Community in Search of Indian Identity*, New Delhi: Indus Pub. Co.

Sivalingam, R.R. (1984) *The Betrayal of Indian Tamils in Sri Lanka*, Tiruchirappalli: Island Trust.

——— (1995) *In the Service of the Displaced*, Kotagiri: Island Trust.

Sreedhar and John Kaniyalil (1993) *Indo-Pak Relations: A Documentary Study*, New Delhi: ABC Publishing House.

Subba, T.B. (1992) *Ethnicity, State and Development: A Case Study of Gorkhaland Movement in Darjeeling*, New Delhi: Vikas Publishing House.

Subba, T.B., A.C. Sinha, G.S. Nepal and D.R. Nepal (eds) (2009) *Indian Nepalis: Issues and Perspectives*. New Delhi: Concept.

Thapan, Meenakshi (ed.) (2005) *Women and Migration in Asia: Transnational Migration and the Politics of Identity*, volume 1, New Delhi: Sage Publications.

Thomas, C.J. (ed.) (2002) *Dimensions of Displaced People in North-East India*, New Delhi: Regency.

Tyagi, Sushila (1974) *Indo-Nepalese Relations (1858–1914)*, Delhi: D.K. Publishing House.

Vamadevan, M. (1989) *Sri Lankan Repatriates in Tamil Nadu: Rehabilitation and Integration*, Madras: Zen Publishers.

United Nations High Commissioner for Refugees (UNHCR) (2014) *Handbook on Protection of Stateless Persons: Under the 1954 Convention Relating to the Status of Stateless Persons*, Geneva: United Nations High Commissioner for Refugees.

van Waas, Laura (2008) *Nationality Matters: Statelessness under International Law*, Antwerp, Oxford, Portland: Intersentia.

Verghese, C.G. and R.L. Thanzawna (1997) *A History of the Mizos*, New Delhi: Vikas Publishing House.

Weiner, Myron (1978) *Sons of the Soil: Migration and Ethnic Conflict in India*, New Delhi: Oxford University Press.

Whyte, Brendan R. (2004) *Waiting for the Esquimo: An Historical and Documentary Study of the Cooch Behar Enclaves of India and Bangladesh*, Research Paper 8, School of Anthropology, Geography and Environmental Studies, Melbourne: University of Melbourne.

Wilson, David (ed.) (1982) *Sight and Sound*, London: Faber & Faber Ltd and British Film Institute (BFI) Publishing.

Articles, Papers and Documents

Acharya, Ram Lal (2006) 'More 105,000 Bhutanese Refugees are becoming Stateless after 15 Yyears in Exile', *al-Majdal*, BADIL Resource Center, Spring, http://www.badil.org/it/annual-al-awda-award/item/968-more-105000-bhutanese-refugees-are-becoming-stateless-after-15-

years-in-exile/968-more-105000-bhutanese-refugees-are-becoming-stateless-after-15-years-in-exile (accessed on 15 June 2015).

Ahmed, Abu Naser Saied (2003) 'Human Rights and the Chakma Problem', in Bolin Hazarika (ed.), *Human Rights in India: Socio-Political and Legal Dimensions*, Jorhat: J.B. College Human Rights Study Cell.

Aman Trust (2005) 'Notes for Internal Evaluation', March, on file with the author.

Asian Centre for Human Rights (ACHR) (2010) 'Hindu and Sikh Refugees from Pakistan: Majority Kashmiris have a Case of Extreme Discrimination to Answer!' *India: Human Rights Report Quarterly*, 2, October–December, http://www.achrweb.org/ihrrq/issue2/hindu_and_sikh_refugees.html (accessed on 15 November 2012).

Association of Human Rights Activists (AHURA) Bhutan (n.d.) 'Government Repression of Southern Bhutanese (Lhotsampas)', Association of Human Rights Activists, Bhutan, http://www.hurights.or.jp/wcar/E/doc/other/Refugee/AHURA.htm (accessed on 15 November 2012).

Banerjee, Paula (2003) 'Aliens in a Colonial World', in Ranabir Samaddar (ed.), *Refugees and the State: Practices of Asylum and Care in India, 1947-2000*, pp. 69–106, Delhi: Sage Publications.

——(2010) 'Aliens in the Colonial World', in *Borders, Histories Existences: Gender and Beyond*, pp. 3–38, New Delhi: Sage Publications.

Bareh, Hamlet (2001) *Encyclopaedia of North-East India*, New Delhi: Mittal Publications.

Basu Ray Chaudhury, Sabyasachi (2003) 'Uprooted Twice: Refugees from Chittagong Hill Tracts', in Ranabir Samaddar (ed.), *Refugees and the State: Practices of Asylum and Care in India*, pp. 249–80, New Delhi: Sage Publications.

—— (2009) 'An Indian Charter for Minority Rights', in Sanam Roohi and Ranabir Samaddar (eds), *Key Texts on Social Justice in India*, pp. 334–72, New Delhi: Sage Publications.

Basu Ray Chaudhury, Sabyasachi and Ashis K. Biswas (1997) 'A Diaspora is Made: The Jummas in North-East India', in Subir Bhaumik, Meghna Guhathakurta and Sabyasachi Basu Ray Chaudhury (eds), *Living on the Edge: Essays on the Chittagong Hill Tracts*, pp. 139–66, Kathmandu: South Asia Forum for Human Rights.

Batchelor, Carol (1996) 'Statelessness and the Problem of Resolving Citizenship Status', Paper presented during United Nations High Commissioner for Refugees Conference on 'People of Concern', 21–23 November.

—— (1998) 'Statelessness and the Problem of Resolving Nationality Status', *International Journal of Refugee Law*, 10 (1–2): 156–83.

Bharatiya Janata Party (BJP) (1992a) 'People Betrayed in Tin Bigha', Pamphlet published by Paras Dutta, General Secretary, BJP West Bengal, Kolkata.

——— (1992b) '"Resist Tin Bigha Transfer', Pamphlet published by Tapan Sikdar, President; Dr Debabrata Singha, Vice-President; Paras Dutta, General Secretary; Smt. Sati Roy, Secretary, BJP West Bengal, Calcutta.

Bhaumik, Subir (1997) 'Strategic Pawn: Indian Policy in the Chittagong Hill Tracts', in Subir Bhaumik, Meghna Guhathakurta and Sabyasachi Basu Ray Chaudhury (eds), *Living on the Edge: Essays on the Chittagong Hill Tracts*, pp. 127–38, Kathmandu: South Asia Forum for Human Rights.

Blitz, Brad K. (2009) 'Statelessness, Protection and Equality', Forced Migration Policy Briefing 3, Refugee Studies Centre, Oxford Department of International Development, University of Oxford, http://www.rsc.ox.ac.uk/publications/policy-briefings/RSCPB3-Statelessness.pdf (accessed on 15 November 2012).

Blitz, Brad K. and Maureen Lynch (2011b) 'Statelessness and the Deprivation of Nationality', in Brad K. Blitz and Maureen Lynch (eds), *Statelessness and Citizenship: A Comparative Study on the Benefits of Nationality*, pp. 1–22, Gloucestershire: Edward Elgar Publishing Limited.

Cahn, Claude (2012) 'Minorities, Citizenship and Statelessness in Europe', *European Journal of Migration and Law*, 14 (3): 297–316.

Calcutta Research Group (CRG) (2006) 'Voices of the Internally Displaced in South Asia', December, http://www.mcrg.ac.in/voices.pdf (accessed on 10 May 2015).

Caplan, Lionel (1991) '"Bravest of the Brave": Representations of the "Gurkha" in British Military Writings', *Modern Asian Studies*, 25 (3): 571–97.

Chakma, Gautam (2005) 'Natives versus Chakma Diaspora in Arunachal Pradesh', in Monirul Hussain (ed.), *Coming out of Violence: Essays on Ethnicity, Conflict Resolution and Peace Process in North-East India*, pp. 86–102, New Delhi: Regency.

Chakraborty, Anup Shekhar (2008) 'Manufacturing of Spaces: The "Others" in Zo/Mizo Politics', *South Asian Journal of Socio-Political Studies (SAJOSPS)* July–December, 9 (1): 39–43.

Chakraborty, Subhas Ranjan (2001) 'Identity, Movements and Peace', in Ranabir Samaddar and Helmut Reifeld (eds), *Peace as Process: Reconciliation and Conflict Resolution in South Asia*, pp. 257–60, New Delhi: Manohar.

——— (2005) 'Silence under Freedom: The Story of Democracy in the Darjeeling Hills', in Ranabir Samaddar (ed.), *The Politics of Autonomy: Indian Experiences*, pp. 173–95, New Delhi: Sage Publications.

Chandran, D. Suba (2007) 'The Forgotten People of Jammu and Kashmir: "Refugees" from PoK', Institute of Peace and Conflict Studies, 8 January, http://www.ipcs.org/article/india/the-forgotten-people-of-jammu-and-kashmir-refugees-from-pok-2182.html (accessed on 15 November 2012).

Chatterji, Joya (1999) 'The Fashioning of a Frontier: The Radcliffe Line and Bengal's Border Landscape, 1947–52', *Modern Asian Studies*, 33 (1): 185–242.

Chawngbuanga, C. (2009) 'Champhai Chanchin', in *Champhai Centenary Souvenir 1990*.

Chhetry, D.B. (2009) 'Nepalis and Bangladeshis: A Comparative Study', in T.B. Subba, A.C. Sinha, G.S. Nepal and D.R. Nepal (eds), *Indian Nepalis: Issues and Perspectives*, New Delhi: Concept.

——— (2012) 'Nepalis and Bangladeshis in Assam: Comparative Historical Analysis of Migration, Identity and Citizenship', in Padam Nepal and Anup Shekhar Chakraborty (eds), *Politics of Culture, Identity and Protest in North-East India*, volumes 1 and 2, pp. 475–87, New Delhi: Authors Press.

Chowdhory, Nasreen (2004) 'Coping with Refugees in India: The Case of Chakma Refugees', in Imtiaz Ahmed, Abhijit Dasgupta and Kathinka Sinha-Kerkoff (eds), *State, Society and Displaced People in South Asia*, pp. 187–205, Dhaka: University Press Limited.

Connor, Walker (1994) 'A Nation is a Nation is a State is an Ethnic Group is a ...' in John Hutchinson and Anthony D. Smith (eds), *Ethnic and Racial Studies*, pp. 377–400, Oxford, New York: Oxford University Press.

Crépeau, François and Ranabir Samaddar (2011) 'Recognizing the Dignity of Migrants', *Refugee Watch*, 37, June: 55–67.

Das, Samir Kumar (2009) 'Governing Minority Rights? The South and South-East Asian Scenario', in Lipi Ghosh (ed.), *Political Governance and Minority Rights: The South and South-East Asian Scenario*, pp. 199–216, New Delhi: Routledge.

Devi, Monimala (2007) 'Economic History of Nepali Migration and Settlement in Assam', *Economic and Political Weekly*, 42 (29), 21–27 July: 3005–07.

Dey, Ishita and Sucharita Sengupta (2010) 'An Interview with Ved Bhasin on Forced Migration in Jammu and Kashmir', *Refugee Watch*, 36, December: 121–26.

Dutta, S. (2002) 'Internally Displaced Persons in Arunachal Pradesh', in C.J. Thomas (ed.), *Dimensions of Displaced People in North-East India*, pp. 201–20, New Delhi: Regency.

English, Richard (1982) *Gorkhali and Kiranti: Political Economy in the Eastern Hills of Nepal*, Ann Arbor: University Microfilms International.

Gamson, William A. (1995) 'Constructing Social Protest', in Hank Johnston and Bert Klandermans (eds), *Social Movements and Culture*, Social Movements: Protest, and Contention, volume 4, pp. 85–106, Minneapolis: University of Minnesota Press.

Gardner, Katy and Filippo Osella (2004) 'Migration, Modernity and Social Transformation in South Asia: An Introduction', in Filippo Osella and Katy Gardner (eds), *Migration, Modernity and Social Transformation in South Asia*, Contributions to Indian Sociology Occasional Studies, volume 11, pp. xi–xlviii, New Delhi: Sage Publications.

Golay, Bidhan (2009) 'Rethinking Gorkha Identity: Outside the Imperium of Discourse, Hegemony, and History', in T.B. Subba, A.C. Sinha, G.S. Nepal and D.R. Nepal (eds), *Indian Nepalis: Issues and Perspectives*, pp. 73–94, New Delhi: Concept.

Golay, Pravesh Jung (2009) 'Ethnic Identity Crisis, History and Cultural Anthropology: Some Reflections', in T.B. Subba, A.C. Sinha, G.S. Nepal and D.R. Nepal (eds), *Indian Nepalis: Issues and Perspectives*, pp. 49–62, New Delhi: Concept.

Goldston, A. (2006) 'Holes in the Rights Framework: Racial Discrimination, Citizenship, and the Rights of Noncitizens', *Ethics & International Affairs*, 20 (3): 321–47.

Goodwin-Gill, Guy S. (1994) 'The Rights of Refugees and Stateless Persons: Problems of Stateless Persons and the Need for International Measures of Protection', in K.P. Saksena (ed.), *Human Rights Perspectives and Challenges*, pp. 378–401, New Delhi: Lancer Books.

Greenblatt, Stephen (1995) 'Culture', in Frank Lestricchia and Thomas Mchaughin (eds), *Critical Terms for Literature Study*, pp. 225–32, Chicago: University of Chicago.

Grossberg, L., C. Nelson and P. Treichler (1992b) 'Cultural Studies: An Introduction', in *Cultural Studies*, London: Routledge.

Hall, S. (1992) 'Cultural Studies and its Theoretical Legacies', in L. Grossberg, C. Nelson and P. Treichler (eds) *Cultural Studies*, London: Routledge.

Human Rights Commission of Pakistan (HRCP) (2012) 'HRCP's Outrage at Minorities' Flight', 10 August, http://www.hrcp-web.org/showprel.asp?id=292 (accessed on 15 November 2012).

Human Rights Law Network (HRLN) (2007) 'Report of Refugee Populations in India', November, New Delhi, http://www.hrln.org/admin/issue/subpdf/Refugee_populations_in_India.pdf (accessed on 15 November 2012).

Human Rights Watch (HRW) (2007a) 'Discrimination against Ethnic Nepali Children in Bhutan', Submission from Human Rights Watch to the Committee on the Rights of the Child, 3 October, http://www.hrw.org/news/2007/10/03/discrimination-against-ethnic-nepali-children-bhutan (accessed on 15 November 2012).

Human Rights Watch (HRW) (2007b) 'Stateless Refugee Children from Bhutan Living in Nepal', Testimony of Bill Frelick to a Joint Briefing for the Congressional Children's Caucus and the Congressional Human Rights Caucus on the Status of Stateless Children, Human Rights Watch, 15 February, http://www.hrw.org/news/2007/02/14/stateless-refugee-children-bhutan-living-nepal (accessed on 8 April 2015).

Hutt, Michael (1988) 'A Hero or a Traitor: Representations of the Gurkha Soldier in Modern Nepali Literature', *South Asia Research*, 9 (1): 21–32.

——— (1994) 'Bhutan's Crisis of Identity', in *The World Book Year Book*, London: World Book Inc.

——— (1997) 'Being Nepali without Nepal: Reflections on a South Asian Diaspora', in David N. Gellner, Joanna Pfaff-Czarnecka and John Whelpton (eds), *Nationalism and Ethnicity in a Himalayan Kingdom: The Politics of Culture in Contemporary Nepal*, London, Amsterdam: Harwood Academic.

Jain, B.K. (1963) 'The Problem of Citizenship Rights of Persons of Indian Origin in Ceylon', *The Indian Journal of Political Science*, 24 (1): 65–78.

Johnston, Hank and Bert Klandermans (1995b) 'The Cultural Analysis of Social Movements', in *Social Movements and Culture*, Social Movements: Protest, and Contention, volume 4, pp. 3–24, Minneapolis: University of Minnesota Press.

KashmirWatch (2012) 'Permanent Settlement of Pak Refugees: Hurriyat (G) Sees Red', 24 August, http://kashmirwatch.com/index.php/2012/08/24/permanent-settlement-8217-of-pak-refugees-hurriyat-g-sees-red.html (accessed on 15 November 2012).

Kerber, Linda K. (2009) 'The Stateless as the Citizen's Other: A View from the United States', in Seyla Benhabib and Judith Resnik (eds), *Migrations and Mobilities: Citizenships, Borders and Gender*, pp. 76–126, New York, London: New York University Press.

Kumar, Ajay (2012) 'Impact of Internal Displacement in Jammu and Kashmir: Study of Pakistan Occupied Kashmir Refugees', *Indian Streams Research Journal*, 2 (3), April: 1–4.

Labh, Kapileshwar (1986) 'The Himalayan Frontier: A Case Study of the Bhutanese Part of the Frontier', in N.R. Ray (ed.), *Himalayan Frontier in Historical Perspective*, pp. 388–99, Calcutta: Indian Institute of Historical Studies.

Ladduwahetty, Neville (n.d.) '"The Need for Building Bridges": Another View', *The Island*, http://www.island.lk/2008/03/26/features4.html (accessed on 22 January 2012).

Lay Lee, Tang (1998) 'Refugees from Bhutan: Nationality, Statelessness and the Right to Return', *International Journal of Refugee Law*, 10 (1–2): 118–55.

Maxym, Maya (2010) 'Nepali-Speaking Bhutanese (Lhotsampa) Cultural Profile', *ethnomed*, 1 March, Health Sciences Library, Harborview Medical Center, University of Washington, https://ethnomed.org/culture/nepali-speaking-bhutanese-lhotsampa/nepali-speaking-bhutanese-lhotsampa-cultural-profile (accessed on 15 June 2015).

Milton, S. (1998) 'Persecuting the Survivors: The Continuity of "Anti-Gypsyism" in Postwar Germany and Austria', in S. Tebbutt (ed.), *Sinti and Roma: Gypsies in German-Speaking Society and Literature*, pp. 35–48, Oxford: Berghahn Books.

Nag, Sajal (2009) 'Fei-ization of the Nepalis of North-East India', in Awadhesh Coomar Sinha and Tanka Bahadur Subba (eds), *The Nepalis in Northeast India: A Community in Search of Indian Identity*, pp. 184–96, New Delhi: Indus Pub. Co.

Ong, Aihwa (2003) 'Cyberpublics and Diaspora Politics among Transnational Chinese', *Interventions: International Journal of Postcolonial Studies*, 5 (1): 82–100.

Piper, Tessa (1995) 'The Exodus of Ethnic Nepalis from Southern Bhutan', 1 April, http://www.refworld.org/docid/3ae6a6c08.html_ftn50 (accessed on 1 July 2015).

Pradhan, K.L. (2009) 'Mizoram Gorkhas: Issues and Problems', in T.B. Subba, A.C. Sinha, G.S. Nepal and D.R. Nepal (eds), *Indian Nepalis: Issues and Perspectives*, pp. 225–36, New Delhi: Concept.

Prasad, Chunnu (2007) 'Chakma-Hajong Refugees and Their Rights', http://www.globalpolitician.com/22651-refugees (accessed on 20 December 2010).

Ramasubramanian, R. (n.d.) 'Refugees Within and Refugees Without', Institute of Peace and Conflict Studies, http://www.ipcs.org/books-review/south-asia/missing-boundaries-refugees-migrants-stateless-and-internally-displaced-persons-in-183.html (accessed on 15 June 2015).

Sen, Arindam Kumar (2003) 'Nei-Manusher Panchali: Chhitmahal Shamashya, Manabadhikarer Lojja' [Chronicles of Absent-Humans: The *Chhitmahal* Conundrum, Shame of Human Rights], Bharatiya Chhitmahaler Chhinnamool o Adhibashi Nagorik Adhikar Shurakkha Shamiti, Kolkata.

—— (2004) 'The Inside and Outside of a Border', in *The Line Between: The Experience of Partitions and Borders*, Kolkata: Seagull Arts and Media Resource Centre.

Sengupta, Sushmita (2002) 'Migration and Ethnic Issues in North East India: An Analysis of the Arunachal Pradesh Situation', in Girin Phukon (ed.), *Ethnicity and Polity in South Asia*, pp. 258–66, New Delhi: South Asian Publishers.

Shrestha, Nanda R. (1991) 'Nepal: The Society and its Environment', in Andrea Matles Savada (ed.), *Nepal: A Country Study*, Washington DC: Federal Research Division, Library of Congress, http://lcweb2.loc.gov/cgi-bin/query/r?frd/cstdy:@field%28DOCID+np0054%29 (accessed on 15 November 2012).

Shrum, L.J. (1994) 'Media Consumption and Perceptions of Social Reality: Effects and Underlying Processes', in Jennings Bryant and Mary Beth Oliver (eds), *Media Effects: Advances in Theory And Research*, pp. 50–73, New York: Routledge.

Singh, B.P. (1987) 'North-East India: Demography, Culture and Identity Crisis', *Modern Asian Studies*, 21 (2): 257–82.

Sinha, A.C. (1982) 'The Nepalese in North-East India: Ethnicity and Resource Appropriation', in J.B. Bhattacharjee (ed.), *Social Tension in North-East India*, Calcutta: Research India Publications.

——— (2003) 'The Indian Northeast Frontier and the Nepali Immigrants', in Awadhesh Coomar Sinha and Tanka Bahadur Subba (eds), *The Nepalis in Northeast India: A Community in Search of Indian Identity*, pp. 31–53, New Delhi: Indus Pub. Co.

Sivapragasam, P.P. (2009) 'From Stateless to Citizenship: Up Country Tamils in Sri Lanka', in Brad K. Blitz and Maureen Lynch (eds), *Statelessness and the Benefit of Citizenship: A Comparative Study*, Oxford: Oxford Brookes University.

Subba, T.B. (2003) 'The Nepalis in Northeast India: Political Aspirations and Ethnicity', in Awadhesh Coomar Sinha and Tanka Bahadur Subba (eds), *The Nepalis in India: A Community in Search of Indian Identity*, pp. 54–66, New Delhi: Indus Pub. Co.

Suryanarayan, V. (2010) 'Indian Tamil Refugees in their Homeland', Paper No. 3856, 11 June, http://www.southasiaanalysis.org/%5Cpapers39%5Cpaper3856.html (accessed on 24 January 2012).

Swindler, Ann (1995) 'Cultural Power and Social Movements', in Hank Johnston and Bert Klandermans (eds), *Social Movements and Culture*, Social Movements: Protest, and Contention, volume 4, pp. 25–40, Minneapolis: University of Minnesota Press.

Talukdar, Ratna Bharali (2008a) 'Livelihood Crisis for Chakma, Hajong Refugees', Centre for North East Studies and Policy Research (C-NES), 14 September, http://www.c-nes.org/nycu/115.html (accessed on 12 January 2011).

Tyagi, Sushila (1986) 'Nepal and the First War of Independence of 1857' in N.R. Ray (ed.), *Himalayan Frontier in Historical Perspective*, Calcutta: Institute of Historical Studies.

United Nations (UN) (2009) 'Note by the Secretary-General with Annex Containing Observations by Governments on Deprivation of Nationality: United Nations Conference on the Elimination or

Reduction of Future Statelessness Geneva, 1959 and New York, 1961', A/CONF.9/10, http://legal.un.org/diplomaticconferences/statelessness-1959/docs/english/Vol_1/14_NOTE_SG_A_conf_9_10.pdf (accessed on 8 May 2015).

United Nations High Commission on Refugees (UNHCR) (2004) 'Final Report Concerning the Questionnaire on Statelessness Pursuant to the Agenda for Protection: Steps taken by States to Reduce Statelessness and to Meet the Protection Needs of Stateless Persons', Department of International Protection, March, hhtp://www.unhcr.org/4047002e4.pdf (accessed on 12 May 2015).

——— (2010) 'The Concept of Stateless Persons under International Law Summary Conclusions', Expert meeting organised by the Office of the United Nations High Commissioner for Refugees, Prato, 27–28 May, http://www.unhcr.org/4cb2fe326.html (accessed on 24 February 2014).

———(2012) '2012 UNHCR Country Operations File—Nepal', http://www.unhcr.org/cgi-bin/texis/vtx/page?page=49e487856&submit=GO (accessed on 15 November 2012).

——— (2013) 'UNHCR Global Appeal 2013 Update: Nepal', http://www.unhcr.org/50a9f82cb.pdf (accessed on 12 May 2015).

van Schendel, Willem (2002) 'Stateless in South Asia: The Making of the India-Bangladesh Enclaves', *Journal of Asian Studies*, 61 (1): 115–48.

van Waas, Laura (2011) 'Nationality and Rights', in Brad K. Blitz and Maureen Lynch (eds), *Statelessness and Citizenship: A Comparative Study on the Benefits of Nationality*, pp. 23–44, Gloucestershire: Edward Elgar Publishing Limited.

Walsh, Rebecca (2003) 'Global Diasporas: Introduction', *Interventions*, 5 (1): 1–11.

Weissbrodt, David and Clay Collins (2006) 'The Human Rights of Stateless Persons', *Human Rights Quarterly*, 28 (1): 245–76.

White, Paul (2009) 'Reducing De Facto Statelessness in Nepal', *Forced Migration Review*, 32, April: 28–29.

Zoramthanga (1998) 'Mizoram Chhunga Nepali/Gorkhali Awmhlun Mipuite Laka MNF Party Intiam Kamna', 14 October, Aizawl.

Newspaper and Magazine Articles

Amrita Bazar Patrika (1953) 'Short Comment on Enclaves', 15 February.

The Arunachal Times (2010a) 'AAPSU to take Chakma issue to National Human Rights Commission', 24 May.

——— (2010b) 'AAPSU Reacts Angrily to Govt's Decision to Issue PRC to Non APST', 8 September.

The Arunachal Times (2010c) 'Government Decision on Grant of PRC to Non-APST draws Flack', 12 September.

——— (2010d) 'Natives vs Non-Natives: Need for a Comprehensive Policy', 28 September.

——— (2010e) 'Arunachal Government Revokes its Decision on PRC to Non-APST', 29 September.

Asian Tribune (2007) 'Issue of Granting Citizenship to 28,500 Sri Lankan Refugees in Tamil Nadu to be Completed Soon—R. Chandrasekaran MP', 31 December, http://www.asiantribune.com/index.php?q=node/8941 (accessed on 12 January 2012).

The Assam Tribune (1994) 'Shoot Chakmas at Sight', 13 September.

Baabar, Mariana (2006) 'Sindh's Stolen Brides', *Outlook*, 23 January, http://www.outlookindia.com/article.aspx?229886 (accessed on 15 November 2012).

Bashir, A. (2012) 'West Pak Refugees, Tibetans in No Man's Land', *Kashmir Monitor*, 17 October, http://kashmirmonitor.org/10082012-ND-west-pak-refugees-tibetans-in-no-man%E2%80%99s-land-34868.aspx (accessed on 17 December 2012).

The Bengal Post (2012) 'Enclave Members Begin Indefinite Hunger Strike', 13 March.

Chakraborty, Arpita (2011) 'She's the Reason for Bangla Enclave on Bengal Poll Map', *The Indian Express*, 17 April.

Chetri, Neel Kumar and Binayak Sundas (2009) 'Identifying Darjeeling as a Part of North-East India', *The Darjeeling Times*, 1, 10 January.

Choudhury, Rabijit (1994) 'Arunachal Chakmas Struggle for their Rights', *The Statesman*, 29 September.

CoochBehar Calling (2011) 'Chhitmahal (Enclave) Dwellers Demand: Enclave Dwellers want to meet Didi [Mamata Banerjee]', 27 June 2011, http://coochbeharcalling.blogspot.in/2011/06/chhitmahal-enclave-dwellers-demand.html (accessed on 29 February 2012).

Daily News and Analysis (DNA) (2014) 'Congress Legislators Walkout from J&K Legislative Council over Refugees Issue', 18 February, http://www.dnaindia.com/india/report-congress-legislators-walkout-from-jk-legislative-council-over-refugees-issue-1963185 (accessed on 22 April 2015).

Dasgupta, Partha (2011) 'In a State of Limbo', *India Today*, 30 September.

Davlin, Melissa (2011a) 'Bhutanese Refugees Adapt to Twin Falls Life: Future of a Forgotten People', *Times-News*, 14 June; http://magicvalley.com/lifestyles/relationships-and-special-occasions/bhutanese-refugees-adapt-to-twin-falls-life/article_5baf46f4-a526-5a57-8108-59d0ec459fa9.html (accessed on 15 November 2012).

—— (2011b) 'Eager for Resettlement, Refugees Endure Harsh Lives in Nepal's Camps Anticipating Idaho', *Times-News*, 24 April, http://magicvalley.com/lifestyles/relationships-and-special-occasions/eager-for-resettlement-refugees-endure-harsh-lives-in-nepal-s/article_8e94fb94-6d2f-11e0-9e64-001cc4c002e0.html (accessed on 15 November 2012).

Deol, Rajesh (2012) 'Pakistani Hindus in India Unwilling to Return', *Deccan Herald*, 5 September, http://www.deccanherald.com/content/86879/pakistani-hindus-india-unwilling-return.html (accessed on15 November 2012).

Dholabhai, Nishit (2007) 'Delhi "Profiles" to Protect: Police Booklet for the Northeast Students Betrays Prejudices', *The Telegraph*, 10 July.

—— (2011) 'Choice of State for Enclave Residents', *The Telegraph*, 25 August.

Ebrahim, Zofeen (2012) 'Why are Hindus from Pakistan Crossing Over to India?' Inter Press Service, 24 August, http://www.ipsnews.net/2012/08/why-are-hindus-from-pakistan-crossing-over-to-india (accessed on 15 November 2012).

FirstPost (2015) 'Assam included in India-Bangladesh Land Swap Agreement: All you Need to Know about the Deal', 6 May, http://www.firstpost.com/india/assam-included-in-india-bangladesh-land-swap-agreement-all-you-need-to-know-about-the-deal-1830365.html (accessed on 24 May 2015).

Ganguly, Tapash (1986) 'Interview: "I'm an Indian": GNLF Chief also swears by Gorkhaland'. *The Week*, 15–21 June.

Greater Kashmir (2007) 'Wadhwa Submits Report on PaK, WP Refugees', 30 November, http://www.greaterkashmir.com/news/2007/Nov/30/wadhwa-submits-report-on-pak-wp-refugees-51.asp (accessed on 22 April 2015).

Hazarika, Sanjoy (1992) 'Bangladeshization of India', *The Telegraph*, 6 February.

The Hindu (2007) 'Tamil Repatriates from Sri Lanka Seek State Help', 22 April, http://www.hindu.com/2007/04/22/stories/2007042217660500.htm (accessed on 20 January 2012).

—— (2008) 'Court Extends Stay on J&K Resettlement Act', 21 February, http://www.hindu.com/2008/02/21/stories/2008022151381300.htm (accessed on 15 November 2012).

Hussain, Kashif (2012) 'A Tale of Migrating Hindus', *The Daily Times*, 20 August, http://www.dailytimes.com.pk/default.asp?page=2012%5C08%5C20%5Cstory_20-8-2012_pg7_10 (accessed on 15 November 2012).

Jagran Post (2011) 'Over 7,500 Pakistanis Overstayed in India: RTI', 14 November, http://post.jagran.com/Over-7500-Pakistanis-overstayed-in-India-RTI-1321253851 (accessed on 15 November 2012).

Joshua, Anita (2012) '"Forcibly Converted" Hindu Women Choose to Stay with Husbands', *The Hindu*, 18 April, http://www.thehindu.com/news/international/article3328893.ece (accessed on 15 November 2012).

Kumar, Manan (2014) 'Why Narendra Modi Made a U-Turn on Land Boundary Agreement?' *DNA*, 2 December, http://www.dnaindia.com/india/report-why-narendra-modi-made-a-u-turn-on-land-boundary-agreement-2040135 (accessed on 24 May 2015).

LankaNewspapers.com (2007) 'Lanka to Give Citizenship to 28,500 Refugees', 8 December, http://www.lankanewspapers.com/news/2007/12/22350.html (accessed on 23 January 2012).

Lelte Weekly (2010) 'Tini Mohini Thapa: Indian Idol 5-ah Golden Card Dawng Chu' (Tini Mohini Thapa: One who got the Golden Card in Indian Idol 5), 26 (37), 12–18 March, Aizawl.

Majumder, Niranjan (1965) 'Cooch Behar Enclaves, Their Past and Future: The Urgency of Demarcation and Exchange', *The Statesman*, 1 May.

Mandal, Caesar (2011) 'Census Begins in Enclaves to Recognize "Stateless" People', *The Times of India*, 17 July.

Masood, Bashaarat (2012) 'Will Oppose Settlement of Pak Refugees, says Geelani', *The Indian Express*, 24 August, http://www.indianexpress.com/news/will-oppose-settlement-of-pak-refugees-says-geelani/992342/ (accessed on 15 November 2012).

Mishra, Sudhanshu (2012) 'Pakistanis in India with Expired Visas under Security Scanner', *Mail Today*, 26 August; http://indiatoday.intoday.in/story/security-on-alert-for-pakistanis-in-india-with-expired-visas/1/214759.html (accessed on 15 November 2012).

Nagchoudhury, Subrata (2011) 'No No-Man's Land: PM and Hasina Mark Border', *Indian Express*, 7 September.

Naqvi, N. (2012) 'Soul Suicide', *Outlook India*, 15 October, http://www.outlookindia.com/article.aspx?282469 (accessed on 14 December 2012).

NDTV (2015) 'Mamata Banerjee Meets Bangladesh Prime Minister Sheikh Hasina in Dhaka', 21 February, http://www.ndtv.com/india-news/mamata-banerjee-meets-bangladesh-prime-minister-sheikh-hasina-in-dhaka-741296 (accessed on 24 May 2015).

OneIndia (2007) 'Wadhwa Committee Submits Report on PoK, West Pak Refugees', 30 November, http://news.oneindia.in/2007/11/30/wadhwa-committee-submits-report-on-pok-west-pak-refugees-1196400922.htm (accessed on 17 December 2012).

—— (2008) 'CYMA against OBC to Mizoram's Gorkhas', 18 July, Aizawl, http://news.oneindia.in/2008/07/18/cyma-against-obc-to-mizorams-gorkhas-1216389950.html (accessed on 2 July 2009).

Outlook (2010) 'Order on PRC to Non-Arunachalees Revoked', 29 September.

Pandey, Shailendra (2012) 'An Uncertain Refuge', *Tehelka*, 5 May, http://www.tehelka.com/story_main52.asp?filename=hub050512UNCERTAIN.asp (accessed on 15 November 2012).

Perera, S. (2007) 'Sri Lankan Success Story', *Refugees Magazine*, volume 147, September.

Prasad, Chunnu (2012) 'The Chakmas Refugees and their Rights', http://nandapriya.blogspot.in/2012/05/chakmas-and-their-rights.html (accessed on 7 May 2015).

Pudaite, Roseim (2006) 'Ramruak Khawvelah: Huat tur haw lo, huat loh tur hua kan ni em?' *ZOlife*, Aizawl, April.

Puri, Balraj (n.d.) 'Refugee Problem in Jammu and Kashmir', *Kashmir Newz*, http://www.kashmirnewz.com/a0002.html (accessed on 15 November 2012).

Ramakrishnan, T. (2012) 'Getting Indian Citizenship a Tough Task for Them', *The Hindu*, 22 February, http://www.thehindu.com/news/article2421605.ece (accessed on 22 January 2012).

Rehman, I.A. (2012) 'Perils of Intolerance', *Dawn*, 16 August, http://dawn.com/2012/08/16/perils-of-intolerance/ (accessed on 15 November 2012).

Roy Chowdhury, Shreya (2010) 'Pak Hindus Narrate 'Citizenship' Woes', *The Times of India*, 28 December, http://articles.timesofindia.indiatimes.com/2010-12-28/pakistan/28255011_1_tourist-visa-long-term-visas-refugee-status (accessed on 15 November 2012).

Samantaray, M.B. (2012) 'Pakistan's Disappearing Hindus', *Open Democracy*, 22 October, http://www.opendemocracy.net/opensecurity/maitreya-buddha-samantaray/pakistan%E2%80%99s-disappearing-hindus (accessed on 13 December 2012).

Sardana, Nandita (1994) 'Chakmas: Living under Notice of Death', *India Today*, 15 November.

Sikand, Yoginder (2009) 'Pakistani Hindu Migrants to India: Demanding to be Heard', *Pakistan Hindu Post*, 30 December, http://pakistanhindupost.blogspot.in/2009/12/pakistani-hindu-migrants-to-india.html (accessed on 15 November 2012).

Sirmed, Marvi (2012) 'Rinkle Kumari: A Test Case for Jinnah's Pakistan', *The Friday Times*, volume 24, no. 15, 25–31 May, http://www.thefridaytimes.com/beta3/tft/article.php?issue=20120525&page=6 (accessed on 15 November 2012).

The Statesman (1960) 'Protest by All-India Convention', 11 December.

——— (1965a) 'Unprovoked Attack by East Pakistan Forces', 19 March.

——— (1965b) 'Uproar over Firing on Border', 20 March.

——— (1965c) 'Situation Worsens on Border', 29 March.

——— (1965d) 'Cease-Fire on Border from Today, Chief Secretaries Likely to Meet on April 9', 31 March.

——— (1965e) 'Shooting Stops on Border: Pakistan Officials Given Visas for Dahagram', 1 April.

——— (1965f) 'East Pakistan Police Enter Dahagram Today: Evacuees also to Start Returning', 2 April.

——— (1965g) 'Appeal Dismissed in Berubari Case', 12 August.

——— (1997) 'Fear of the Foreigner', 22 February.

Talukdar, Ratna Bharali (2008b) 'Human Rights: State of Denial', *Frontline*, 29 August.

The Telegraph (1994) 'Chakma Plea to Assam', 1 October.

Tawrh Bawm (2010) 'Indian Idol nihna chuh turin Tini Mohini Thapa-in Golden Card a dawng' (Tini Mohini Thapa gets the Golden Card in Indian Idol), 8 March, Aizawl.

Thapa, Saurav Jung (2011) 'Bhutan's Hoax: Of Gross National Happiness', *Wave Magazine*, no. 187, July, http://www.wavemag.com.np/issue/article3775.html (accessed on 15 November 2012).

The Times of India (1994) 'Saikia Opposes Move to Settle Refugees in N-E', 11 October.

——— (2007) 'Do's and Don'ts Irk N-E Students: IPS Officer's Booklet Reinforces Stereotypes', 16 July.

Vij-Aurora, Bhavna (2012) 'No Country for Pakistani Hindus', *India Today*, 27 April, http://indiatoday.intoday.in/story/pakistani-hindu-refugees-feel-betrayed-by-india/1/186304.html (accessed on 15 November 2012).

WebIndia123 (2007) 'Mizoram Refuses to Recognize its Gorkhas as OBC', 11 May, http://news.webindia123.com/news/ar_showdetails.asp?id=705110554&cat=&n_date=20070511 (accessed on 2 July 2009).

Websites

Asian Indigenous and Tribal Peoples Network (AITPN) (1997) 'Rajya Sabha Committee On Petition: Hundred And Fifth Report—On the Petition Signed by Smt. Snehadini Talukdar of Mizoram and Shri Subimal Chakma of Delhi on the Petition Pertaining to Problems being Faced by the Chakma Tribal Population in Mizoram and Arunachal Pradesh', 14 August, http://www.aitpn.org/StatelessIPs/Rajyasabha.pdf (accessed on 8 July 2014).

Baba Ramsaa Peer (n.d.) http://babaramsaapeer.com/history.html (accessed on 15 November 2012).

Coonoor.com (n.d.) http://www.coonoor.com/about.htm (accessed on 7 May 2015).

Election Commission of India (ECI) (n.d.-a) 'Election Results: Full Statistical Reports', http://eci.nic.in/eci_main1/ElectionStatistics.aspx (accessed on 29 February 2012).

——— (n.d.-b) 'Party-Wise Comparison Since 1977: Cooch Behar Parliamentary Constituency', http://www.eci.nic.in/eci_main/electionanalysis/GE/PartyCompWinner/S25/partycomp01.htm (accessed on 29 February 2012).

——— (n.d.-c) 'Partywise Comparison Since 1977: Dinhata Assembly Constituency', http://eci.nic.in/archive/ElectionAnalysis/AE/S25/Partycomp07.htm (accessed on 29 February 2012).

——— (n.d.-d) 'Partywise Comparison Since 1977: Mekliganj (SC) Assembly Constituency', http://eci.nic.in/archive/ElectionAnalysis/AE/S25/Partycomp01.htm (accessed on 29 February 2012).

——— (n.d.-e) 'Partywise Comparison Since 1977: Sitai Assembly Constituency', http://eci.nic.in/archive/ElectionAnalysis/AE/S25/Partycomp06.htm (accessed on 29 February 2012).

Empowering India (n.d.-a) 'Constituency: Dinhata, West Bengal Assembly Election 2011', http://www.empoweringindia.org/new/constituency.aspx?eid=736&cid=7 (accessed on 29 February 2012).

——— (n.d.-b) 'Constituency: Sitai, West Bengal Assembly Election 2011', http://www.empoweringindia.org/new/constituency.aspx?eid=736&cid=6 (accessed on 29 February 2012).

——— (n.d.-c) 'Constituency: Sitalkuchi, West Bengal Assembly Election 2011', http://www.empoweringindia.org/new/constituency.aspx?eid=736&cid=5 (accessed on 29 February 2012).

Government of Pakistan (n.d.) 'Population by Religion', Population Census Organization, http://www.census.gov.pk/Religion.htm (accessed on 15 November 2012).

Internet FAQ Archives (n.d.) 'World Directory of Minorities: Hindus of Pakistan', http://www.faqs.org/minorities/South-Asia/Hindus-of-Pakistan.html (accessed on 15 November 2012).

Kashmir-Information.com (n.d.) 'State Subject Definition Notification dated the 20th April, 1927', Legal Document no. 44, http://www.kashmir-information.com/LegalDocs/44.html (accessed on 15 November 2012).

Pakistan Hindu Council (n.d.) 'Population of Hindus in Pakistan', http://pakistanhinducouncil.org/hindupopulation.asp (accessed on 15 November 2012).

Parliament of India (2012) 'One Hundred and Forty-Ninth Report on the Citizenship (Amendment) Act 2011 (Presented to the Rajya Sabha on March 28, 2012) (Laid on the Table of Lok Sabha on March 28, 2012)', Department-Related Parliamentary Standing Committee on Home Affairs, Rajya Sabha Secretariat, March, New Delhi, http://www.prsindia.org/uploads/media/Citizenship/SCR%20Citizenship%20Amendment%20Bill%202012.pdf (accessed on 15 November 2012).

PhotoVoice (n.d.) 'Bhutanese Refugees: The Story of a Forgotten People', PhotoVoice and the Bhutanese Refugee Support Group, http://www.photovoice.org/bhutan/index.php?id=3 (accessed on 15 November 2012).

South Asian Politics and Governments (2013) 'Tamil Migration to Sri Lanka, 1830–1950', 21 February, http://southasianpoliticalsystem.blogspot.in/2013/02/tamil-migration-to-sri-lanka-1830-1950.html (accessed on 9 April 2015).

Tamil Nadu Tea Plantation Corporation (TANTEA) (n.d.) 'History', http://tantea.co.in/org.html (accessed on 10 November 2012).

TamilNet (2009) 'Restriction on Upcountry Tamils Traveling to Colombo to be Lifted', http://www.tamilnet.com/art.html?catid=13&artid=30847 (accessed on 12 January 2012).

United Nations (n.d.) 'United Nations Treaty Collection', http://treaties.un.org/pages/ViewDetails.aspx?src=TREATY&mtdsg_no=V-4&chapter=5&lang=en (accessed on 12 March 2012).

——— (1954) 'United Nations Conference on the Elimination or Reduction of Future Statelessness'.

United Nations High Commissioner for Refugees (UNHCR) (n.d.) http://www.unhcrwashington.org/atf/cf/%7Bc07eda5e-ac71-4340-8570-194d98bdc139%7D/PUBLIC_PGRN2012.PDF (accessed on 15 November 2012).

——— (2011) 'Projected Global Resettlement Needs 2012', 17th Annual Tripartite Consultations on Resettlement, 4–6 July, Geneva, http://www.unhcr.org/4f0fff0d9.pdf (accessed on 17 March 2015).

Unpublished Papers/Theses

Bhushan, Bharat (2013) 'Citizens, Refugees, or Aliens? Ambiguous Identity of Hindu Migrants from Pakistan', Unpublished, On file with the author.

Corsellis, Tom (2001), 'The Selection of Sites for the Temporary Settlements for Forced Migrants', PhD Dissertation, Department of Architecture, University of Cambridge, http://www.shelterproject.org/downloads/thesis/c7nepal.pdf (accessed on 15 November 2012).

Dey, Ishita (2007) 'Migration and Entrepreneurship: Chinese Community in Calcutta,' MPhil Dissertation, Delhi School of Economics, University of Delhi.

Weis, Paul (1961) 'Elimination or Reduction of Future of Statelessness,' Speech delivered at the United Nations Conference, 25 August.

Notes on the Contributors

Paula Banerjee is Associate Professor, Department of South and Southeast Asian Studies, University of Calcutta; and President, Mahanirban Calcutta Research Group, Kolkata.

Sahana Basavapatna is a human rights activist; Advocate, Supreme Court of India, New Delhi; and member, Mahanirban Calcutta Research Group, Kolkata.

Subhash Ranjan Chakraborty is an eminent historian, and member, Mahanirban Calcutta Research Group, Kolkata.

Anup Shekhar Chakraborty is Assistant Professor, Department of Political Science, St Joseph's College, University of North Bengal, Darjeeling.

Anasua Basu Ray Chaudhury is Fellow, Observer Research Foundation, Kolkata.

Samir Kumar Das is Dean, Faculty of Arts, and Professor, Department of Political Science, University of Calcutta; and member, Mahanirban Calcutta Research Group, Kolkata.

Atig Ghosh is Assistant Professor of History, Visva-Bharati, Santiniketan; and Honorary Researcher, Mahanirban Calcutta Research Group, Kolkata.

Pravina Gurung is National Programme Officer, International Organization for Migration Nepal, Kathmandu.

Suhit K. Sen is an independent researcher, currently associated with the Indian Council of Historical Research, New Delhi.

Index